Women as Leaders in Education

Women as Leaders in Education

SUCCEEDING DESPITE INEQUITY, DISCRIMINATION, AND OTHER CHALLENGES

VOLUME 2: WOMEN'S LEADERSHIP IN CLASSROOMS, SCHOOLS, AND K–12 ADMINISTRATION

Jennifer L. Martin, Editor

Women and Careers in Management
Michele A. Paludi, Series Editor

 PRAEGER

AN IMPRINT OF ABC-CLIO, LLC
Santa Barbara, California • Denver, Colorado • Oxford, England

Copyright 2011 by ABC-CLIO, LLC

Library of Congress Cataloging-in-Publication Data

Women as leaders in education : succeeding despite inequity, discrimination, and other challenges / Jennifer L. Martin, editor.

p. cm. — (Women and careers in management)

Includes bibliographical references and index.

ISBN 978–0–313–39169–9 (hard copy : alk. paper) — ISBN 978–0–313–39170–5 (ebook)

1. Women school administrators—United States. 2. Women college administrators—United States. 3. Sex discrimination in higher education—United States. 4. Educational leadership—United States. I. Martin, Jennifer L. II. Title. III. Series.

LC212.862.W64   2011

378.1′2082—dc22   2011009216

ISBN: 978–0–313–39169–9
EISBN: 978–0–313–39170–5

15 14 13 12 11   1 2 3 4 5

This book is also available on the World Wide Web as an eBook.
Visit www.abc-clio.com for details.

Praeger
An Imprint of ABC-CLIO, LLC

ABC-CLIO, LLC
130 Cremona Drive, P.O. Box 1911
Santa Barbara, California 93116-1911

This book is printed on acid-free paper ∞
Manufactured in the United States of America

Contents

Series Foreword

Ma muaka kite a muri
Ma muri ka ora a mua
(Those who lead give sight to those who follow,
Those who follow give life to those who lead)

—Pauline Tangiora

Welcome to the *Women and Careers in Management* Series at Praeger. This series examines the status of women in management and leadership and offers discussions of issues women managers and leaders face, including:

Differences in leadership styles

Traditional gender roles reinforcing women's subordinate status in the workplace

Obstacles to advancement and pay

Benefit and resource inequity

Discrimination and harassment

Work/life imbalance

This series acknowledges that gender is one of the fundamental factors influencing the ethics, values, and policies of workplaces and that the discrimination against women managers and leaders explains the pervasiveness of institutionalized inequality. This series also discusses interconnections among equality issues: sex, race, class, age, sexual orientation, religion, and disability. Thus, this series brings together a multidisciplinary and multicultural discussion of women, management, and leadership.

Women and Careers in Management encourages all of us to think criti-cally about women managers and leaders, to place value on cultural expe-riences, and to integrate empirical research and theoretical formulations with experiences of our family, friends, colleagues, and ourselves. It is my hope that the books in *Women and Careers in Management* serve as a "life raft" (Klonis, Endo, Crosby, & Worrell, 1997), especially for the Millennial and subsequent generations.

I am honored to have Dr. Jennifer Martin's two-volume set published in the *Women and Careers in Management Series*. Dr. Martin was instrumen-tal in bringing together noted educators and scholars to address women as leaders in K–12 and in higher education. The volumes are essential read-ing for students preparing for a career in teaching and education administration, school and college administrators, and human resource personnel. Dr. Martin offers her readers a "paper mentor" in her edited volumes. As such, these volumes share Pauline Tangiora's sentiment:

> Those who lead give sight to those who follow, Those who follow give life to those who lead.

—Michele A. Paludi
Series Editor

Reference

Klonis, S., Endo, J., Crosby, F., & Worrell, J. (1997). Feminism as life raft. *Psychology of Women Quarterly, 21,* 333–45.

Acknowledgments

Do not follow where the path may lead. Go instead where there is no path and leave a trail.

—Muriel Strode

I dedicate this book set to veteran feminist leaders. I thank you for making the road a little less rocky for the women behind you. I honor your work and celebrate your strength. Your work informs and inspires mine and has led me to this point in my thinking about women and leadership. You have carved your own path; because of your work, mine is possible. It is with you in mind that I bring together this group of diverse voices.

I have had the distinct pleasure of collaborating with colleagues, friends, students, and mentors on this project. I have also been given the unique opportunity to meet many feminist scholars who were interested in sharing their work. These new colleagues have taught me much from their writing and their scholarship. I thank you for your contributions to this book set. This process has been a true collaboration in the spirit of transformational leadership; all of the authors have brought much to the discussion on women and leadership and have assisted me greatly throughout this process.

I thank my parents, John and Dolores Martin, and my sister Elizabeth Martin for their help and support throughout this process. Tremendous thanks go to my husband Peter Midtgard, my greatest sounding board, cheerleader, and provider of reassurance and support; no one believes in me as much as he.

I acknowledge several special friends whose encouragement has been instrumental throughout this process: Annie James, Elizabeth Schuch, and Karissa Williams. Special thanks go to Alice Kondraciuk for technological support without which this project would have been much more laborious, and Ken VanDerworp for his keen wordsmithing. I also thank the Women of Words writer's group, especially Coralie Johnson and Karen Simpson, for allowing me to share my thoughts and providing me with guidance, feedback, friendship, and mentoring.

My students continue to inspire me and make me strive to be a better person and educator. I thank my students from the Women and Gender Studies and Education Specialist programs at Oakland University and my high school students at Tinkham Alternative High School. My students have informed my praxis, my research, and my writing.

I have been fortunate enough to have many mentors throughout my career. These inspiring people continue to help me and advise me in my work. I honor and thank Dr. Duane Moore, Dr. Heather Neff, Dr. Mary Otto, Dr. Dawn Pickard, Dr. Julia Smith, and especially Dr. Jo Reger and Dr. Dyanne Tracy.

To my friends at Michigan NOW, thank you for your support and wisdom. Your feminist leadership continues to inspire me.

I thank Brian Romer, Senior Acquisitions Editor at Praeger, for supporting my work and my vision for this project. His helpful guidance has been instrumental in the completion of this series.

Finally, I give special thanks to my mentor and friend Dr. Michele Paludi, who always believed in my abilities as a scholar, teacher, and writer. She has provided me with tremendous opportunities to grow as a person and as a professional. Without her, this book set would not have been possible.

—Jennifer L. Martin

Introduction

Given that our educational institutions are so deeply invested in a banking system, teachers are more rewarded when we do not teach against the grain. The choice to work against the grain, to challenge the status quo, often has negative consequences.

—bell hooks

Education either functions as an instrument which is used to facilitate integration of the younger generation into the logic of the present system and bring about conformity or it becomes the practice of freedom, the means by which men and women deal critically and creatively with reality and discover how to participate in the transformation of their world.

—Paulo Freire

Without acknowledging the presence of students, one cannot have a discussion about education, let alone educational leadership. The dreams, standpoints, and values of students should be at the forefront of any discussion of education and every dialogue on curriculum, pedagogy, and classroom research. Teachers are an essential resource in bringing these perspectives to the conversation. But in reality, teacher knowledge, and by extension student voice, is largely absent from the dialogue. Teachers are expected to rely on outside experts to inform them of best practices, despite the fact that they know their students best. Teaching, particularly in the public sector, has lost much of its professional caliber beginning in the late twentieth century. Teachers are increasingly being viewed as technicians as opposed to professionals. This impacts teacher effectiveness, for when teachers are devalued, their impact diminishes.

Many teachers are experts in curriculum, pedagogy, and research; thus, they can and should contribute to the production of knowledge in partnership with their students. For this to occur on a larger scale, we must work to change how the teaching profession is perceived from the outside and strive for the empowerment of teachers by valuing their expertise. This will be beneficial to both teachers and students. Since the passage of No Child Left Behind (2001), academic freedom for teachers has decreased. This law punishes instead of supports low-performing schools. The media also participate in presenting teachers and schools in a negative light. For example, the film *Waiting for Superman* exacerbates teacher scapegoating by indicting the tenure system and teacher unions for failing schools. Fortunately, there are recourses for these challenges. Teacher educators sharing their tools with teachers in the field instead of viewing them as the objects of study and requiring courses in research methods for beginning teachers will help. According to Christianakis (2008), "Self-definition enacted through teacher research has the power to free teachers from the unchallenged academic gaze, and more specifically from generalized outsider expertise" (p. 104). For changes to occur in the public's perception of the profession, advocacy and teacher training are necessary.

If learning is to be an emancipatory and democratic process, it must be based on the development of trusting, caring, and reciprocal relationships between teachers and students. These relationships are crucial in the collaborative process of knowledge production and transfer and in valuing student voice. It is therefore imperative that teachers insert themselves in the dialogues about what students need to know and how they can learn.

In addition to these crucial issues facing educators today, this volume brings together a wide array of topics that are relevant to classroom pedagogical practices, school reform measures, and social justice work by including diverse perspectives informed by standpoints of gender, race, class, and sexuality. Women in the field tell rich stories of participating in true counter-hegemonic projects, teaching to transgress, and advocating for those "on the margins." This volume gives voice to those who have been systematically silenced because they do not represent the tone of the majority. It presents the field of education as requiring advocacy at its core. To raise awareness of the problems of marginalization within the student population and within the teaching ranks is crucial; to fight for solutions is paramount. This text will provide inspiration to current and future educators and educational leaders to take up the fight for the inclusion, safety, and success of all students and to fight for the future of the profession.

My students have inspired me to put together this collection of essays, for it is always with them in mind that I seek to improve my practice and to contribute to the field by passing on what I have learned from them. Additionally, during my work on this volume, I was inspired by classic texts from the tradition of critical pedagogy. The current increase of social and political conservatism affecting public education is perhaps most clearly illustrated by Arizona's ban on ethnic studies, HB 2881, indicating that some in positions of power do not want all to be equally represented. Every story is a necessary element in the creation of an accurate portrait of American life; systematic omissions or deletions of student voices represent a false reality. Critical pedagogy thus remains a timely and relevant discourse for today's educators. Strong leaders are also a necessary resource in these contentious times.

Many women are transformational leaders who work for social justice, but their stories and struggles are also largely absent from the formal conversation on educational leadership in K–12 schools today; this volume seeks to rectify this by dealing specifically with women's unique experiences as leaders in education, for they have much to bring to the conversation. For example, if feminism is defined as the eradication of sexism (hooks, 2000) and other forms of oppression, then feminist leadership is necessary in education. It is not only necessary to add nonhegemonic stories to the conversation about education and leadership but also to problematize their omission and advocate for the general inclusion of diverse voices. The male as human universal is still the paradigm in the field, with texts on leadership often delegating a single chapter to gender or other nondominant narratives. These textual omissions are metaphors for the absences of women and other minorities from proportional representation in positions of leadership.

Because women traditionally hold less power, they are thought to be less deserving of positions with high status where power may be achieved (Miner-Rubino & Cortina, 2004). Belenky, Clinchy, Goldberger, and Tarule (1997/1986) argue that women find it more difficult than men to not only assert authority but also to consider themselves authorities in their fields. This is certainly true in the field of education. Although an increasing number of women are qualified for positions in educational administration, many are not taking on these roles. It is more difficult for them to be taken seriously; their goals may not be supported because they run counter to the status quo, and their authority may be questioned because of their gender. In fact, they may not even seriously consider themselves capable leaders, and instead are pushed into leadership roles. To complicate these issues, some current and aspiring women leaders do not see these challenges as systemic. "I find the antifeminist attitudes of some women administrators perplexing. . . . It is perplexing that women who have faced overt bias and discrimination refuse to call it bias and discrimination. Why do some women deny the fact that they have been discriminated against?" (Schmuck, as cited in Gupton & Slick, 1996, p. viii).

Women who deny systemic injustice perpetuate it by blaming the victim: to do so is to distance themselves from other women and thus from themselves. They may not support other women but support those who have reached the levels of success to which they aspire: men. They minimize issues of privilege and discrimination by perpetuating the bootstrap myth. Ignoring inequities based on gender will not eradicate them. Because women administrators still face discrimination, sexual harassment, trivialization, and microaggressions, I have included the stories of women administrators who have had to grapple with these issues but eventually created their own success and personal career fulfillment.

This volume contains chapters written by teachers in the field who practice social justice leadership in the classroom for, as Freire and hooks remind us, the classroom should embody the *practice* of freedom; teachers must create a community of learners where all are on the road to self-actualization. Empowerment is necessary for true learning to occur. However, teachers must be empowered themselves in order to empower others. Therefore, the need for advocacy is stressed throughout many chapters.

Social justice education is not often rewarded. Feminist leaders and social justice advocates are frequently considered "trouble makers" because they challenge the status quo and force people from their comfort zones. As hooks (1994) indicates, " . . . it is painfully clear that biases that upload and maintain white supremacy, imperialism, sexism, and racism have distorted education so that it is no longer about the practice of freedom" (p. 29). Thus, counterhegemonic projects may be resisted. But advocates do not engage in this work out of a desire for accolades; they do this work out of love for their students and for the principles of justice. This work is difficult; it involves risk, and it requires courage.

Many chapters in this volume deal directly with teachers in K–12 classrooms and schools and with the disconnection between teachers in the field and professors in the academy. In an attempt to bridge this gap, I have included work that discusses how higher education interacts with the field of education. Specifically, I have included work by educational leaders who have made the transition to higher education as well as work that situates the challenges women leaders in education have faced in a historical context. I have also included chapters that detail policies and practices within education that disadvantage women and other minorities. I have concluded this volume with a chapter on mentoring because this process is essential in shaping women as future leaders.

Education, if it is to be transformative, must be participatory. Students must be involved in the development of a critical consciousness, question their own beliefs and the existing hegemony, and critique the very nature of education itself. Making these higher-order processes a priority is required for a successful and competitive workforce, but this is not the current trend in education. No Child Left Behind requires low-level multiple-choice assessments that necessitate diverging from higher-order thinking toward scripted curricula, pacing guides, and a standards-based "one size fits all education" (Darling-Hammond, 2010). Freire indicts this banking system of education where students are "passive consumers," as opposed to creators of knowledge. This is hardly the prototype of a free and democratic society, but it characterizes much of our present system. Such educational policies will contribute to the United States continuing to trail other industrialized nations in knowledge and skill.

In order to improve our public schools and prepare our students to compete in a global economy, we must respect what students know, what they can bring to the classroom dialogue, and what they can teach us. We must have the same respect for teachers. Students must feel safe enough to question their education and to insert themselves within the process to be truly active in their own learning. As teachers, we must create this empowering type of classroom environment. However, empowerment comes with a price; the true counterhegemonic project is bound to challenge the established hierarchy and make people, including students, uncomfortable. It is not easy to broach issues of marginalization that may hit close to home with students, to challenge students to think for themselves, and, as teachers and teacher leaders, to advocate for academic freedom. But we have to "respect that pain" as bell hooks suggests; it is difficult to engage in this work. It is painful. It is risky, but required.

—Jennifer L. Martin

References

Belenky, M. F., Clinchy, B. M., Goldberger, N. R., & Tarule, J. M. (1997/ 1986). *Women's ways of knowing: The development of self, voice, and mind*. New York: Basic Books.

Christianakis, C. (2008, fall). Teacher research as a feminist act. *Teacher Education Quarterly*, 99–115.

Darling-Hammond, L. (2010). *The flat world and education: How America's commitment to equity will determine our future*. New York: Teachers College Press.

Freire, P. (1970). *Pedagogy of the oppressed*. New York: Continuum.

Gupton, S. L., & Slick, G. A. (1996). *Highly successful women administrators: The inside stories of how they got there*. Thousand Oaks, CA: Corwin.

hooks, b. (1994). *Teaching to transgress: Education as the practice of freedom*. New York: Routledge.

hooks, b. (2000). *Feminism is for everybody: Passionate politics*. Cambridge, MA: South End Press.

Miner-Rubino, K., & Cortina, L. M. (2004). Working in a context of hostility toward women: Implications for employees' well-being. *Journal of Occupational Health Psychology, 9*(2), 107–22.

1

Toward a Conceptual Model of Feminist Leadership in American Education

Jennifer L. Martin

One of the most difficult tasks for women is overcoming the "imposter syndrome"—the feeling that we aren't good enough, don't have the necessary background, or don't deserve leadership opportunities. We feel like we need one more credential, one more bit of experience, et cetera. Men do not have this problem. They take the job and figure out how to do it later. We need to adopt some of their sense of entitlement to leadership.

—Martha Burk

Men are taught to apologize for their weaknesses, women for their strengths.

—Lois Wyse

Introduction

Feminist pedagogy, feminist leadership, and even *feminism* in general are terms one rarely hears in K–12 education. Perhaps because the word *feminism* itself has become so stigmatized, people are reluctant to broach any subject with which the term is associated. However, feminist practices, which have at their core the eradication of sexism, social justice reform, equity, and collaboration, are crucial to educational leadership today. This chapter, in fact this series, helps to rectify feminism's omission from education.

There are many different conceptions of leadership and what defines a leader, both inside and outside of education. Strodi (1992) defines leadership as "the influence a person asserts upon the behavior of others . . . the quality of a person to motivate people to change individual behavior to cooperative group behavior and to give direction and purpose to the lives of other people" (p. 3). Some find leadership difficult to define, but they "know it when they see it." Wahlstrom and Seashore Louis (2008) note that " . . . teacher, custodian, education assistant, specialist, office support staff—they all seem to know good (and bad) leadership when they experience it. Furthermore, most people can identify particular behaviors of school leaders that they remember as being effective" (p. 459). Some theorists distinguish between leadership and management (Antonakis, Cianciolo, & Sternberg, 2004; English, 2008). Others attempt to conceptualize leadership (Northouse, 2010); and still others provide applications of leadership in practice, pulling ideas from business and applying them to education (Bolman & Deal, 1997). However, in popular texts on leadership used in university schools of education and educational leadership, most do not make mention of women's leadership, how gender plays a large part in people's conceptions of leaders, how authentic leaders appear to their followers (which is often impacted by gender and other uncontrollable characteristics such as race, class, sexuality, etc.), the unique challenges women face as leaders in education, or feminist leadership. What I have learned through my research and practice in educational leadership is that gender constantly matters, as does one's standpoint in general; it informs our points of view and often either enables or inhibits our goal attainment.

In this chapter, I will sort through current views of leadership and discuss the obstacles to women's leadership in order to define and conceptualize feminist leadership in educational theory and practice. A model of feminist leadership or models of leadership that include the perspectives of women in general are lacking in the literature (Chin, 2007a). I have brought together interdisciplinary research on leadership, feminist theory and ethics, the psychology of gender, and social justice education in order to create a model of feminist leadership for educators. This chapter serves two purposes. The first purpose is to change the negative perceptions of feminism that are held by many by clearly defining feminism and theorizing feminist leadership in practice. The second purpose is to provide a call to feminist educators and feminist leaders to voice their ideas about equity and social justice toward a new, more inclusive model of educational leadership in today's schools. In other words, I advocate for and my work represents feminist educational leadership.

There are myriad approaches to researching and understanding leadership stemming from both theory and practice; some of these include the trait school, the behavioral school, leader–member exchange, transactional leadership, and transformational leadership. The trait approach to leadership suggests that there are several psychological traits associated with effective leadership (Korabik & Ayman, 2007). Often, these traits, such as agency and assertiveness, are viewed as exclusively male characteristics or are characteristics that are not valued when exhibited by women. The behavioral school involves studying the behaviors leaders enact and analyzing how leaders treat their followers. Leader–member exchange describes the relationship between leaders and followers and examines the meaning behind such reciprocal relationships.

Transactional leadership involves meting out consequences, incentives, and rewards for productivity or lack thereof. This is a system of bartering for results; ethics and beliefs do not necessarily play a part in this type of leadership. Transformational leaders are leaders who seek to empower others in the implementation of their vision for a school. A transformational leadership model may include transmitting the vision of the leader in order to give direction to and inspire others, communicating high expectations, empowering others, and nurturing the growth of others through nonhierarchical strategies, mutual respect, and trust (Shapiro & Leigh, 2007). It is also defined as "enlightened power" (Coughlin, 2005), because these leaders encourage divergent and diverse perspectives and open dialogue in an attempt to gain insight and results.

Relational-cultural theory accords quite nicely with the transformational leadership model and provides for relational leadership and value for the communal, for mentoring, and for establishing a sense of connection between people. In fact, the most effective style of leadership is transformational leadership, which builds empowerment in a mutual and collaborative context (Eagly, Johannesen-Schmidt, & van Engen, 2003; Eagly, Karau, & Makhijani, 1995; Hopkins, O'Neil, Passarelli, & Bilimoria, 2008). The transformational approach to leadership is the style most practiced by women leaders, particularly feminist women (Chin, 2007a). Thus, it would seem that more women would be moving into the upper echelons of leadership in the corporate, educational, and political realms. But, as of yet, we are not seeing this. Transformational leaders are role models, but women need more role models of their own in order to transition to these high levels of leadership with greater frequency.

The field of educational leadership is predicated on the analysis of these and other varying schools of thought on leadership in order to determine which work best for schools. Often, these schools and theories leave gender entirely out of the discourse. However, gender is relevant to how one is perceived, how one views herself, and the choices one makes in defining her leadership practices. More specifically, often missing from the dialogue are the implications of what leaves certain individuals out of the discussion and why the authenticity of certain leaders is questioned: the latter not because of a lack of education or qualification, but because of factors beyond their control such as gender.

Feminist leaders face the challenges of overcoming the perceptions of others who may view their position as incompatible with their gender or of being perceived as "too political" in their advocacy work within schools or both. Feminist values will not always be endorsed in schools, which contributes to difficulties for feminist leaders. However, feminist leaders must, in spite of their value for collaboration, communicate a "clear-cut exercise of authority. Leaders who are inflexibly collaborative can be poorly prepared to exert directive, autocratic leadership when it is needed" (Eagly, 2007, p. xviii). Feminist leaders must maintain this delicate balance.

Leadership in American education has been quintessentially male throughout its history. When the teaching profession changed from predominantly male to predominantly female, the prestige of the profession dwindled as more men entered the ranks of administration. As Baker indicates, "There's a trend in American history that when women enter a particular activity or profession, men then often think less of that domain. When something becomes feminized, the pay diminishes, the stratification in the work increases, and the status diminishes" (as cited in Wilson, 2007, p. 118). The percentage of female teachers began to increase dramatically in the 1800s; at this time the expectations and duties for the profession changed to accord with societal expectations for women. Likewise, the expectations for male educators shifted as well; men entered the ranks of management and administration. As Newton (2006) states, "By the late 19th century, men, who filled virtually all superintendent's positions, had separated themselves 'socially, intellectually, economically, and politically from the largely feminized profession' " (p. 557). In essence, "Men manage, women teach" (Newton, 2006, p. 557).

This divide continued through the late twentieth century. To exacerbate this stratification, male philosophical paradigms remain present in educational theories and in the embodiment of the American educational leader (i.e., the "great man" paradigm). This traditional "trait" view presumes that leadership is innate, born into a "great man." We still live with the repercussions of this. Male educational leaders historically transitioned from positions as coaches and teachers. Through traditional male gender socialization and sports, men were taught not to show weakness or fear, not to show vulnerability or emotion of any kind; they were socialized to project an aura of confidence. The result is that male leaders may not know what they are doing, but they project confidence regardless; it is a logical extension of patriarchal entitlement. Women, on the other hand, traditionally socialized to admit their insecurities, ask if they need help; they do not tend to hide these feelings. Traditional gender socialization contributes to the perceived greater authenticity of male leaders; male leaders are still often seen as more "natural" leaders whether they are effective or not.

All of the above factors have made it more difficult for women leaders to be taken seriously as principals, central office administrators, and especially as superintendents. Women represent 65 percent of the workforce in education; however, they only make up 14 percent of superintendent positions (Newton, 2006). According to Newton (2006), "By some estimates, men continue to be more than 40 times more likely than women to advance from teaching to the superintendency . . . " (p. 552). Feminist educational theorists have attempted to account for the discrepancies at high levels of leadership: among these theories are pipeline theory, work/family conflict, and deficits theory, which holds that there are formal and informal barriers that prohibit advancement. These include discrimination based on race and sex, homophobia, sexual harassment (and the tolerance of it), a sexist climate, and so forth (Settles, Cortina, Malley, & Stewart, 2006).

Barriers to Women's Leadership: The Labyrinth

Although leadership is still largely considered to be a male trait, we have moved beyond the view that leadership skills are innate. Leadership traits are all acquirable; however, they are more easily acquired by some than by others. Women have more obstacles that prevent them from being taken seriously as leaders and to being viewed as authentic leaders. Women in education who attempt to transition to leadership positions often find it difficult to be seen as authentic leaders. Unfortunately, some women have difficulty viewing themselves as authentic leaders and thus do not seek leadership positions at all (Gupton & Slick, 1996). Teaching is still seen, in large part, as a traditional female job. Historically, women were not considered viable candidates for leadership positions because of their gender or were viewed as less effective in leadership and administration positions because they were judged by male standards. "Traditions are masculine, and women are at risk for seeming unqualified and having others resist their efforts to exert influence" (Eagly, 2007, p. xix). To illustrate, both women and men have shown a preference for male bosses. According to Gupton and Slick (1996):

> Attitudinal studies consistently show a bias against women compared with men for school administrative positions. This bias is found among teachers, school board members, and superintendents. . . . Furthermore, the literature is replete with claims of sex role stereotyping as the major barrier to women seeking entry into or advancement in educational administration. (p. xxix)

It is not just women who are subject to the constraints of gender. Men are also subject to gender role norms. If women exhibit assertive behaviors in their roles as leaders, they may be perceived as "bitchy," whereas men who exhibit the same characteristics in the same situation will be lauded. Likewise, men who act out of their prescribed role, by showing any vulnerability, for example, may be perceived as weak. However, if women leaders behave in ways that are perceived to be traditionally feminine, they may also be perceived as weak. Thus, it is more difficult for women to find the balance between gender role expectations and the characteristics of authentic leaders. Society's dictates for women are still much more rigid, with the expectation that women be more nurturing and selfless. For example, when contemplating what constitutes a hero, my undergraduate students over the years have indicated that men are viewed as heroes for what they give. Women are viewed as heroes for what they give up. This is never something that is analyzed prior to emerging through discussion. Students provide examples such as, "My mother is my hero because she gave up her dream of college to raise six kids," or "LeBron James is my hero because his athletic ability is unprecedented." It is only when I point out the difference in these two examples that students begin to recognize and understand the problem. Clearly, feminist analysis is important in education.

Contrary to popular belief that the gender gap has largely been filled and that the glass ceiling has been shattered, women make up only 16 percent of college and university CEOs, less than 5 percent of public school superintendents, and only 20 percent of principals (Lott, 2007). Women are also underrepresented in union leadership as representatives and stewards, positions that serve as pipelines to higher offices. Minority women are even less represented than white women (Lott, 2007). Women make up the majority of degree recipients in educational leadership; however, most are not funneling through the pipeline to actual positions of leadership in schools. For example, according to the Digest of Education Statistics, in 2007 to 2008, women received 12,142 of the master's degrees awarded in educational leadership and administration and 2,017 of the doctoral degrees awarded, whereas men received 7,007 of the master's degrees awarded in educational leadership and administration and 1,131 of the doctoral degrees awarded (Digest of Education Statistics, 2009). Women are awarded degrees much more frequently than men, yet men are still achieving the majority of the employment positions in school leadership.

One of the reasons for this is that women continue to be judged based upon gender-biased notions of their abilities to juggle home life and career and whether they can "sustain the traditional roles of women (wife, mother) as well as their skill as a school leader" (Williamson & Hudson, 2003, p. 7). Other reasons include traditional notions of gender and leadership of those responsible for hiring decisions, a lack of informal and formal networking opportunities for women, and few women mentors in higher ranks of educational leadership. The current metaphor used to describe these and other barriers to career advancement women face is the "labyrinth" (Eagly & Carli, 2007): the inability to see what obstacles lie in one's path or what barriers exist that prevent one from successfully transitioning to positions of leadership.

Such barriers include entering a culture with hidden norms and practices. Women leaders who attain formal positions of leadership are still faced with entering a traditional male realm, replete with a male organizational culture and male norms that may be completely foreign to them. Williamson and Hudson (2003) found that successful women superintendents were aware of this culture and the expectations placed upon them as women. As Gupton and Slick (1996) previously found, "The problems for women are not the formal, tangible barriers, such as education or certification, but the intangible, informal ones that require an aspirant to be accepted as 'one of us' by those already at the apex of the organization" (p. 1). Although some women go into school leadership positions fully aware of the male culture that still predominates, many do not. Women lack the informal networks that are available to men and often lack formal mentoring by other women who can point out the gender barriers that they may face (Gupton & Slick, 1996). Again, it is not that women do not have the qualifications; in fact, more women are qualified in terms of sheer numbers than their male counterparts for positions of educational leadership. The problem is still one of bias. As Wilson indicates (2007):

> We often find resistance to women's leadership because they are not seen as tough enough, both due to the male-oriented definition of "leader" and the entrenched "cultural ideal" of female: sensitive and warm, self-sacrificing and nurturing, good wife and mother. These assets, while valued in the home, become reasons to marginalize women on the job. (p. 22)

A second invisible barrier explaining women's limited success in leadership positions is biased evaluations. Women's credentials and performances are often not evaluated in an equitable manner; leadership qualities, such as agency and assertiveness, may be viewed less favorably when exhibited by a woman (Eagly, Makhijani, & Klonsky, 1992). Eagly, Makhijani, and Klonsky (1992) found that women leaders were devalued in comparison to male leaders when the leadership was carried out in a stereotypically masculine manner. This devaluation was exacerbated when women leaders occupied positions in male-dominated realms and when male evaluators were used:

> Because placing women in leadership positions upsets the traditional societal gender hierarchy, male subjects might, in a sense, have more

> to lose by approving female leadership because their status vis-à-vis women would decline. Thus, male subjects may be more prone than female subjects to reject female leaders. (p. 7)

This system of evaluation has much to do with male privilege and male instinct, whether conscious or not, to maintain it (Chin, 2007a).

Self-promotion (an agentic quality) tends to be unsuccessful for many aspiring women leaders (Eagly & Karau, 2002). Historically, women have been punished when they "act out" of their prescribed roles; they may experience negative results when exhibiting behaviors outside the dominant sexual script because the expectation is that women be self-effacing. Standpoint theory stresses that women's experiences should be included in the conversation about leadership; although women and men are not essentially different in their styles, they possess very different *lived experiences* based upon the expectations of educational institutions and the gender stereotypes and discrimination within school cultures today. These are the stories that need to be told. Feminist leaders seek to end marginalization and to eradicate sexism, to have the difficult conversations about privilege, about the intersections of ability, class, color, gender, heterosexism, race, and sexuality. Feminist leaders can aid in ending the barriers to women's leadership within schools. According to Pratch and Jacobowitz (1996):

> Whereas the details of female leaders' behaviors may be scrutinized because of their role conflict, male leaders are not ordinarily constrained by the attitudinal bias of their coworkers. Hence, men are freer to carry out leadership in a variety of masculine or feminine styles without encountering negative reactions because their leadership is ordinarily perceived as legitimate. (p. 205)

Women should have the freedom to be who they are: to be self-promoting, to be ambitious.

A third invisible barrier that prevents women from achieving success as school leaders deals with voice and perceived confidence levels. Eagly and Karau (2002) indicate that women tend to prefer female speakers who come across confidently, whereas men prefer tentative female speakers. Women exhibit more tentativeness in speech in general: they tend to ask more tag questions, exhibit more hesitations, space fillers, and qualify their statements with questions such as, "you know?" Or, "does that make sense?" Women are socialized to exhibit a more relational nature and thus are more concerned about making connections in conversations; thus, women are perceived to lack the confidence of men in general when making their voices and opinions heard. Women are interrupted more than men in conversations; this fact impacts both leaders and emergent leaders. Women's lack of societal privilege in comparison to men's has consequences for their speech and communication that affect their style of leadership and their sense of authenticity within leadership roles.

Visibility, to be seen as qualified within the organization, is important for leaders. However, when one is relegated to token status, visibility can be negative: it is to be seen as different, to be viewed as marginal in the eyes of the dominant group culture. One is then subject to the controlling gaze of the majority. This situation becomes even more difficult for those who possess double minority status. "Ethnic minority women leaders are often questioned in subtle and indirect manners that question their competence or assume they got to where they did because of affirmative action, not because they can do the job" (Chin, 2007a, p. 357). However, the same is not true for men who often benefit from token status. According to Simpson and Lewis (2005), " . . . the invisibility that men experience signifies not an absence or a 'real presence' as in the case of women, but a 'strong presence' in that invisibility emanates from the transparency that accompanies the norm" (p. 1263). As such, men are not seen in terms of their gender; likewise, whites are not seen in terms of their race. In fact, the privileges people enjoy because of their maleness or whiteness often are not deconstructed, which allows for them to continue unchecked.

The male gender role and its associated privileges are often taken for granted and not questioned or challenged (Collinson & Hearn, 1994). Feminist analysis is crucial in the dismantling of privilege and in contributing to a more equitable educational environment by and for all, but it is not only gender that concerns feminist leaders. As Suyemoto and Ballou (2007) state, "In creating feminist leadership that embraces the diversity of women, we must resist overemphasizing the ways in which we are similarly oppressed (i.e., gender) and underemphasizing the ways in which we may simultaneously be differently privileged (e.g., race, ethnicity, nationality, social class, sexual orientation, ability, etc.)" (p. 37). The task of feminist leaders is to include all discourses to improve schools, which will benefit everyone—not just women.

Because we still experience inequity in a variety of forms within our schools, feminist leaders are instrumental in dismantling stereotypes and advocating for greater equity within both employee and student populations. Feminist awareness presupposes an ethic of care for disenfranchised groups and an awareness of intersectionality: the interlocking oppressions of ableism, class, gender, race, sexuality, and trans status. Feminist leaders are also experts at recognizing privilege and how it functions to oppress; this is key to creating more equitable school environments.

I have previously discussed some of the dominant discourses of femininity: the expectation is that women be self-effacing, nurturing, and non-aggressive. However, there are additional discourses that prevent women from achieving success in leadership positions. Women are still depicted as sexual objects and therefore simultaneously vulnerable and dangerous (Gordon, Iverson, & Allan, 2010, p. 87). No matter what the dominant discourse, when women fail to fulfill society's expectation of them, they are met with criticism and are labeled as "noncompliant, incompetent, disruptive, and controversial" (Gordon, Iverson, & Allan, 2010, p. 87). If a man is controversial, this will not necessarily be perceived negatively.

These stringent expectations and the resulting criticism for failure to comply are harsher for women leaders, who tend to be more visible (and vulnerable) because they are sparser than male leaders. Thus, it is clear that gender bias still exists; the whole range of human emotions is not available to women: they have less freedom to fall naturally within this range. Rather, their behavior is relegated to specific stereotypes. The same is true for other oppressed groups. People of color are far more limited than are whites to engage in certain behaviors for fear of reprisal; for example, African American women and men are more limited in expressing anger, for they are more likely to be labeled disruptive, overemotional, hysterical, unstable, militant, and even crazy if they do so. As Frye (1983) reminds us:

> One of the most characteristic and ubiquitous features of the world as experienced by oppressed people is the double bind. . . . For example, it is often a requirement upon oppressed people that we smile and be cheerful. If we comply, we signal our docility and our acquiescence

in our situation. . . . On the other hand, anything but the sunniest coun-
tenance exposes us to being perceived as mean, bitter, angry or dangerous. This means, at the least, that we may be found "difficult" or
unpleasant to work with, which is enough to cost one one's livelihood;
at worst, being seen as mean, bitter, angry or dangerous has been
known to result in rape, arrest, beating and murder. (p. 85)

Feminist leaders in education must navigate between two tightropes of
gender bias without a net (which speaks to the inherent dangers of this
proposition): that of the leader and the other of the feminist (the double/
double bind). That is, the tightrope of the feminist leader is such that she
must straddle the line between what is expected of her gender and what
is expected of a leader. For women, these expectations are largely incompatible. Although transformational leadership is inherently feminist,
incorporating a philosophy of empowering others and sharing leadership,
there are negative aspects to this form of leadership. Feminist leaders
who work to build consensus can be seen as weak and unable to make
decisions on their own. Furthermore, feminist leaders must walk the tightrope of equity; advocating for the dismantling of stereotypes, hierarchical
thinking, and systems of privilege; and that of politics, taking care not to
alienate members of the organization who may not share feminist goals
for fear of what they personally will lose. A new metaphor is more useful
in examining these complexities: fire walking. Fire walking has been practiced by a variety of cultures for thousands of years and is performed as an
act of faith or initiation involving walking barefoot over hot coals. This
daring prospect is tantamount to what feminist leaders face. Feminist leadership in schools takes courage and a leap of faith. Perhaps most importantly, feminist leaders must persevere—faith in the ultimate goal will
shepherd them through. Rice (2007) offers helpful advice in dealing with
one of the coals over which feminist leaders must walk, politics:

One does not avoid politics, but uses the political process as a way of
effecting positive social change for equity. To get buy-in from men as
well as women, the feminist leader articulates shared purposes, joint
goals, and respectful disagreement. This is then another aspect of
feminist collaboration and leadership which we might call transformational in that it seeks to transform relationships between men and

women by including men in the vision of a changed society and a syn-
thesis of power that is advantageous to both sexes. (p. 130–131)

In sum, women's paucity at high levels of school leadership deals more
with the perceptions of others and the informal and often invisible barriers
that prevent their acceptance into positions of leadership or derail their
advancement and success in formal leadership positions than with their
desire to lead, their qualifications, or their motivation to succeed. Feminist
leadership is necessary in education to bring these truths to light and to
create more equitable schools. Working with men to advance these causes
will bring them about more readily. Feminists remind us that women are
not a universal category: that there are more differences within the category of women in general than between women and men. This is yet
another issue that feminist leaders can bring to the forefront: women are
not diametrically different from men; rather, they should be assessed on
their individual merits.

Co-Opting Feminist Leadership

In *The Flat World and Education: How America's Commitment to Equity
Will Determine Our Future* (2010), Darling-Hammond argues that if more
resources (such as adequate healthcare, food, and housing) are not allocated to help prepare students to enter the classroom ready to learn, then
the achievement gap will never close. The United States will continue to
lag behind other developed nations in terms of reading and math test
scores and will cease to be a leader in the global economy if we continue
to spend more on incarcerating people than on educating them. Darling-
Hammond argues for a deep commitment to equity, investing in schools
and teachers, and focusing on higher-order thinking and performance
skills. Feminist leaders are necessary in education because they are
already committed to such changes in policy and practice. Feminist leadership for social justice is necessary to improving our schools from within,
to valuing and respecting the diversity of all students, and to meeting their
social, behavioral, academic, physical, and aesthetic needs.

Much research has been conducted since the mid-1970s on women's
ways of knowing and on how women's experiences can contribute to educational leadership, such as the feminist theories of Carol Gilligan, bell hooks,

and Belenky, Clinchy, Goldberger, and Tarule (1986). However, these theories have been co-opted and repackaged, not as feminist theories, but as pared-down and simplified "how-tos" of school improvement and leadership in general. Women's leadership styles are valued but called something else: Peters's "pay attention to employees," Senge's "learning organizations," Collins's "good to great" all stem from the prototype of the "nurturing leader," which without women's contributions would not be possible (Wilson, 2007, p. 112). When women do the work of leadership, whether formally or informally, it is often not seen as leadership, especially if it is done in a style that does not typify what traditional male leadership looks like. Many theorists have taken these ideas to add to their own visions of leadership, often without mention of women's contributions to the field. In fact, most books on leadership do not discuss feminist leadership, even if they discuss women (Lott, 2007).

The main obstacle to feminist leadership in K–12 education is fear. Women may be hesitant to focus on activist leadership to avoid being pigeonholed as feminists. Many people, both inside and outside the academy and those far removed from activist circles, hold misconceptions of feminism; some who understand feminism distance themselves from it in fear that it will alienate others. Several studies on feminist identification suggest that people are hesitant to self-identify as feminists in large part because of the negative connotations associated with the term; people also tend to express feminist ideas without labeling themselves feminists (Henderson-King & Stewart, 1994; Morgan, 1995; Percy & Kremer, 1995; Renzetti, 1987; Rupp, 1988; Stacey, 1987; Weis, 1990). Burn, Aboud, and Moyles (2000) found that although many people may agree with the goals of feminism, they may also avoid self-identification with the term for fear of being associated with the stigmatized label.

As I examined the literature for this book, the question that came to mind was, "how are feminist women leaders different from women leaders?" Marie Wilson of the White House Project argues that if there is a pipeline of women leaders to bring us to critical mass, then women will be able to change the world (Wilson, 2007). However, it is a bit more complicated than that. Not all women leaders are feminist leaders, for being female and feminist are not necessarily the same (Chin, 2007a). Some women fail to see themselves as members of a group who face the historical and present problem of inequitable and oppressive treatment. Not all women support other women, and many are not advocates for causes that would benefit all women in general. Malveaux (2005), in a discussion of female leaders, addresses the queen bee syndrome that pits women against each other:

> The Queen Bee, of course, is the woman who gets some psychic pleasure by being the first and only. She doesn't give other women a break because no one ever gave her one. She did it the hard way, by golly, and everyone else had better do the same. She forgets that some queens, like Marie Antoinette, end up with no one to protect them and their heads on a plate. (p. 55)

These women fail to identify with other women and obtain their sense of power from their identification with males and the traditional male power structure; their negative views of other women are an extension of this. Ultimately, this is a position of powerlessness for women.

There is a wealth of literature concerning women not supporting other women, women who are unable to get along with other women, and women who compete against women to attain the few positions that are open to them (Malveaux, 2005; Wilson, 2007). As Ginn (1989) indicates, "One of the explanations for this phenomenon ... had to do with power. Because a large portion of women have been excluded from the power structure of 'out of home' decision-making, they become anxious that there is not enough power to go around" (as cited in Gupton & Slick, 1996, p. 92). In other words, this phenomenon stems from women's lack of formal power. As Wilson (2007) argues, " 'Women are our own worst enemies,' because sometimes we don't join as we should in the workplace, supporting female leaders and bringing others along. It's a function of powerlessness, the view that there's precious little room at the top and the competition is fierce" (p. 74). The feminist leader, on the other hand, seeks to nurture leadership in other women and to work with others to achieve shared goals; this is true empowerment (Malveaux, 2005).

Defining Feminist Leadership

hooks (2000) defines feminism as, " ... a movement to end sexism, sexist exploitation, and oppression" (p. viii). My view of feminist leaders in education springs from this. Feminist leaders challenge the status quo and thus make life better for women, and, arguably, for men as well—men are also harmed by sexism and limited gender roles. Feminist leaders address the gendered nature of the organization and bias in evaluations, advocate for the dismantling of stereotypes, and provide strategies to advance equity. In general, feminist leaders tend to play the role of facilitator as opposed to one of authority figure within schools; they focus on consensus building and empowering others toward a counterhegemonic project. Feminist leaders examine and are critical of the school, the school system, and how these systems operate in order to make positive change to advance educational equity.

In order to gain additional insight into the philosophy of feminist leadership, I created a weblog with a variety of questions addressing the concerns facing women leaders in education. I posted the call for participants on two educational listservs and I used snowball sampling (Gobo, 2004; Patton, 2002), suggesting that those reading the call also pass it on to interested friends and colleagues. The questions that were most useful to this discussion were as follows:

> Define feminist leadership. What are some examples of feminist leadership? What are the competencies that feminist leaders should have? What sets feminist leadership apart from other forms of leadership? Is a feminist leader inherently more apt to possess the qualities that successful leaders possess?

I received a variety of responses from women working in education, either as leaders or aspiring leaders. This is how they defined feminist leadership:

1. I think feminist leadership is done by anyone who identifies as feminist who leads. This leadership can be done just within her family, in a work setting, or in the public sector. A feminist leader should be sensitive to intersectionality and make a very strong effort to not marginalize those around her.

2. I think feminist leadership is accomplished from the standpoint of being a feminist. It can happen anywhere . . . in the workplace, home, etc. My own experience is that I find myself struggling to create community wherever I am . . . in the classroom, in the college, leading meetings,

etc. This sense of community means everyone has a voice. I am very interested in creating democratic communities whenever I can.

3. Feminist leadership involves questioning the norms of structure and organizations and putting women more at the center versus the margins. Feminist leadership is not limited to women, as all leadership operates on a continuum. What differs in this case is a recognition of more equal power bases and less reliance on hierarchy. Feminist leaders recognize the value of all followers and work to provide nurturing environments for success. I think collaborative leadership is a form of feminist leadership. . . . Feminist leaders are more participatory, generative, and collaborative than hierarchical leadership of the past.

4. Feminist leadership takes on a different approach that derives from a sense of inclusion and teamwork rather than traditional assumptions of leadership that seek to identify an authority figure and guide others. For example, the classroom displaces a powerful teacher-figure by engaging all participants as both teachers and learners in a layering form in order to overcome the dichotomous roles. Feminist leadership also incorporates a social justice perspective in both theory and practice. A feminist leader in my opinion utilizes the position to include others, give voice to those individuals who are often excluded from participation, and to accomplish a task by actively engaging, critically examining, and listening in order to develop discussions and conclusions.

5. Feminist leadership is smart, inclusive, thoughtful. Feminist leaders consider the big picture and the smaller parts that comprise it. They are collaborative. They are courageous, willing to lead in different ways. Strong feminist leaders seek to understand meanings in different ways, using different tools and with a heightened awareness of context, silences, and omissions. . . . I think "successful leadership" has been (traditionally) characterized as autonomous, patriarchal, and hierarchical. Many schools still operate in this way, making genuine feminist contributions/leadership rare, often unwelcome, and largely silenced. In the schools I've worked at, no one has EVER discussed feminism, feminist leadership, or "strayed" outside of the traditional hierarchical norm.

6. [F]eminist leadership [sic] is a woman that is capable of leading in any capacity. This leader should have vision, a personality, be caring,

resilient, and can handle challenges; they fight for a cause and/or for change. Feminist leadership is set aside from others, because these women understand the power of a woman. A successful leader is anyone who is great at what they do *and* they create lasting impacts on the lives of others. I think all feminist leaders (according to my definition of the term) inherently possess these qualities.

7. Often, people interchange the words *leadership* and *management*. Leadership is about motivating others to take action. Thus, feminist leadership is about applying the principles of feminism: celebration, challenging power/privilege, respecting intersectionality, and shared power to one's ability to motivate others toward action. . . . I do not think that someone needs to define themselves as a feminist to be a good leader; however, I do believe that feminist leadership has the capacity to change the way that we see leadership in our country.

8. When I think of feminist leaders, I think of women who fought to create equity for women in the workplace. I know there are feminist leaders in all parts of society, but that is the stereotype that I have. These women fight for change. In general, I think leaders should be able to motivate people to do more than they believe they can do, have integrity and values, and stay focused on achieving their goals. These characteristics should be true for all leaders. Feminist leaders probably have to be more diplomatic than other leaders, so they are not seen as too threatening. If they are seen as too threatening, they turn people off.

Feminist leaders possess a strong commitment to social justice education and practice; their style is transformational. They share power with others in their leadership by bringing stakeholders together to engage in decision making and by utilizing the skills of others within the school. Feminist leaders empower others through collaboration and mentoring. Feminist leaders possess both the knowledge and the courage to break free from traditional notions of schooling and create new alternatives to the traditional top-down structure.

Social justice is a feminist proposition because it inherently requires examining and dismantling the system of privilege that rewards some to the detriment of others. Part and parcel of examining and dismantling systems of privilege, feminist leaders possess a sense of cultural competence that is displayed in their leadership. They seek to eradicate sexism, racism, and other forms of discrimination. They bring "everyone to the table;" they pay attention to the conversations that are happening, those that are not but should be, and to the silences (which also have meaning). Reflection is a critical part of this dialogue.

The eight definitions of feminist leadership listed above provide the necessary pieces that, when combined, truly convey a concise picture of feminist leadership. Feminist leaders must possess a commitment to feminist principles and social justice in general; they must not fear the word *feminism* or being perceived as political and therefore dangerous. All leadership is political. The difference is, more traditional leaders are not viewed as dangerous because they maintain the status quo. Feminist leaders are aware of systemic oppressions of people based on class, race, gender, and sexuality as well as the interlocking oppressions of multiple identities. Feminist leaders work to end all forms of oppression including examining their complicity in the oppression of others via their personal privilege.

There are three precepts that define feminist leadership stemming from the commitment to feminism and social justice: to empower, to challenge, and to collaborate. Feminist leaders *empower* others by practicing a non-hierarchical style and by viewing all persons as members of a community where all are valued for their strengths. *To challenge* the status quo toward building a vision of a more egalitarian school, which can then contribute to a more egalitarian society is another requirement of feminist leadership. However, because such work may be threatening to school personnel who are in positions of privilege, feminist leaders must also be prepared to be challenged (Rice, 2007). Feminist leaders do not stand alone in creating, working, and leading; they incorporate multiple perspectives in building and realizing a vision and *collaborate* with all stakeholders: students, community members, administrators, and teachers. They value this process and maintain it over time through constant dialogue. As Jones, Webb, and Neumann state (2008), "Social justice leadership demands that organizational members consciously attempt to engage in dialogue about a level playing field. The collective group, rather than any individual, determines the vision that is established through the dialogue. The dialogue must remain critical in nature with an ongoing goal of identifying inherent biases and inequities in the community" (p. 13–14). In sum, feminist leadership is the practice and the process of doing social justice work in a collaborative environment.

The requirements of feminist leadership (a commitment to empowerment, a commitment to challenging the status quo, and a commitment to collaboration) can be combined and conceptualized into three major leadership areas: vision, reflection, and advocacy. These three areas are linked to the requirements of feminist leadership through praxis[1] and build upon, interact with, overlap, and influence one another, as I will illustrate.

Vision

A crucial leadership skill is the ability to develop a vision. If a leader does not have a vision in terms of where to take the school, then lacking direction or a specific focus, members may travel in different directions, pulling the organization apart. A successful leader leaves the organization stronger than it was. In order to do this, a leader must know herself and her stakeholders.

A feminist leader's vision must incorporate the goals of inclusion, diversity, and equity. Inclusion requires that the feminist leader involve all stakeholders in the development of the vision and empower all in the service of the vision. A feminist vision for school improvement should celebrate and embrace diversity; this includes hiring a diverse staff and requiring that all curricula and pedagogy are culturally responsive. The feminist vision values equity with the goal of closing the achievement gap, advocates for all students, and protects them from harm, bullying, and harassment.

Empowering others will assist a feminist leader in the service of her vision; to do so, she must share power, work collaboratively, have the ability to pick the right people for the right positions, and nurture talent in others through guidance and mentoring. It is crucial that the feminist leader possess a sense of cultural competence and the ability to constantly compare her standpoint against her vision for the school.

---

[1]Praxis, as defined by hooks (1994) is "action and reflection upon the world in order to change it" (p. 14). I define praxis as the bridging of theory and practice with a goal in mind, one of progress. Praxis is required when using knowledge in the service of others. Praxis is performative; it is a process. It requires taking action.

Reflection

Reflection is a requirement for a feminist leader; examining her stand-point, her position of privilege (or lack thereof), and institutional power dynamics, all impact her leadership. She must be aware of who her stakeholders are, what the needs and strengths of stakeholders are, and how these needs are being met and these strengths utilized by the school. A feminist leader must also reflect on the status quo of the school, the privileged, and how to create a nonhierarchical, egalitarian environment. She must be aware of the "bootstrap myth," how the perpetuation of this does not help anyone gain empowerment; she must communicate these facts to staff and advocate for nonmajority and at-risk populations in the school to ensure that staff believe all children can achieve no matter where they come from, what they look like, or how they behave.

Feminism is about empowering everyone, including men. Feminists are aware that traditional stereotypes are limiting and damaging to men as well as to women. Feminist leaders are aware that power over others is dangerous not only to the individual but also to the group, for it omits valuable perspectives from the dialogue. This is why it is so important to involve all stakeholders in decision making. According to Shapiro and Leigh (2007):

> Culturally competent women leaders must learn to understand these workings of power by becoming self-reflective about our own histories of internalized oppression, and the ways these vulnerabilities can be exploited by others. However, knowing ourselves, and appreciating our vulnerabilities to cultural messages of our lower value as women or members of a non-dominant group, is only a first step in acting as leaders in ways that are safe and effective in promoting change. (p. 96–97)

It will take more time to gather all information when making shared decisions. Staff and stakeholders will likely be more invested in decisions because of this process. Gaining community involvement can be tricky, but feminist leaders make this a priority. It is imperative to have such involvement and support when working in a school. This can be broached by building trust through respecting and valuing all cultures. According to Lott (2007), "Feminist leadership in community organizations has been described as encouraging the voices of those who are vulnerable and promoting skills needed to effectively question authority and end social injustice" (p. 27).

Advocacy

Advocacy involves speaking out in order to create systemic change and is another integral aspect of feminist leadership. Feminist educational leaders advocate for all stakeholders: for students and parents, staff, and community members. They also strive for the creation and implementation of fair and equitable policies and empower other leaders, teachers, and students to do the same. Feminist leaders are allies; through them social justice can become institutionalized within schools. There are current school practices that most people do not even think about, let alone critique, that perpetuate dominant gender discourses that are harmful for both women and men. For example, many schools have "sunshine committees," which are groups within schools that handle the party planning and other recognitions such as birthdays, holiday celebrations, and other non-work-related functions. These volunteer duties primary fall on women, whether it be secretaries, paraprofessionals, or teachers. These committees are a throwback to a time when secretaries would shop for gifts for their bosses' wives, facilitate staff recognitions, and provide setup and cleanup for events. The expectation is that women will do this work for free in addition to their other paid duties. Often, women hesitate to decline their "duty" for such work because they will then be seen as acting outside of the dominant discourse of femininity and thus as difficult, noncompliant, and even militant. Women also complete these duties because they do not believe they will be completed otherwise. When feminist leadership is present in a school, such division by sex is acknowledged, problematized, and dismantled; additional work is rewarded, not expected.

Part of feminist advocacy should involve dismantling systems of privilege such as the sunshine committee and inequitable treatment of certain groups of students, for example, practicing informal discipline policies where popular or more academically inclined students are given more lenient consequences for behavior infractions, or recognizing that the student suspension rate is disproportionately high for students of color.

Dismantling privilege involves limiting the privilege of some for the benefit of the whole. As Suyemoto and Ballou (2007) state:

> Those of us with relatively more privilege than others will need to limit some of our privilege in order to build coalitions and allies and enable all coactors to feel connected to the process. The privilege of taking space to speak, for example, may need to be limited in order to actively make space for others whose experiences don't afford them the privilege to "take" space without invitation. (p. 51)

Listening to and valuing diverse voices and absences in voice is a necessity in recognizing where a school needs to change and where inequitable environments exist. Incorporating nondominant discourses into policy is a requirement in the development of more equitable school environments.

Discursive practice within the organization tends to privilege certain terms and forms and people's access to them; thus, there are many important issues within schools that are evaded. There is silence around issues of sexuality, pregnancy, and sexual harassment (Simpson & Lewis, 2005). Sexual harassment, for example, is seen primarily as a "woman's problem." A sexist environment decreases levels of felt influence, job satisfaction, and productivity; tolerance for sexual harassment is a better predictor for job satisfaction and psychological health than personal experiences with the phenomenon (Fitzgerald, Drasgow, & Magley, 1999; Settles, Cortina, Malley, & Stewart, 2006). These issues affect everyone in some way. Moreover, the dialogue of the school reinforces the status quo, often excluding those possessing token or minority status, " . . . privileged discursive regimes are based largely on hegemonic understandings of masculinity and suppress or silence ideologies of femininity" (Simpson & Lewis, 2005, p. 1262). The issue is that women's discourse, women's issues, are seen to only affect women. Feminist leaders have been instrumental in advancing dialogue and defining women's rights issues as human rights issues that affect the organization as a whole. Feminist leadership is necessary to continue this and various other dialogues and to bring them to the educational forefront: through the law, through policy, through consciousness raising.

Other areas in need of advocacy are issues of parenting for students, teachers, and leaders, both in terms of child bearing and child rearing. According to Chin (2007a), "Female managers experienced 'emotional stress,' primarily because of the pressure to meet expectations of being responsible and caring for people both inside and outside of their home. In contrast, male managers tended to focus on themselves and regard other things as beyond their control or responsibility" (p. 356). I argue that all female employees feel this sense of stress, not just leaders, and these are areas that can be addressed by feminist leadership. Women's time spent away from career on child rearing and other family commitments is often perceived as representing a lesser commitment to their careers (Chin, 2007a). Feminist leaders work to change these ideas and to dismantle stereotypes of women as the sole, or primary, caretakers in the family and to advocate for childcare within educational institutions; they must also advocate for sexual harassment awareness and prevention and the inclusion of the LGBTQ community in policies to prevent harassment both among the employee and student populations.

Feminist leaders are, first and foremost, educators. Thus, educational advocacy in the areas listed above is their first priority. Children cannot learn and adults cannot work successfully when an environment is unsafe. A major priority of the feminist leader is the establishment of a healthy school culture through the education of students, the training of staff, and the creation of inclusive policies. For example, antidiscrimination policies must enumerate protected categories such as race, ethnicity, religion, ability, real or perceived sexual orientation, real or perceived gender identity, and trans status to truly protect all students and employees; they should also include an antiretaliation statement. These policies should be written in student-friendly terminology and consequences should be posted. Violations of such policies should be clearly detailed and publicized. Leaders should designate at least one staff member to whom students can report incidents of harassment and gain information about the issue, including details of their legal rights and the resources that are available to them. Title IX of the 1972 Civil Rights Act protects students from sex discrimination in federally funded educational institutions; gendered harassment based on sex, sexual orientation, and gender identity (real or perceived) falls under the umbrella of sex discrimination. Most states have antibullying laws in place, of which students and parents should be made aware as well.

Feminist leaders advocate for, create, and promote trainings for staff to become educated on these issues, to implement the aforementioned policies, and to promote an open dialogue about ableism, race, class, gender, sexuality (etc.) so that all voices are heard and any problems that are occurring can be addressed. This can be done in staff meetings, but opportunities for employees and students to address concerns anonymously must also be provided; this can be done by conducting anonymous surveys on school climate and culture. Feminist leaders include the entire community of learners: students, teachers, administrative colleagues, community members, and board members in all trainings and surveys when feasible. Finally, feminist leaders encourage and participate in mentoring and institute mentoring programs for teachers and students with the goal of social justice advocacy. Students can be the best advocates for themselves if they are provided a little guidance.

Practice, Teaching, Research

To further complicate the picture of feminist leadership, it is crucial that feminist leaders implement their vision, their reflection, and their advocacy (through praxis) into their daily practice, their teaching, and their research. Feminist leaders practice counterhegemonic projects: they write brave policies that protect *all* students and employees. They do not simply protect the privileged few who benefit from maintaining the status quo. They desire mutuality in student–teacher relationships, work toward equity in the curriculum at all levels, value diversity in their hiring practices, celebrate diversity within the student body, critique stereotypic notions, and provide training for staff to these ends as well.

Feminist leaders question policies and research that promote essentialist notions and those absent a critique of privilege, power, and an analysis of intersectionality. They facilitate open dialogues on issues of race, class, gender, sexuality, and ableism. Feminist leaders also work toward full Title IX compliance within schools, which includes designating a Title IX coordinator at the district level to oversee complaints and to publish contact information so that parents and students know where to go with questions or claims of Title IX violations. Since feminist leaders strive to go beyond the minimum of what the law requires, they may designate a Title IX contact person on site, or a compliance officer. They also train staff on Title IX regulations to prevent the harassment of employees and students.

Practice

Feminist leaders apply their vision, their advocacy, and their reflection, which possess the goals of empowering, challenging, and collaborating, into their day-to-day activities. The second-wave notion "the personal is political" is fitting to feminist leaders in this regard. They live their lives according to these principles. Feminist ethics with the goal of social justice enter into every decision, dialogue, and interaction. Their practice, in terms of their leadership and their interactions with others, is informed by content knowledge of policy, curriculum, pedagogy, and empathy. They stay current with new educational ideas and discourses and insert themselves into these dialogues. They read journals, are aware of current research and theory, and join and participate in professional organizations and professional learning communities. Attending and presenting at conferences is crucial in maintaining the knowledge that is necessary in becoming a true educational leader. Feminist leaders also work to establish and maintain connections within their building and district and make connections on the state, national, and even international level; they network with other leaders and activists in order to keep current and relevant. When leading in meetings and trainings, they practice the principles of inclusion and empowerment by involving all voices in the dialogue in a collaborative manner. Finally, feminist leaders continually evaluate their standpoints and take an inventory of their personal mission and goals against those of the school.

Teaching

Feminist leaders are first and foremost educators, although they may no longer be in the classroom full time. Feminist teaching involves the establishment of relationships; relationships are crucial in developing emancipatory and democratic classrooms: students play active roles in their educations and work with teachers to provide and produce higher-order thinking and culturally relevant instruction. Feminist leaders facilitate the building of relationships between teachers and students. Because they understand that no learning will occur without an ethic of care, they advocate for the teaching of students, not standards. According to Williamson and Hudson (2003):

> ... in schools headed by women, relationships with others are central to all actions. The leaders spend more time with people, communicate more, care more about individual differences, are more concerned with teachers and marginal students, and devote more energy to motivating others. In these schools, teaching and learning is the major focus, perhaps because women tend to know more about and be more personally involved in the teaching/learning process. (p. 6)

Feminist leaders are true educational leaders as opposed to managers. Feminist leaders resist discriminatory practices such as tracking and "dumbing down" the curriculum for certain groups of students. They have high expectations for all and help students meet these by empowering and supporting teachers and providing them with adequate resources. Writing grants to supplement school funding, adding support staff, and creating programs to meet the needs of high-risk students are all priorities for feminist leaders.

Creating interventions to meet the needs of struggling students is a part of the feminist leader's mission. Attending professional development trainings to keep up on pedagogical techniques and new curricula will aid in this endeavor. Feminist leaders are involved in the teaching and learning process in general. They serve as support for teachers and advocate for learning to be democratic and participatory as opposed to autocratic and passive. They communicate the goal of participatory learning to teachers in their buildings and practice it in meetings and trainings.

Research

Feminist leaders conduct research in their own schools, both traditional and action research, on student achievement: on school culture, on levels of sexual, gender, and sexual orientation harassment, on levels of bullying and cyber bullying. They also conduct evaluations on the effectiveness of programs within their schools and study academics and behavior. They share their findings and involve all stakeholders, including community members, in strategies for improvement. This process is a continuous cycle.

Feminist leaders advocate for all teachers to conduct research in their classrooms. This will enable teachers to become more active in the educational process. Teachers are often asked to use materials that they have no part in creating, forced to use educational scripts and pacing guides, and asked to cover content without stopping and reteaching so that all students achieve mastery. They are commonly viewed as objects within educational research and are expected to enlist outside "experts" to inform them of what works best for their students. Teacher research not only empowers teachers but also improves student performance because it is geared to responding to individual student need; thus teacher research can improve teaching practices (Christianakis, 2008). As Bullock argues, " . . . teacher research is revolutionary; it upsets the educational hierarchy, much like feminism upsets the patriarchal hegemony" (as cited in Christianakis, 2008, p. 99).

Feminist leaders approach research from an insider standpoint. People they study are participants as opposed to subjects; they involve participants at every stage of the research process. In this sense, feminist research in education is democratic and participatory. Because the goals of involving teachers in the research process are to advance equity and improve schools from within, this research is also emancipatory. Feminist leaders will advance this agenda by conducting collaborative professional development and supporting professional learning communities where teachers work together to identify problems areas, devise strategies, and eventually create interventions to address the needs of students and schools. This work will contribute to the perception of teachers as experts in the field. For a conceptual model of feminist leadership, please see: http://tinyurl.com/jlmartin.

Conclusions and Recommendations

Feminist leaders working to transform schools can expect to face resistance. Being strong and definitive may be seemingly incompatible with feminism; however, where there is change, there is conflict. Feminist leaders should not shrink in the face of struggle but understand, although at times uncomfortable, this is how change is enacted. It is only through this process that we can improve our schools. As Madden (2005) reminds us, "May a shared vision, a strong sense of the importance of the mission, and faith in the power of collective action give us the energy and determination to persist" (p. 12).

Diverse feminist leaders, both women and men, are needed to improve our schools from within. Feminist leaders can change how we view leadership in general and the field of leadership specifically. Perseverance is necessary in the realization of this challenging mission and in achieving success and overcoming obstacles (Gupton & Slick, 1996). Feminist leaders must not abandon their vision and its implementation; aspiring feminist leaders must continue to strive for authenticity.

The following are recommendations that may assist aspiring feminist leaders in finding a formal position of leadership and in achieving success in their endeavors (adapted from Gupton & Slick, 1996).

1. Feminist leaders and aspiring leaders believe in women's abilities in general and in their own abilities specifically; they must also believe that they have something to contribute to education.

2. Feminist leaders treat other women well (as opposed to treating them as competitors) so that more women will have the opportunities to lead.

3. Feminist leaders persevere in their endeavors; social change is not for the weak willed.

4. Feminist leaders and aspiring feminist leaders obtain mentors and mentor other women. This process allows women to learn and understand the hidden rules of the school, which is instrumental to their success. Mentoring and being mentored provide great systems of support when one may feel nothing is changing or when one faces resistance. It always helps to process with another person in the field.

5. Feminist leaders avoid gender stereotypes and traditional notions of gender and share these ideas with others in the school community; this will be beneficial for current and future women leaders, whether feminist or not.

6. Feminist leaders and aspiring feminist leaders plan career goals and provide a timeline for the fulfillment of goals.

7. Feminist leaders and aspiring feminist leaders network with people in the field, both inside and outside of their schools and districts. This can help leaders navigate organizational culture, find new mentors, collaborate, learn of innovative research and techniques, find new

resources, and gain allies. Attending and presenting at state and national conferences can help with these endeavors. Conferences are a great vehicle for making professional contacts.

8. Feminist leaders and aspiring feminist leaders create support systems both within and outside of the school community. This is instrumental in dealing effectively with occupational stress and surviving the pitfalls of educational leadership. Friends and family can provide needed support during trying times.

9. Feminist leaders and aspiring feminist leaders are comfortable with navigating the school politically.

10. Feminist leaders and aspiring feminist leaders advocate for gender equity to be taught in teacher education programs, particularly with regard to gender stereotypes, visions of leadership, and compliance with Title IX. For insight into feminist leadership in practice, see Martin's "Teacher Leaders Working for Social Justice: Contributing to the Field" (in this volume).

11. Feminist leaders conduct research in their schools and encourage and support teacher research in classrooms. It is through this research that teachers will become active participants in the production of knowledge. This process will contribute to changing the perception of teachers as technicians to teachers as true experts in the field of education.

Some leaders in education are hesitant to claim their feminism. They feel it will be either detrimental to their careers to do so or that it will alienate others. However, it is the brave pioneers standing up in the face of such conflicts who have facilitated positive educational and social change. I implore the reader to do the same.

References

Antonakis, J., Cianciolo, A. T., & Sternberg, R. J. (Eds.). (2004). *The nature of leadership*. Thousand Oaks, CA: Sage.

Belenky, M. F., Clinchy, B. M., Goldberger, N. R., & Tarule, J. M. (1986). *Women's ways of knowing: The development of self, voice, and mind*. New York: Basic Books.

Bolman, L. G., & Deal, T. E. (1997). *Reframing organizations: Artistry, choice, and leadership.* (2nd ed.). San Francisco, CA: Jossey-Bass.

Burn, S. M., Aboud, R., & Moyles, C. (2000). The relationship between gender social identity and support for feminism. *Sex Roles, 42*(11/12), 1081–1089.

Chin, J. L. (2007a). Conclusion: Transforming leadership with diverse feminist voices. In J. L. Chin, B. Lott, J. K. Rice, & J. Sanchez-Hucles (Eds.), *Women and leadership: Transforming visions and diverse voices* (pp. 355–62). Malden, MA: Blackwell.

Christianakis, C. (2008, fall). Teacher research as a feminist act. *Teacher Education Quarterly*, 99–115.

Collinson, M., & Hearn, J. (1994). Naming men as men: Implications for work, organization and management. *Gender, Work and Organization, 1*(1), 2–22.

Coughlin, L. (2005). Women are transforming leadership. Retrieved July 30, 2010, from http://www.forbes.com/2005/08/03/opinion -leadership-women-cx_lc_0803coughlin.html.

Darling-Hammond, L. (2010). *The flat world and education: How America's commitment to equity will determine our future.* New York: Teachers College Press.

Digest of Education Statistics. (2009, July). *Bachelor's, master's, and doctor's degrees conferred by degree-granting institutions, by sex of student and discipline division: 2007–08.* Retrieved August 13, 2010, from http://nces.ed.gov/programs/digest/d09/tables/dt09_275.asp.

Eagly, A. (2007). Foreword. In J. L. Chin, B. Lott, J. K. Rice, & J. Sanchez-Hucles (Eds.), *Women and leadership: Transforming visions and diverse voices* (pp. xvi–xix). Malden, MA: Blackwell.

Eagly, A., & Carli, L. L. (2007). *Through the labyrinth: The truth about how women become leaders.* Boston: Harvard Business School Press.

Eagly, A. H., Johannesen-Schmidt, M. C., & van Engen, M. L. (2003). Transformational, transactional, and laissez-faire leadership styles: A meta-analysis comparing women and men. *Psychological Bulletin, 129*(4), 569–91.

Eagly, A. H., & Karau, S. J. (2002). Role congruity: Theory of prejudice toward female leaders. *Psychological Review, 109*(3), 573–98.

Eagly, A. H., Karau, S. J., & Makhijani, M. G. (1995). Gender and the effectiveness of leaders: A meta-analysis. *Psychological Bulletin, 117* (1), 125–45.

Eagly, A. H., Makhijani, M. G., & Klonsky, B. G. (1992). Gender and the evaluation of leaders: A meta-analysis. *Psychological Bulletin, 111*(1), 3–22.

English, F. W. (2008). *The art of educational leadership*. Los Angeles, CA: Sage.

Fitzgerald, L. F., Drasgow, F., & Magley, V. J. (1999). Sexual harassment in the armed forces: A test of an integrated model. *Military Psychology, 11*(3), 329–43.

Frye, M. (1983). Oppression. In S. Shaw & J. Lee (Eds.), *Women's voices, feminist visions: Classic and contemporary readings* (pp. 84–86). Boston: McGraw Hill.

Gilligan, C. (1982). *In a different voice: Psychological theory and women's development*. Cambridge: Harvard University Press.

Ginn, L. W. (1989). A quick look at the past, present, and future of women in public school administration. Research in Education (RIE Document Reproduction No. ED 310 498).

Gobo, G. (2004). Sampling, representativeness, and generalizability. In C. Seale, G. Gobo, J. F. Gubrium, & D. Silverman (Eds.), *Qualitative research practice* (pp. 435–56). Thousand Oaks, CA: Sage.

Gordon, S., Iverson, S. V., & Allan, E. J. (2010). The discursive framing of women leaders in higher education. In E. J. Allen, S. V. Iverson, & R. Ropers-Huilman (Eds.), *Reconstructing policy in higher education: Feminist poststructural perspectives* (pp. 81–106). New York: Routledge.

Gupton, S. L., & Slick, G. A. (1996). *Highly successful women administrators: The inside stories of how they got there*. Thousand Oaks, CA: Corwin.

Henderson-King, D. H., & Stewart, A. J. (1994.) Women or feminists? Assessing women's group consciousness. *Sex Roles, 31*(9/10), 505–16.

hooks, b. (1994). *Teaching to transgress: Education as the practice of freedom.* New York: Routledge.

hooks, b. (2000). *Feminism is for everybody: Passionate politics.* Cambridge, MA: South End Press.

Hopkins, M. M., O'Neil, D. A., Passarelli, A, & Bilimoria, D. (2008). Women's leadership development: Strategic practices for women and organizations. *Consulting Psychology Journal: Practice and Research, 60*(4), 348–65.

Jones, L. C., Webb, P. T., & Neumann, M. (2008). Claiming the contentious: Literacy teachers as leaders of social justice principles and practices. *Issues in Teacher Education, 17*(1), 7–15.

Korabik, K., & Ayman, R. (2007). Gender and leadership in the corporate world: A multiperspective model. In J. L. Chin, B. Lott, J. K. Rice, & J. Sanchez-Hucles (Eds.), *Women and leadership: Transforming visions and diverse voices* (pp. 106–24). Malden, MA: Blackwell.

Lott, B. (2007). Introduction. In J. L. Chin, B. Lott, J. K. Rice, & J. Sanchez-Hucles (Eds.), *Women and leadership: Transforming visions and diverse voices* (pp. 22–34). Malden, MA: Blackwell.

Madden, M. E. (2005). 2004 division 35 presidential address: Gender and leadership in higher education. *Psychology of Women Quarterly, 29*, 3–14.

Malveaux, J. (2005, April 7). Nurturer or queen bee? *Black Issues in Higher Education*, 55.

Morgan, D. (1995). Invisible women: Girls and feminism. In G. Griffin (Ed.), *Feminist activism in the 1990s* (pp. 125–36). London: Taylor and Francis.

Newton, R. M. (2006). Does recruitment message content normalize the superintendency as male? *Educational Administration Quarterly, 42*(4), 551–77.

Northouse, P. G. (2010). *Leadership: Theory and practice* (5th ed.). Los Angeles, CA: Sage.

Patton, M. Q. (2002). *Qualitative research and evaluation methods* (3rd ed.). Newbury Park, CA: Sage.

Percy, C., & Kremer, J. (1995). Feminist identification in a troubled society. *Feminism and Psychology, 5*(2), 201–22.

Pratch, L., & Jacobowitz, J. (1996). Gender. Motivation, and coping in the evaluation of leadership effectiveness. *Consulting Psychology Journal: Practice & Research, 48,* 203–20.

Renzetti, C. M. (1987). New wave or second stage? Attitudes of college women toward feminism. *Sex Roles, 16*(5/6), 265–77.

Rice, J. K. (2007). Introduction. In J. L. Chin, B. Lott, J. K. Rice, & J. Sanchez-Hucles (Eds.), *Women and leadership: Transforming visions and diverse voices* (pp. 127–139). Malden, MA: Blackwell.

Rupp, R. (1988, January–March). Is the legacy of second-wave feminism postfeminism? *Socialist Review,* 52–57.

Settles, I. H., Cortina, L. M., Malley, J., & Stewart, A. J. (2006). The climate for women in academic science: The good, the bad, and the changeable. *Psychology of Women Quarterly, 30,* 47–58.

Shapiro, E. R., & Leigh, J. M. (2007). Toward culturally competent, gender-equitable leadership: Assessing outcomes of women's leadership in diverse contexts. In J. L. Chin, B. Lott, J. K. Rice, & J. Sanchez-Hucles (Eds.), *Women and leadership: Transforming visions and diverse voices* (pp. 88–105). Malden, MA: Blackwell.

Simpson, R., & Lewis, P. (2005). An investigation of silence and a scrutiny of transparency: Re-examining gender in organization literature through the concepts of voice and visibility. *Human Relations, 58*(10), 1253–75.

Stacey, J. (1987). Sexism by a subtler name? Postindustrial conditions and postfeminist consciousness in the Silicon Valley. *Socialist Review, 17*(6), 7–28.

Strodi, P. (1992, March). *A model of teacher leadership.* Paper presented at the Eastern Educational Research Association Annual Meeting, Hilton Head, SC.

Suyemoto, K. L., & Ballou, M. B. (2007). Conducted monotones to coacted harmonies: A feminist (re)conceptualization of leadership addressing race, class, and gender. In J. L. Chin, B. Lott, J. K. Rice, & J. Sanchez-Hucles (Eds.), *Women and leadership: Transforming visions and diverse voices* (pp. 35–54). Malden, MA: Blackwell.

Wahlstrom, K. L., & Seashore Louis, K. (2008). How teachers experience principal leadership: The roles of professional community, trust, efficacy, and shared responsibility. *Educational Administration Quarterly, 44*(4), 458–95.

Weis, L. (1990). *Working class without work: High school students in a deindustrializing economy.* New York: Routledge.

Williamson, R., & Hudson, M. (2003, April). *Walking away: New women school leaders leaving the career track.* Paper presented at the Annual Conference of the American Educational Research Association, Chicago, IL.

Wilson, M. C. (2007). *Closing the leadership gap: Add women and change everything.* New York: Penguin Group.

2

From Rags to the Riches of Radcliffe: A Historical Study of Female Graduate Leaders from Poor and Working-Class Backgrounds

Jennifer O'Connor

Introduction

The purpose of this chapter is to open a lens into the previously uncovered experiences of working-class females who were intellectual leaders in their high schools and were selected to attend the most prestigious women's college in the country, Radcliffe College, between the years 1940 and 1970. These women were raised in poor and uneducated families but succeeded in becoming student leaders on the Ivy League campus and following graduation in their respected professions. These Radcliffe students (otherwise known as Cliffies) reached high levels of educational achievement despite gender and class barriers, and their legacy is as powerful in the twenty-first century as it was fifty years ago, given today's remaining inequity in education. Their story can provide current and future generations of women students from low-income backgrounds a deeper understanding of successful strategies and pathways to upward mobility and leadership feats through education.

A secondary analysis was conducted on an archived study at the Henry A. Murray Center, *The Radcliffe Centennial Survey,* originally conducted by Martina Horner in 1977. The purpose was to pursue my research interest (the relationship between leadership, academic, and professional development among low-income Cliffies) that was distinct from that of the original work, which sought to gather basic demographic data of alumnae. I accomplished this by analyzing a subset of the original data sample from the analytical lens of social class and measured student leadership capacities postgraduation through career achievement. To enrich my interpretations of the quantitative findings, a historiography was conducted at the Radcliffe Institute for Advanced Study and the Schlesinger Library Second; a content analysis of students' and alumnae's personal records including letters, diaries, reminiscences, periodicals, yearbooks, athletic and health reports, and the minute books of clubs and associations, alumni magazines, reunion notes, and college catalogs documenting leadership opportunities, positions, and academic life were also reviewed.

As the field of women in education achieves legitimacy and popularity, new questions need to be asked about the history of gender in America's institutions of knowledge, specifically concerning women's access to higher education and the academic experiences of minority women and their potential to become leaders in our society. This in-depth historical understanding of working-class women will provide insights into how gender, education, and personal background shaped and impeded leadership prospects. This chapter chronicles an important period in the unfinished revolution in higher education equity for women from lower income brackets. To maintain and propel a momentum for equality, it is vital to understand the enduring complexities and challenges for working-class women. By illuminating their struggles and progress, the resulting knowledge will strengthen institutions in taking the next steps toward true equality and demand closer examination of working-class women reaching a new threshold of opportunity in the twenty-first century. Class consciousness and historical awareness can assist campus communities in embracing leadership opportunities for working-class women as undergraduates and alumni in the workforce.

Women have been marginalized in research and practice in general and in historical research of higher education in particular (Woyshner & Kuo Tai, 1997). The experiences of working-class female students in higher education during the middle years of the twentieth century have never been analyzed. Within the last decade, feminist scholars have encouraged further investigation into the history of women in education. The following questions have been raised: What were the educational experiences of marginalized women such as linguistic, cultural, racial, and/or ethnic minorities? In an attempt to begin filling the knowledge gap about working-class students, this study investigates the unexplored conditions that have affected lower-socio-economic women's college experiences and opportunities for leadership during and after their time as students.

In 1997, Harvard College dedicated a gate into the Old Yard to celebrate the twenty-fifth anniversary of housing female students in the dorms. Intended as a symbol of opening, it was also a reminder of women's historical separation at the institution. During the last half-century, female students have raised their aspirations and moved away from marginality and discrimination in the social and academic realms of Crimson life and turned to increasing positions of leadership on campus. Heightened attention has been given to trailblazing women who redefined gender expectations and equity at the College. Harvard's relationship with women has been analyzed from the perspectives of Radcliffe and Harvard students, alumnae, faculty, and administrators. The historical relationship between gender and race at the institutions has further been acknowledged, but to a lesser extent. However, the College has yet to tell the historical story of the relationship between social class and gender. "Womanless history has been a Harvard specialty" (Ulrich, 2004, p. 10); the dismissal of class culture has been a joint project on behalf of both Harvard and Radcliffe. More importantly, this chapter reveals the untold story of how a Radcliffe education led to professional leadership opportunities for graduates.

Historical Context

> Abigail Adams said to her husband John Adams, "If you complain of neglect of education in sons, what shall I say with regard to daughters, who every day experience the want of it."
>
> —Adams, 1776

Higher education, over the last two hundred years, has profoundly influenced American women's lives (Grahm, 1989; Schuster, 1993; Schwager, 1997; Solomon, 1985; Woyshner & Kuo Tai, 1997). While the impact of women's higher education has had revolutionary implications for American society, educated women have still not achieved equal status with men within the sphere of education (Glazer, 2000; Glazer, Benisom, &

Townsend, 1993; hooks, 1994; Martinez Aleman & Renn, 2002; Sadker & Sadker, 1994). The following brief historical overview of women's higher education will present the advancements as well as the remaining oppositions for American women in achieving the promises of equality in America's academies (Glazer, 2000; hooks, 1994).

By the mid-nineteenth century, the expansion of higher education for women in the United States finally emerged (Faragher & Howe, 1998; Faust, 2001; Graham, 1989). Advocacy grew, in large part, because women's education proved advantageous to society. Significantly, women's special roles as mothers of male citizens offered the first powerful rationale for higher education (Solomon, 1985). Similarly, the justification of the function of women as schoolteachers emerged (Solomon, 1985; Weiler, 1997; Woyshner & Kuo Tai, 1995). Thirdly, women gaining political power with the right to vote began to seek opportunities outside the roles of mothers and wives and included themselves under the Jeffersonian principle that every individual should rise according to his/her abilities (Glazer et al., 1993; Schuster, 1993; Schwager, 1995; Solomon, 1985).

In 1837, Oberlin College was the first to admit women, and Mount Holyoke was founded the same year (Faust, 2001; Martinez Aleman & Renn, 2002; Newcomer, 1959; Woody, 1929). The democratization of higher education facilitated by such landmark legislation as the Morrill Acts of 1862 and 1890 vastly increased women's attendance (Newcomer, 1959; Nidiffer, 2002; Solomon, 1985; Woody, 1929). Vassar opened in 1865 as a college exclusively for women; Cornell accepted an endowment for a college for women in 1872; Smith and Wellesley opened for women students in 1875 (Micheletti, 2004; Newcomer, 1959). By 1880, 20,000 women were enrolled in college representing 33 percent of the college population (Harwarth, Maline, & DeBra, 1997; Micheletti, 2004). Between 1890 and 1910, enrollment at women's colleges increased by 348 percent and female matriculation at coeducational colleges increased by 438 percent (Woody, 1929).

By the turn of the twentieth century, coeducation for women had become the norm (Harwarth et al., 1997; Newcomer, 1959; Solomon, 1985; Woody, 1929). The 1920s were a high point for women's education; female students represented 47 percent of the student body in colleges and universities. During this decade, 74 percent of colleges and universities were coeducational and the vast majority of female students attended these institutions

(Lasser, 1987; Martinez Aleman & Renn, 2002; Solomon, 1985). Unlike women graduates of earlier generations, those of the 1920s and 1930s knew that they would either take a job or pursue further study in preparation for professional work (Newcomer, 1959; Solomon, 1985). Despite marriage and a family, these women carried an awareness of expanding options in postwar, postsuffrage America. Even the Depression in the thirties did not completely extinguish younger women's quests for achievement; for a variety of reasons, the more education a woman had, the more she determined to use it in gainful employment and in voluntary services.

However, the gains that women had made as a percentage of the college population in the 1930s were reversed in the following decades. The percentage of women among undergraduates dropped precipitously from 1930 (44%) to 1950 (30%). The 1950s and 1960s represented a historically depressed level of women in higher education. Women represented 41.3 percent of college graduates in 1940, slipping to 23.9 percent in 1950, and remaining at a low of 35.0 percent in 1960 (U.S. Bureau of the Census, 1975). Beginning in the postwar period and continuing into the 1950s, the expansion of scientific and technological fields at the universities throughout the nation brought large numbers of men back for further education (Solomon, 1985). The same period saw college women diverted from their own graduate work for early marriage and jobs, which they took to support husbands in their undergraduate and graduate studies. After such employment, these women turned to life at home and the raising of families, putting aside aspirations of their own professional lives (Harwarth et al., 1997; Howells, 1978).

During this time period, there was a general lack of awareness and assistance for Radcliffe students from lower-socio-economic backgrounds (Radcliffe College, 1944–45). Prior to financial aid and diversity recruitment, admissions partly depended on a student's financial status (Radcliffe College, 1954). Students were selected on achievement and promise with regard to financial need. Many talented young women from low-income families could not compete with their more affluent peers in affording the price of tuition (Radcliffe College, 1954–55). It was considered a student's responsibility to overcome significant financial obstacles if she wanted to attend the College (Radcliffe College, 1955–56). Consequently, many working-class women declined their invitations for admission because they did not believe they could dedicate their full attention to academics while working in full-time jobs (Radcliffe, 1940). This persistence of inequality contributed to the gap between the daughters of different economic backgrounds in matriculating and graduating. Hence, the low percentage of working-class women who did graduate from Radcliffe were leaders during their undergraduate days as many of them held part-time and full-time jobs, maintained academic rigor in their courses, and were involved in extracurricular leadership positions on campus such as class secretary, president of the ethics society, and director of a community service organization. This academic and social training helped them develop their capacity for leadership in their postgraduate careers (Radcliffe College, 1954).

During the 1960s and 1970s, even the most prestigious exclusively male institutions finally began to admit women. According to Busenberg and Smith (1997), women were initially the stepchildren of affirmative action because they were not originally included as a protected class under Title VII of the Civil Rights Act of 1964. Following lobbying by feminists, Title IX of the Educational Amendments Acts of 1972 finally included sex as a discriminatory category, banning sex discrimination in federally funded educational programs whether in athletics or academics (Lasser, 1987; Martinez Aleman & Renn, 2002). In 1974, Congress also passed the Women's Educational Equity Act, which made provisions for the technical and federal monetary support of local efforts to eliminate obstacles for females in every area of education (Harwarth et al., 1997; Micheletti, 2004). Women's share of degrees climbed steadily during the 1970s and 1980s (Karen, 1991), during a period when the fraction of college-age young adults enrolled in school increased slowly but steadily. By 1982, women surpassed men in the number of bachelor's degrees earned. Women have garnered more bachelor's degrees than their male counterparts ever since.

Women in Higher Education Today

One of the striking features of education in the United States today is the predominance of women among college students. In 1999, women received 61 percent of associate's degrees, 56 percent of bachelor's degrees, 57 percent of master's degrees, and 42 percent of the doctoral degrees award (Guido-DiBrito, 2002). Unless a dramatic shift occurs, women in the United States will soon receive more doctorates than U.S. men, making women the number-one recipients of all degrees in U.S. colleges and universities at all educational levels (Guido-DiBrito, 2002).

Some factors that have contributed to the distinctive position of women in higher education in the United States are the decentralized structure of higher education (Jenks & Riesman, 1968), with more than 3,000 public and private institutions, which allowed for the creation of specialized colleges for women. Second, the existence of the social space for the independent political mobilization of women enabled them to create some of the first schools for women. Finally, women successfully exploited the ideology of individual opportunity to justify their pursuit of higher education.

Feminist activism is responsible for much of the expansion in opportunities for women at Radcliffe and Harvard as well as other elite schools (Solomon, 1985; Woody, 1929). From the ongoing organizing activity of the American Association of University Women (AAUW; Levine, 1995) to Betty Friedan's (1963) influential critique of the narrow options available to college-educated women to the passage of equal educational opportunity legislation for women (Stromquist, 1993), women's access to higher education emerged because women successfully demanded a place.

The parity women have achieved in higher education is a recent phenomenon; yet there is still progress to be made (Bashaw et al., 1995; Lasser, 1987; Martinez Aleman & Renn, 2002; Sadker & Sadker, 1994; Weiler, 1997; Woyshner & Kuo Tai, 1997). While women are more likely to attend community colleges, they are less likely to find themselves at the most selective colleges (Nidiffer, 2002). For example, there are several prestige hierarchies that exist within higher education, and within them women are better represented at the lower levels of the hierarchy in schools of education, nursing, and social work (Glazer, 2000; Martinez Aleman & Renn, 2002). Similarly, women hold fewer full professor positions and are underrepresented in all levels of basic science, technology, business, and engineering departments (Glazer et al., 1993; Solomon, 1985).

Women are not equally represented at top-tier institutions. Hearn (1990) and Persell, Catsambis, and Cookson (1992) reported, based on an analysis of data on 1980 high school seniors, that women were disadvantaged in access to elite schools. While women have made progress since 1980, they remain slightly overrepresented in schools with higher acceptance rates, lower faculty/student ratios, lower standardized test scores, and lower fees (Karen, 1991). The small remaining sex gap at top-tier schools is due to two factors: the relative scarcity of women in schools with large engineering programs and the tendency of women to enroll in school part-time—lower-status institutions are more likely to accept part-time students (Monthly Forum on Women in Higher Education, 1995).

Methodology

For the purpose of this study, a secondary analysis was conducted on an archived study at the Radcliffe Institute of Advanced Study's Henry A. Murray Center, *The Radcliffe Centennial Survey,* originally conducted by Matina Horner in 1977. As part of its centennial celebration, Radcliffe College undertook and financially sponsored this comprehensive survey of the life experiences of its alumnae from the classes of 1900 through 1975. The survey included questions about their family background and current family status, occupational and educational histories, and major life activities.

Since historical research relies on existing sources of data typically found in archives, I began my search at the Henry A. Murray Research Archive as a secondary researcher. I had to determine the "fit" between the purpose of my analysis, which was to learn about the relationship between a Cliffie's social class background and her leadership opportunities postgraduate from Radcliffe, and the nature and quality of the original data, which was predominantly to collect demographic data about alumni (Thorne, 1990).

My Secondary Analysis: Data Collection and Analysis

During the thirty-year time period (1940–1970) under investigation for this secondary analysis, 3,354 alumnae participated in the survey. For individual classes, response rates ranged from 29 percent to 76 percent. Seven hundred seven (23.1%) respondents were graduates from the 1940s. At the time of the survey, these women were between the ages of 48 and 57 years and had been out of college for 26 to 37 years. One thousand eighty-nine respondents (32.7%) were graduates from the 1950s. In 1977, when responding to the survey, these women were between the ages of 36 and 47 years and had been out of college for 16 to 27 years. One thousand four hundred seventy-two (44.2%) respondents were graduates from the

1960s. These women were between the ages of 26 and 35 years at the time of the survey and had been out of college for 6 to 17 years.

The sample consists almost entirely of white women and thus a limitation to this study is that social class is not strongly confounded with ethnicity. More than 50 percent of the respondents were first-born children. Graduates increasingly received advanced degrees over the thirty-year period. The number of women who married peaked in the 1950s at 95.3 percent and then dropped in the 1960s to a relative low of 86.1 percent. Similarly, the number of Radcliffe women who became mothers peaked in the 1950s at 88.9 percent and then dropped in the 1960s to a relative low of 65 percent. However, the low marital and motherhood percentages are misleading given that graduates of the 1960s were still single women of traditional marriage age and had yet to reach their peak fertility years by the time of the survey in 1977. Student diversity also increased over the thirty-year period. There was a significant increase in immigrant students, non–Anglo Saxon students, and students whose parents were not born in the United States.

The concept of socio-economic status has been variously defined and measured (Betz & Fitzgerald, 1987). This data set includes two of the most standard social class indicators: fathers' educational level and occupational status (Coleman & Rainwater, 1978; Hollingshead & Redlich, 1958). A combination of these two variables is used to determine students' social class background. Using this information for the purpose of the secondary analysis, women were considered to be working class if their fathers had a high school degree or less. These fathers had occupations such as refrigeration mechanic in an ice cream plant, depot agent on the railroad, campus security officer, laborer, and electrician. Women were considered to be non-working-class if their fathers had a college or advanced degree. These fathers had occupations such as engineer, chemist, professor, dentist, lawyer, and banker. Given that their fathers had been college educated, it can be assumed that this group of women had been exposed to embodied cultural capital in childhood. Their fathers probably had higher incomes, attaining occupational prestige with colleagues with high cultural and social capital.

During the middle decades of the twentieth century, higher education was not necessarily a prerequisite to professional status; thus for the group of women whose fathers attended some college, the social class categorization was determined by prestige level of occupation. Clearly a limitation to this analysis is that the study is constrained by the relatively small percentage of working-class women who attended Radcliffe and by the rudimentary categorizations of social class. Yet even with approximately 8 percent of working-class survey respondents, the analysis provided an important perspective on gender, social class, and career development.

Of the 3,354 women who graduated between the years of 1940 and 1970, 87 did not list enough information to determine social class by neither citing their father's educational level and/or his occupation. Of the remaining women, 3,009 (92.1%) classify as non-working class. Two hundred fifty-eight (7.9%) women classify as working class. During the 1940s, there was a total of 84 (11.4%) working-class students. During the 1950s, there was a total of 89 (8.9%) working-class students. During the 1960s, there was a total of 84 (5.8%) working-class students.

The number of working-class students basically did not change across the three decades even though the population of the student body increased in size. Similar to the demographic trends based on decade of attendance, more than 50 percent of all students were first born. There were also significantly more immigrant students from working-class backgrounds. Women from both class backgrounds were just as likely to marry, partner with upper-class husbands, and become mothers.

To measure leadership opportunities postgraduation in the professions, the Hollingshead and Redlich Occupation Scale (1958) was used to categorize the occupational status and leadership attainment of the study's participants. The scale ranges from the low evaluation of unskilled physical labor toward the more prestigious use of skill, through the creative talents, ideas, and management of individuals. The seven positions on the scale include: (1) executives and proprietors of large concerns and major professionals, (2) managers and propitiators of medium-sized business and lesser professionals, (3) administrators of medium-sized business and lesser professionals, (4) owners of small business, clerical and sales workers, and technicians, (5) skilled workers, (6) semiskilled workers, and (7) unskilled workers.

Since the 1960s, studies have been conducted on women's career orientation (Matthews & Tiedeman, 1964). The early studies suggested that the majority of young women did not plan to work outside the home. Studies in the early 1970s strongly suggested that the majority of young women planned to combine marriage and career, thereby replacing the centrality of marital and motherhood roles in the lives of women (Rand & Miller, 1972; Watley & Kaplan, 1971).

Due to the growing number of young women planning to combine career and marriage and the growing number of women holding leadership positions in society, the homemaking versus career orientation distinction decreased in usefulness as a dependent variable. Rather, it was necessary to describe the nature and degree of career orientation to understand women's career choice behavior. Another major approach to the description of women's career development utilizes the concept of career patterns originally developed by Super (1957) and first used in the study of male career development. A myriad of scales have been developed to extend the theory of women's career orientation based on differing levels of vocational participation and occupational prestige (Betz, 1984; Harmon, 1967; Wolfson, 1976; Zytowski, 1969).

For the purposes of this analysis, the following scale, originally designed by Matina Horner for *The Radcliffe Centennial Survey,* was used to determine the career involvement of participants. Horner created the following scale to measure the graduates' participation in paid and volunteer jobs: 0. No Information, 1. No Work, 2. Part-time volunteers, 3. Full-time volunteers, 4. Part-time paid work, 5. Full-time paid work.

To measure career involvement based on social class, ANOVA was employed. The following statements explain the statistical tests. For graduates from the 1940s, 1950s, and 1960s, ANOVA measured differences in career intensity by social class background.

To measure professional attainment based on social class, a chi-square test was computed for students' age and level of job prestige on the 1958 Hollingshead and Redlich Occupational Scale. The following statements explain the statistical tests. For graduates from the 1940s, 1950s, and 1960s, a chi-square test measured differences in professional status by respondents' years of age: twenties, thirties, forties, and fifties. For graduates from the 1940s, 1950s, 1960s, a chi-square test measured differences in professional status by respondents' social class background.

Findings: Leadership in the Family and Work

Throughout their postcollege lives, women from working-class backgrounds were more likely to have higher involvement in their careers than their peers from non-working-class backgrounds. Although career involvement for women during their twenties and thirties by social class background was not statistically significant by social class background, overall, women from non-working-class backgrounds were less likely to work than their peers from working-class backgrounds.

Career involvement for women in their forties by social class background was statistically significant, F (1, 3261) = 8.501, $p < .05$, (Eta = .003, power = .830). Career involvement for women in their fifties by social class background was statistically significant, F (1, 3264) = 8.494, $p < .05$, (Eta = .003, power = .830). Overall, women from working-class backgrounds volunteered more and worked in the paid labor force more than their non-working-class peers at midlife. They were leaders in their communities and careers. Regardless of social class background, women's career involvement score was highest immediately postgraduation and decreased sequentially by age.

There was significant difference on professional status attainment for women in their twenties by social class background, $X_{(7)}$ = 25.371, $p = .001$. A higher percentage of non-working-class graduates than working-class graduates achieved leadership positions at the top three professional status levels immediately following graduation. As they approached midlife, graduates from working-class backgrounds eventually achieved equal professional heights in comparison to their non-working-class graduates. It may have taken women from working-class backgrounds longer to achieve top leadership professional status, but their long-term dedication reflects their professional motivation and talent.

A statistical analysis was conducted to determine the highest Hollingshead ranking that the graduates from working-class and non-working-class backgrounds ever achieved. Overall, only 8 percent of working-class graduates achieved the top professional status as top professionals in comparison to 21 percent of non-working-class graduates. Sixty-seven percent of working-class graduates achieved the second status level as minor professionals in comparison to 63 percent of non-working-class graduates. Hence, the percentage of women from working-class backgrounds who achieved major professional status was not as high as the percentage from non-working-class women. However, the percentage of women from working-class backgrounds who became minor professionals and administrators was higher than the percentage of non-working-class women.

Working-class women may have actively resisted what has been referred to as some of the gender-based traps of middle-class family life. Women from working-class backgrounds wanting to avoid the kind of domestic subordination they observed in their mothers (who most likely were not college educated, had limited career prospects, and were financially dependent upon their husbands) may have been reluctant to ascribe to the gender ideology demanded by the upper-class Radcliffe culture to become supportive wives, dedicated mothers, and upstanding members of their communities. Hence they were more likely to choose to continue involvement in the work force as opposed to becoming full-time homemakers during their midlife in comparison to their peers from non-working-class backgrounds.

Despite their humble origins, the women from working-class backgrounds apparently succeeded in their efforts to achieve professional success. These women clearly had talent and a drive to move away from their family's social class environment. Their success in doing so is reflected in the fact that at midlife they were indistinguishable (at least in terms of leadership in the professions) from their more privileged sisters. The only significant difference among the women was in their twenties immediately following graduation, when non-working-class women achieved significantly more top positions in the work field.

There were no significant differences in professional status attainment for women from the two social class backgrounds in their thirties, forties, and fifties. Non-working-class women's faster postbachelor start in the work force and attainment of more top-level jobs during their twenties might have resulted from greater economic and social capital/networks and possibly their upper-class habitus (an embodied aspect of cultural capital). In order to level out any advantages that non-working-class women would have had due to cultural capital and family connections, working-class women may have needed to attain advanced degrees. Working-class women would most likely have been in graduate school during their twenties and thus achieved equal professional standing to non-working-class graduates in their thirties.

In following their mothers' paths, these working-class daughters *chose* to continue to work while raising a family despite the lack of financial necessity for such reasons as embodying the self-sufficiency displayed by their mothers. Although their mothers may have been trapped in lower-tier employment, such jobs enabled working-class women to have an identity outside their families. Radcliffe daughters of these working-class women may have been reluctant to be defined solely as wives and mothers in typical upper-class fashion. Having the model of their mothers, working-class Cliffies may have felt fortunate to have both the opportunity for more stimulating work than their mothers *and* their acquired knowledge to resist the trappings of the feminine mystique personified by their wealthy classmates.

Conclusion

Overall, the results of the analyses detail a portrayal celebrating the resilience of Radcliffe women who overcame gender stigmas and class-based obstacles along their educational and professional journeys to become leaders in their communities and careers postgraduation. The midpoint of the twentieth century was a pivotal period of change, resistance, progress, and backlash for American women in higher education (Hartman, 1982; Harvey, 1993; Schuster, 1993; Solomon, 1985). World War II—a watershed event in American history and in particular for American women—offered greater access to higher education and increased employment opportunities and undermined long-standing beliefs about women's and men's distinct gender roles (Hartman, 1982; Harvey, 1993; Solomon, 1985). The contradictions and cultural tensions for Radcliffe women during the postwar years, the domestic 1950s, and the feminist 1960s have largely been told from the perspective of middle-class white sisterhood (Crimson, 1948, 1969; Eisenmann, 1995; Faust, 2001; Harwarth et al., 1997; Levine, 1964). A common thread of Radcliffe's history during this period ignores the deluge of evidence and argument about differences among women in terms of class and that an elite degree could lead to many professional leadership opportunities for low-income women (Harwarth et al., 1997; Howells, 1978).

With the addition of this historical perspective highlighting the generational experiences of working-class women, current higher education practitioners and administrators can examine how much progress has been made in the last half-century to accommodate the particular needs of this student population. Hopefully, this study will trigger such significant questions as when the intersection of structural variables such as social class, gender, and leadership opportunities will be treated with the same recognition on college campuses as other minority classifications.

This work will teach a new generation about a more diverse and contextualized history of educated American women and their leadership development. Working-class Radcliffe students (Cliffies) were path breakers for future generations of lower-socio-economic women at elite institutions. The question remains, as higher education practitioners and administrators, what have we learned from their stories to assist and improve the leadership possibilities for lower-socio-economic women in higher education today as they prepare for the labor force?

References

Bashaw, C. T., Clifford, G. J., Palmieri, P., Perkins, L., Schwager, S., Eisenmann, L., et al. (1995). *Ten years after a classic: Historical research and teaching on women's higher education a decade after Barbara Solomon.* Paper presented at the American Educational Research Association, San Francisco.

Betz, E. (1984). Need fulfillment in the career development of women. *Journal of Vocational Behavior, 24,* 249–64.

Betz, N. E., & Fitzgerald, L. B. (1987). *The career psychology of women.* Orlando: Academic Press.

Busenberg, B., & Smith, D. (1997). Affirmative action and beyond: The woman's perspective. In M. Garcia (ed.) *Affirmative action's testament of hope: Strategies for a new era in higher education* (pp. 149–80). Albany, NY: State University of New York Press.

Coleman, R. P., & Rainwater, L. (1978). *Social standing in America: New dimensions of class.* New York: Basic Books.

Crimson. (1948, Tuesday, April 27). Women will share Radcliffe privileges: Summer school maps plan to lure feminine students. *Harvard Crimson.* Retrieved March 25, 2006, from http://... www.thecrimson.com/ .../1948/4/27/summer-school-maps-plan-to-lure/.

Crimson. (1969, Monday, January 20). Harvard-Radcliffe policy committee report: Coeducation at Harvard. Retrieved March 27, 2006, from http:// www.thecrimson.com/.../1969/.../20/h-rpc-report-coeducation-at -harvard-pbcboeducation/.

Eisenmann, L. (1997). Reconsidering a classic: Assessing the history of women's higher education a dozen years after Barbara Solomon. *Harvard Educational Review, 4*, 689–717.

Faragher, J. M., & Howe, F. (1998). *Women and higher education in American history.* New York: W.W. Norton.

Faust, D. G. (2001). Mingling promiscuously: A history of men and women at Harvard. In L. Ulrich (ed.) *Yards and gates: Gender in Harvard and Radcliffe history* (pp. 317–28). New York: Palgrave Macmillan.

Friedan, B. (1963). *The feminine mystique.* New York: Dell.

Glazer, J. S. (2000). Affirmative action and the status of women in the academy. In B. Ropers-Huilman, B. K. Townsend, & J. Glazer-Raymo (Eds.), *Women in higher education: A feminist perspective* (pp. 170–80). United States of America: ASHE Reader Series.

Glazer, J. S., Benisom, E. M., & Townsend, B. K. (1993). *Women in higher education: A feminist perspective.* Needham Heights, MA: Ginn Press.

Graham, P. A. (1989). Expansion and exclusion: A history of women in American higher education. In L. S. Goodchild & H. S. Weschsler (Eds.), *ASHE reader on the history of higher education* (pp. 413–24). Needham Heights, MA: Simon & Schuster.

Guido-DiBrito, F. (2002). Overview. In A. M. Martinez Aleman & K. A. Renn (Eds.), *Women in higher education: An encyclopedia* (pp. 249–61). Santa Barbara, CA: ABC-CLIO.

Harmon, L. W. (1967). Women's working patterns related to their SVIB housewife and "own" occupational scores. *Journal of Vocational Behavior, 14*, 299–301.

Hartman, S. M. (1982). *The home front and beyond: American women in the 1940s.* New York: Barnard College, Presidents' Report, 1942.

Harvey, B. (1993). *The fifties: A woman's oral history.* New York: HarperCollins.

Harwarth, I., Maline, M., & DeBra, E. (1997). *Women's colleges in the United States: History, issues, and challenges.* Washington, DC: U.S. Government Printing Office.

Hearn, J. C. (Ed.). (1990). *Pathways to attendance at the elite colleges.* Albany, NY: SUNY Press.

Hollingshead, A. B., & Redlich, F. C. (1958). *Social class and mental illness: A community study.* New York: John Wiley & Sons.

hooks, b. (1994). *Teaching to transgress: Education as the practice of freedom.* New York: Routledge.

Howells, D. E. (1978). *A century to celebrate, 1879–1979.* Cambridge, MA: Radcliffe College.

Jenks, C., & Riesman, D. (1968). *The academic revolution.* Chicago: University of Chicago Press.

Karen, D. (1991). The politics of class, race, and gender: Access to higher education in the United States, 1960–1986. *American Journal of Education, 99,* 208–37.

Lasser, C. (1987). *Educating men and women together: Coeducation in a changing world.* Urbana: University of Illinois Press.

Levine, F. (1964, May 9). Coeducation. *Harvard Crimson.* Retreived March 28, 2006, from: http://www.thecrimson.harvard.edu/. . ./1964/ . . ./9/coeducation-pbcboeducation-by-any-other-name/.

Levine, S. (1995). *Degrees of equality: The American Association of University Women and the challenge of twentieth-century feminism.* Philadelphia: Temple University Press.

Martinez Aleman, A., & Renn, K. A. (Eds.). (2002). *Women in higher education: An encyclopedia.* Santa Barbara, CA: ABC-CLIO.

Matthews, E., & Tiedeman, D. V. (1964). Attitudes toward career and marriage and the development of lifestyle in young women. *Journal of Counseling Psychology, 11,* 374–83.

Micheletti, L. M. (2004). Coeducation. In A. Martinez Aleman & K. A. Renn (Eds.), *Women in higher education: An encyclopedia* (pp. 21–25). Santa Barbara, CA: ABC-CLIO.

Monthly Forum on Women in Higher Education. (1995). Enrollment ratios of first-year women students at the nation's highest ranked college and universities. *Monthly Forum for Women in Higher Education, 1*(1), 6–8.

Newcomer, M. (1959). *A century of higher education and American women.* New York: Harper.

Nidiffer, J. (2002). Overview. In A. Martinez Aleman & K. A. Renn (Eds.), *Women in higher education: An encyclopedia* (pp. 3–14). Santa Barbara, California: ABC-CLIO.

Persell, C. H., Catsambis, S., & Cookson, P. W., Jr. (1992). Differential asset conversion: Class and gendered pathways to selective colleges. *Sociology of Education, 62*, 208–25.

Radcliffe College. (1944–45). Scholarships, loans, and financial aid. *Annual Report.* Cambridge, MA: Radcliffe College.

Radcliffe College. (1954). *Scholarships and other financial aid.* Cambridge, MA: Radcliffe College.

Radcliffe College. (1954–55). Scholarships and other financial aid. *Annual Report.* Cambridge, MA: Radcliffe College.

Radcliffe College. (1955–56). Scholarships and other financial aid. *Annual Report.* Cambridge, MA: Radcliffe College.

Radcliffe College. (1940). *Annual Report.* Cambridge, MA: Radcliffe College.

Rand, L. M., & Miller, A. L. (1972). A developmental cross-sectioning of women's career and marriage attitudes and life plans. *Journal of Vocational Behavior, 2*, 317–31.

Sadker, M., & Sadker, D. (1994). *Failing at fairness: How our schools cheat girls.* New York: Simon & Schuster.

Schuster, D. T. (1993). Studying women's lives through time. In K. D. Hulbert & D. T. Schuster (Eds.), *Women's lives through time: Educated American women of the twentieth century* (pp. 32–60). San Francisco: Jossey-Bass.

Solomon, B. M. (1985). *In the company of educated women.* New Haven: Yale University Press.

Stromquist, N. P. (1993). Sex equity legislation in education: The state as promoter of women's rights. *Review of Educational Resources, 63*(4), 379–407.

Super, D. E. (1957). *The psychology of careers.* New York: Harper & Row.

Thorne, S. (1990). Secondary analysis in qualitative research: Issues and implications. In J. M. Morse (Ed.), *Critical issues in qualitative research.* London: Sage.

Ulrich, L. T. (Ed.). (2004). *Yards and gates: Gender in Harvard and Radcliffe history.* New York: Palgrave Macmillan.

U.S. Bureau of the Census. (1975). *Historical statistics of the United States: Colonial times to 1970.* Washington, DC: US Government Printing Office.

Watley, D. J., & Kaplan, R. (1971). Career or marriage? Aspirations and achievements of able and young college women. *Journal of Vocational Behavior, 1*, 29–43.

Weiler, K. (1997). Reflections on writing a history of women teachers. *Harvard Educational Review, 4*(67), 635–57.

Wolfson, K. P. (1976). Career development patterns of college women. *Journal of Counseling Psychology, 23*, 119–25.

Woody, T. (1929). *A history of women's education in the United States.* New York: Science Press.

Woyshner, C. A., & Kuo Tai, B. H. (1997). Symposium: The history of women in education. *Harvard Educational Review, 67*(4), v–vii.

Zytowski, D. G. (1969). Toward a theory of career development of women. *Personnel and Guidance Journal, 47*, 660–64.

3

Shirking the Maternal Shroud: A Call to Arms in Reinscribing Women Compositionists and Their Feminist Classrooms

Rachel Grimshaw

Recently I had the opportunity to work as a T.A. in a course on gender and sexuality in film and literature, and my duties included a weekly meeting with the two instructors and other assistants. At one of these meetings, the subject of the glass ceiling came up. Several female colleagues and myself began to banter about the physical consistency of the infamous ceiling, and while we joked about its morphing construction from one of concrete or steel to one of opaque glassiness, it became clear to me that not one of us, though we differed in age and professional experience— an undergraduate gender studies major, two English graduate students, and a nontenured instructor of gender studies and English—was under the impression that the glass ceiling no longer existed. While the mood at that meeting was lighthearted, the subject of sex and gender discrimination in the workplace is anything but light, and as a female student on the verge of completing my graduate degree, the presence and implications of that glass ceiling are quite daunting. As an individual who one day hopes to teach English inside of academia, I have no way of knowing precisely where I will end up professionally. As a female student who specializes both in literature and composition, however, I can say with some certainty that my academic path, at least initially, will likely lead me to the door of basic-level writing and first-year composition. Because I believe this is where my professional career will begin, and because I am aware that composition has its own unique gendered implications, it has become increasingly important for me not only to understand these disciplinary nuances but also to formulate some sort of response to them ahead of time.

Composition, as a discipline, in many ways has always been a "woman's" field, and in some respects, that is a fortunate set of circumstances for my current position (I will likely find a job), but in many more respects, I feel discouraged by both the historical and current climate of composition studies, its classrooms, and what I fear lies in store for a young, feminist composition teacher: a teacher with strong opinions not only about what constitutes the effective teaching of writing but also of what practices, methods, characteristics, and pedagogical formulations constitute an effective teacher who can be held accountable not only for the writing coming out of her class but also for the social awareness and critical ideas of the students compiling that writing. In order to become the professor I desire and envision, I will undoubtedly have to confront a very prevalent notion widely held by students and academics alike—that the female composition teacher is supposed to be nurturing and maternal—while simultaneously etching out an alternate identity and set of practices that I can not only be proud of but that I can also defend against a potential backlash of student and administration distaste for innovative and boat-rocking ideas and manifestations.

I would first like to portray the current composition climate as I see and understand it in order to establish just exactly what it is I see as problematic and what it is I am already fighting against long before even stepping foot into my first college classroom. Composition has long been and continues to be a gendered discipline, and one reason is the continued trend of individuals defining not only the instruction of writing but also the act itself using gendered terms and along gendered boundaries. Academic writing in almost every other discipline is constructed through observation, analysis, interpretation, fact, data, argument, and so forth, and while composition encourages, elicits, and emphasizes each of these elements— and more—in the instruction of conventions and crafting of persuasion, it is arguably the only discipline that also invites emotion, feeling, and personal response and validates them as methods of expression inside the university. Gail Corning (1997) explains, "Disregarded as a strategy for making knowledge, emotion lurks largely ignored at the bottom of the academic hierarchy, partly at least, because it's gendered female; even the word 'discipline' implies a male domain of rigorous, orderly, rational, and pure mental process" (p. 46). Composition, as an act, therefore, is not only coded female, but as a subject, it is not always validated in the same ways or by the same standards as other disciplines. Moreover, the field is sometimes regarded as an unfortunate but necessary training ground so students may become equipped with the tools necessary for engaging in real academic or more scientific undertakings.

The other and more pressing reason composition remains gendered is the majority of composition teachers are female, and the majority of these females are part-time or non-tenure-track employees. These two seemingly simple and straightforward statistics are problematic in and of themselves because they imply that while women have and find a ready place inside the English department or writing program, they are not privy to the same professionalism or salary as their male counterparts. While I find these hiring practices to be unfair and uncouth, they lie outside the scope of this project. What I am concerned with here, however, are the ways in which women compositionists are regarded inside the university, not because this is more problematic per se, but because these are the very formulations that will directly and negatively impact me once I get my foot inside the door.

In explaining why female composition instructors are in high demand, Eileen E. Schell (1991) claims, "Many administrators and full-time faculty members believe that women make ideal candidates for teaching writing because the same qualities necessary for motherhood—patience, enthusiasm, and the ability to juggle multiple tasks—are qualities that effective writing teachers possess" (p. 79). While collaborative learning, portfolio assessment, writing across the curriculum, and other student-centered approaches have come to be seen by many as ideal classroom practices concerning student writing, one aspect from composition's past has not seemed to lose its prevalence, and it is the main tenet of current composition climate that will be addressed here: the idea and expectation of female composition teacher as mother in the classroom.

Schell refers to this role that is both assumed by students and taken up by female compositionists—sometimes painstakingly and begrudgingly—as an "ethic of care" and explains, "for women teachers caring is not merely a natural instinct or impulse, it is a socially and historically mandated behavior" (p. 78). Part of this social construct and academic pressure comes from administration, but an even larger part comes from students. Schell further claims, "Ethnographic studies and surveys of feminist classrooms demonstrate that students, both male and female, expect their women teachers to act as nurturing mother figures," yet she cautions, "There is often conflict between that expectation and the teacher's need to be taken seriously as a teacher and intellectual" (p. 78). Schell is certainly not alone in witnessing this conflict, however, as can be seen by Robin D. Crabtree and David Alan Sapp (2003) who, in their essay, share their unique experiences in their separate classrooms guided by a shared feminist orientation. In conveying the way her students have seen her over the years, Crabtree writes:

> Only after ten years, with increasing weight, graying hair, and other signs of aging, has this objectification diminished substantially. Of course, I now find that I am increasingly called on as a nurturer and mother figure, a concern my older female colleagues have often noted of their experiences. (p. 136)

Crabtree's options, then, fall right in line with prevalent expectations and assumptions. When she first entered the academy as an instructor, a fresh-faced, female, Ph.D., she was seen as an anomaly—a sexual object that differed from the staunch, white, tenured male instructor—and once she acquired a decade of teaching experience, instead of being taken at face value or being appreciated for her innovative approaches, she was, instead, expected to take her place as the maternal figure.

One issue that is very much at play here is the fact that many of the factors informing student-centered approaches, particularly a collaborative learning environment, are some of the same tenets feeding into feminist pedagogy, which both simultaneously eases tensions and hopelessly complicates them. Susan C. Jarratt (1998) explains, "Composition and feminism, then, currently share to some degree an institutional site, and educational mission, and a conflicted relation to both" (p. 2). Jarratt further claims, "For both feminism and composition, the question of the subject has particular resonance and complexity" (p. 4). Composition aims to have students find their personal identity, form a distinct voice that develops at the same time processes and conventions are learned, and train that voice so that it can speak to and about social issues and concerns. Feminism, in much the same way, seeks to analyze and deconstruct those social conventions and distributions of power in order to separate the "I" from sublimation, domination, structures of power, and systems of hierarchy. While they may appear quite different on the surface, both feminism and composition work to give credence to a voice and subject that might not otherwise be heard, because as Jarratt points out, "Both woman and writing, it seems, are made, not born" (p. 8).

Collaborative learning environments have proven quite effective for student writers in the composition classroom because they allow students the opportunity to be more hands on and responsible for their own success, and I subscribe to their effectiveness. There is one aspect of collaborative settings, however, that lends itself to the maternal categorization of women and is therefore, at least in part, detrimental to the female compositionist. One marked characteristic of most, if not all, collaborative classrooms is a shared sense of authority. Instead of lectures, students form small groups for the sake of discussion, sharing ideas, offering feedback, asking questions, and so forth, and the instructor exists more as a facilitator and a source than the voice of authority. In this type of setting, Schell writes, "cultural feminists deemphasize a model of communication based on argumentation and endorse a rhetoric of mediation, conciliation, and shared authority" (p. 76). When applied to the feminist classroom, Schell further explains, "maternal thinking encourages writing teachers to create a supportive, nonhierarchical environment responsible to students' individual needs and cultural contexts" and "an ethic of care can counteract patriarchal pedagogy's 'emphasis on hierarchy, competition, and control'" (p. 77). For the feminist instructor, this type of approach certainly seems to fit the bill as it allows each student to form and articulate a voice, free from the constraints of hierarchy, patriarchy, or oppression, while simultaneously allowing differences to be not only highlighted but celebrated in a community-inspired setting. This type of feminist approach can also work toward putting students at ease, particularly those belonging to groups that have been traditionally and historically marginalized or silenced.

On the surface, this type of thinking and subsequent classroom approach seemingly supports both a collaborative environment and a feminist ideology, but to the detriment of students and feminist instructor alike, it can also simultaneously work toward supporting the very mechanisms it seeks to undo. While the benefits of these types of practices have already been addressed, it is important to mention that inside these arguments, there does not seem to be any recognition of the potentially negative stigma this approach can create for the women who support and utilize it nor any mention of the tendency toward inequitable hiring practices the implementation of this approach often enables. Christy Desmet (1998) claims, "a refusal to classify writers by gender obscures the operations of power in the writing classroom and the academy in general" (p. 156), and feminist instructors "who unilaterally refuse to play judge in their classrooms therefore may occupy the panopticon unwittingly" (p. 157). To this issue of gender, I would also add formulations of class, ethnicity, race, language, and sexuality to compile the list of identity markers that can, and often do, become problematic in the composition classroom. When these markers are downplayed or ignored in the feminist-driven classroom in order to alleviate tension, hierarchy, or systems of power in an attempt to create a community in spite of diversity, these efforts, while formed from good intentions, can actually leave students feeling marginalized and encouraged to continue denying those aspects of self that do not fit the perceived or actual norm. To complicate the matter, students may come to see the feminist instructor as the perpetuator of the marginalization, and because the university is often still foreign to composition students, in particular, these practices can not only serve to insert the instructor into the watch tower but may even create the very interpretations of societal and collegiate norms feminism strives to fight against and overturn. Gail Stygall (1991) explains, "Liberal ideology in both cases assumes that the classroom is a free, open forum, because the instructor can mediate inequalities by articulating, modeling, and enforcing the rules of respectful, relevant exchange and development of positions," but she also cautions, "in both the composition and feminist versions of collaboration, when the instructor withdraws, hierarchy and inequality may reappear" (p. 253). For this reason, composition instructors, feminist-oriented ones in particular, need to be cognitively and critically aware of our students, our assumptions, and our practices as they relate to the way we think about both the teaching of writing and the identities of the students compiling that writing.

Many basic-level and first-year composition students are new to the university setting, and as such, they have not yet learned the discourse, codes, and proper conduct conducive to academic success. While student-centered approaches such as portfolios—which allow students to avoid the risk of assessment early on—and small-group discussion—which allows students to avoid the risk of large-group criticism and potential embarrassment—can create a low-stakes and comfortable environment for students, when these approaches are combined with a nonauthoritative, noncombative, supportive, praising, available, and doting female instructor, student and teacher roles and expectations can become skewed beyond the point of recognition. Crabtree and Sapp (2003) an instructor who subscribes to and utilizes feminist pedagogy in her classrooms, describes a collaborative course she taught wherein students were encouraged to negotiate their own learning goals, and per their request, she lectured less and allowed them more group time to hash out ideas. At the end of the semester, not only did students resent the fact that they actually had to be assessed (because they had learned not to see her as authoritative) but many wrote on their evaluations that they did not feel like she "taught" the class and wished she had lectured more (Crabtree & Sapp, 2003, p. 138). Crabtree laments:

> Students sometimes write in their evaluations that I hate men, because I challenge gendered language and social structures; that I am too opinionated, because I have and articulate my own opinions; or that I am too intimidating, because I am intelligent and articulate and speak passionately. (Crabtree & Sapp, 2003, p. 138)

Both of these types of student responses come from this shared sense of authority, which may work toward students developing ownership of their writing and of their academic success but certainly seem to have negative repercussions for the female teacher who struggles to gain and keep respect. Along this line, Crabtree cautions, "Women who practice feminist pedagogy, then, run the risk of undermining the very social power we have fought so hard to obtain, and with additional professional consequences" (Crabtree & Sapp, 2003, p. 138). Here we see firsthand some of the ramifications of an ethic of care. Crabtree, in an effort to share classroom authority with her students and in an effort to have them articulate their own needs for academic success, has not only created an environment where her expertise and ability are questioned by students but has also inspired student evaluations that could impede her professional advancement.

By looking at the experiences of Crabtree's male colleague, David Alan Sapp (Crabtree & Sapp, 2003), who shares her feminist approach and pedagogy, we can begin to see, understand, and articulate the gendered professional consequences to which Crabtree refers. Sapp holds many of the same ideals as Crabtree, utilizes many of the same practices as she, and yet, he has had very different experiences with his students. He writes, "Most of my male students, oddly enough, also seem to appreciate the noncompetitive relationship they have with me" (Crabtree & Sapp, 2003, p. 136). He further claims:

> This provides me with the delicate task of making sure that my authoritative position is not just replaced by another male student voice, that space is available for a variety of student voices, and, in the process, that I do not also reassert myself as the ultimate authority. (Crabtree & Sapp, 2003, p. 136)

In spite of his classroom resembling Crabtree's, the result is very different. Sapp states, "I realize that as a male teacher, I have automatic and unquestioned authority, even though, as a self-identified feminist, I attempt to diminish it through classroom rhetoric and practices" (Crabtree & Sapp, 2003, p. 138). What we see, then, is that for the female feminist teacher who strives for collaboration and shared authority, respect dwindles, and for the male feminist teacher with the same ambitions, respect and authority are given automatically, in spite of their undesirability.

I have seen this same sort of categorization along sex and gender lines in my work as a writing tutor at the University Writing Center. For many of the basic-level writers I tutor, English 1000 (Introduction to Composition) is their first college course. Several things become quite clear early on: these students have very little idea of what they are doing, of what is expected of them, but they also have preconceived expectations of instructor performance, and these expectations break down neatly along gendered lines. Students expect their female teachers to be kind, gentle, compassionate, understanding, lenient, and supportive. When teachers act in these ways, all is right in the world of composition. When students' gendered expectations of female instructors are not met, however, these instructors are described or regarded as mean, unsympathetic, unfeeling, uncaring, or possessing a desire to see students fail. Conversely, male teachers are expected to be knowledgeable, strict, authoritative, instructive, and direct. When male teachers fall into these guidelines, they are described or regarded as professional, smart, experienced, knowledgeable, and academic, and these teachers are readily respected, even when they appear harsh or gruff. When a male teacher is kind, gentle, or compassionate, however, that is an added bonus, and students are more likely to approach that teacher, but the respect earned by or given to that male instructor does not fluctuate based on a deviance from the students' gendered expectations.

Student expectations and university hiring practices are particularly problematic for my professional future precisely because my personality and pedagogy posit me as opposite—or in opposition to—what is expected of a female composition instructor. What, then, is at stake for an individual, like myself, who does not see the merit in coddling, but who, instead, desires to push students critically, to awaken activism, to expose them to texts that will make them question their truths and analyze their assumptions, to have them question their identities and the identities they have constructed for others? What do I risk losing by refusing to conform to gendered expectations of who I am, what I believe in, and how I operate in the classroom? What options are available for me and my future classroom when I know that my pedagogy and personality, while similar to those of male colleagues, are irrevocably irreconcilable with the maternal compositionist and gendered student expectations? The remainder of this essay will explore these personal and pertinent questions.

Throughout my years as a student, writing tutor, and teaching assistant, it has become quite clear to me that while I enjoy working with literature on a personal and academic level, I have a genuine passion regarding composition. The ability to express one's ideas clearly and cohesively is absolutely critical in having one's voice heard and one's ideas understood and appreciated, and there is something fundamentally satisfying in knowing one's life work has visible and tangible personal and social impacts. Conversely, there is a particular tragedy that exists in formulating a substantial idea but lacking the tools or ability to articulate that idea to the outside world. Thus, teaching composition necessitates a certain amount of compassion for the writer and passion about the writing. While I do feel that I am a compassionate individual, I do not see how that compassion need be misinterpreted or misconstrued as a maternal instinct nor do I believe that the continuation of this maternal categorization and expectation of women compositionists can be anything other than detrimental to myself, my female contemporaries who will soon be entering the university as instructors, and the writers we teach. In response to those who favor an ethic of care, Schell (1991) concedes, "If a feminist teacher adopts a maternal stance, she may better conform to her students' expectations" but also asks, "what if her pedagogy favors critical challenge and intellectual vigor, not overt encouragement and nurturance?" (p. 78). This question is pertinent to my future as an instructor because I have no desire to cater to students' whims and desires nor do I think it benefits them to be coddled, particularly because this action has no place anywhere else inside the university.

Academia teaches, encourages, and rewards critical thinking, questioning, and responding among its active participants—both by instructors and students—but too often, these skills exist as an honor bestowed upon students at the culmination of their education. In other words, students are not privy to disciplinary nuances or discourse until they have proven their worth through time, labor, and achievement. Although professors can and should be aware of how students are acclimating to university life and its inherent expectations of performance, that awareness need reveal itself through clearly articulated course goals and objectives, guidelines, policies, directions, and assignments. Being more concerned about students' emotional state and comfort level than with their intellectual vigor and academic voice and performance serves only to distance students both from their collegiate peers and from the rest of their academic journey. Because composition teachers often receive students at the very beginning of—or near to—their academic endeavors, it becomes our responsibility to act as the example of and not the exception to the rest of academia. That is not to say that we should favor bad teaching practices or unsound pedagogy but that in spite of our individual ideology, political orientation, or social views, academic integrity and vigor should remain central to teaching practices, regardless of which discipline students are actively pursuing or how long they have been a member of the university. Part of setting an example and encouraging critical vigilance, for me, comes in the form of utilizing a feminist approach inside the composition classroom.

Even when students are not comfortable subscribing to feminism or self-identifying as feminists, once they understand how feminism functions and what it is arguing for and against, many will find favor with or strongly support the ideology that informs the movement. While part of this initial unease and resistance likely stems from unfamiliarity, an even greater amount will stem from preconceived notions of what constitutes feminism, or more pointedly, deep-seeded formulations of the sorts of people who would call themselves feminists. Sharon Bohn Gmelch (1998) states, "In one survey, 71 percent of the more than 350 male and female students at Michigan State University who were asked to define 'feminism' defined it favorably" (p. 3; see Gmelch, 1998 Jackson, Fleury, & Lewandowski, 1996, for complete data). Gmelch further explains, "But when the same students were asked to define a 'feminist,' fewer responses were favorable, and far fewer students were willing to attach the label to themselves" (p. 4). These findings directly correlate with my own experiences both inside and outside of academia. Feminism as a political or sociological standpoint or orientation is often viewed more favorably and forgivably than the actual feminists who subscribe to it. Gmelch contends, "Given widespread stereotypes of feminists as radical 'feminazis' or angry 'male-bashers' and lesbians, it is not terribly surprising that many students do not readily apply the label to themselves" (p. 4). While it is not necessarily surprising, it is certainly unfortunate that so many individuals fear the social reprimand that often accompanies a self-imposed identity as feminist. What is particularly striking is how many women readily and publically subscribe to the ideology and nuances of feminism but how the majority shy away from being associated with or identifying themselves as feminists.

Fortunately for myself and the students who will enter my classroom, the university has a more positive view toward and a more enlightened definition of what constitutes feminism, although that is not to say that misinterpretations and misrepresentations do not occasionally occur. "In academia—the world of higher education and scientific research—feminism refers to scholarship and theoretical perspectives that place gender at the center of analysis and usually seek to explain the persistence of gender inequality" (Gmelch, 1998, p. 8). Feminism inside the university does not merely exist as a theoretical perspective, however, as many individuals who subscribe to this way of thinking about the world also find it necessary to be both socially and politically active in order to question, analyze, and ultimately undo patriarchal and hierarchal oppression.

It becomes important, then, when using this sort of formulation in the composition classroom, not only to define what feminism means to the instructor and academically but also to facilitate a discussion of that definition with students, so they can start with a clean slate and begin to formulate and articulate their own working notions of feminism. Noted feminist scholar bell hooks (2000) offers a simple but effective definition of feminism as "a movement to end sexism, sexist exploitation, and oppression" (p. viii). Put into such simple and straightforward terms, this articulation of feminism readily lends itself to interpretation and incorporation within the classroom.

Here I would like to describe several aspects of my personal feminist pedagogy that I hope will allow me to shirk maternal expectations and develop a student-centered and facilitative classroom that will not require my authority as an instructor to be nonexistent but to be channeled into the development of culturally and socially literate writers and vocalizers of resistance. Composition courses at the university I attend are richly diverse along lines of race, ethnicity, religion, politics, sexuality, class, language, geography, and so forth, and this diversity not only creates a rich pool of potential narratives but also necessitates some maneuvering of personal, private, and often uncomfortable differences in identity and preconceived, misunderstood, and misconstrued notions about those identities. David M. Weed (1997) states, "To rejuvenate the notion of citizenship for post modernity, I think involves arguing for the idea that individuals have a stake in culture and a responsibility to understand its social and political implications" (p. 28). Creating socially, culturally, critically, and academically literate student thinkers and writers is a hefty and complex task, but it is my belief that navigating this sometimes-murky terrain is most effectively accomplished by utilizing feminist theory and pedagogy, but it cannot be a successful endeavor under false pretenses or through polite silences.

College classrooms, which by their very nature are full of diversity, are referred to as "contact zones" by Wendy S. Hesford (1998), and she borrows the term from Mary Louise Pratt, who defines them as "space[s] in which peoples geographically and historically separated come into contact with each other and establish ongoing relations, usually involving conditions of coercion, radical inequality, and intractable conflict" (p. 134). Hesford claims, "When applied to the academy, Pratt's concept of the contact zone challenges images of colleges and universities as stable and unified cultural sites where the principles of cooperation and equality obtain"

(p. 134). University students often see academia as a place of freedom and acceptance in terms of identity, speech, and ideology, and this is an understandable perception since the conservative current often does not ripple the visible surface of university life and operations. One long-standing trend in feminism has more recently become a part of many composition classrooms, and I find it problematic precisely because it uses the same masking features as the university: the viewing of debate as a form of dominance and exertion of power. Susan Jarratt (1991) expounds, "Some feminists vigorously reject argument on the grounds that it is a kind of violence, an instrument specific to patriarchal discourse" and for "some composition teachers, creating a supportive climate in the classroom and validating student experience leads them to avoid conflict" (p. 106).

Oftentimes, this supportive climate is pursued and desired because current composition pedagogy stresses reading and writing as social acts, and to create an environment of shared social interaction is to create a literacy community.

While I do subscribe to the benefits of regarding and approaching reading and writing as social activities, and while I do think student writers will function to their highest potential when active members of a literacy community, I do not believe a genuine community can be constructed when individuals are asked to leave their identities at the door in order to form a tentative and tenuous relationship built upon perceptions of sameness. It is important to mention that although I do not encourage or allow confrontational or oppressive debate in the classroom, I do believe that because composition requires students to draw upon and articulate their personal experiences, and because those experiences often relate to, are informed by, or are complicated because of identity constructs, those constructs need be welcome or visible in the classroom. Laura Gray-Rosendale (1997) asserts, "Attention to how students can challenge and resist the many identities constructed for them as well as how they can exercise their power of response should increasingly become a greater part of the process of writing education" (p. 155). In addition to understanding the identities that have been constructed for them, students also need to begin to understand the identities they have constructed for others.

Identity visibility, then, necessitates students' willingness and ability to see, understand, and empathize with classmates' identities that will sometimes be foreign, intimidating, or even disconcerting, but it is an integral and essential step in becoming socially and culturally literate citizens. Hesford (1998) asserts:

> In an era defined by a plethora of conflicts related to identity; by the blurring of national, cultural, and disciplinary boundaries; and by backlash against reforms that benefit women and men of color (e.g., affirmative action), it seems more pressing than ever to focus on how social differences intersect and are mobilized in campus politics and to examine the consequences of that intersection and that mobilization for particular communities. (p. 133–134)

In forming a genuine community of literacy, it is not only important that students recognize and respect each other's genetic, social, and cultural identity constructs, but it is also imperative that they begin to understand the ways in which these constructs connect to, interact with, and are complicated by each other, particularly when considering how hierarchy and oppression function within society.

One critical text that helped me understand the interconnectedness of identity formulations when I was still new to the world of academia, and one I plan to implement into my composition courses, is a short but concise and critically vigilant piece by Audre Lorde (1999). In this essay, she claims that her identities include being "black, lesbian, feminist, socialist, poet, mother of two including one boy and a member of an interracial couple," and she claims, "I usually find myself part of some group in which the majority defines me as deviant, difficult, inferior or just plain 'wrong' " (p. 1). Lorde is certainly no stranger to the complexity of interconnected identities, but she also understands that in order to form a genuine sense of self, each of her personal identities must be given due attention, and none can be downplayed or silenced in order to please the majority or to earn acceptance in mainstream society. From her "membership" in so many diverse groups, Lorde has come to realize:

> Oppression and the intolerance of difference come in all shapes and sizes and colors and sexualities; and that among those of us who share the goals of liberation and a workable future for our children, there can be no hierarchies of oppression. (p. 1)

Several of the formulations that make up Lorde's identity are the very ones I feel need to be addressed, understood, and validated in the composition classroom as acceptable and belonging inside academia, and these—not surprisingly—are the very same patriarchal and hegemonic formulations feminism seeks to reformulate and rearticulate: gender, sexuality, class, and race. In speaking of the interconnectedness of identity, Dorothy Allison (1994) writes, "What I know for sure is that class, gender, sexual preference, and prejudice—racial, ethnic, and religious—form an intricate lattice that restricts and shapes our lives, and that resistance to hatred is not a simple act" (p. 23). Resistance to outwardly imposed articulations of self is admittedly no easy task, but this refusal to conform or be subservient to systems of domination or power is inherent to a feminist pedagogy, and as such, we cannot be afraid to incorporate it into our classrooms or unwilling to extend an invitation to our students to join the ongoing discussion. We cannot stop there, however, as it is crucial that we also arm students with the tools to dissect and analyze the conversations they are witnessing and to understand the power of language. Corning (1997) eloquently describes language as "an act we wield as forcibly as a club on one another, chiefly to establish certain versions of reality" (p. 48). As we introduce students to new and challenging modes of discourse concerning language and identity, some student writers will undoubtedly be uncomfortable with encountering and reading about, entering into a communal and critical discourse with, and writing academic essays concerning these topics, precisely because for many, they will be uncharted terrain and an unexpected addition to the curriculum.

It becomes our job, then, not only to structure course material and assignments with this acknowledgment in mind but also to possess a willingness to facilitate discussions that recognize and ease tensions about student qualms, fears, and feelings of inadequacy or discomfort. Hesford (1998) posits, "Feminists should develop writing pedagogies that reflect experiences and languages of traditionally oppressed groups and simultaneously bear witness to social constructions of whiteness and to the way such constructions shape reader–writer and student–teacher relations" (p. 148). In spite of—or arguably because of—students' unfamiliarity with or resistance to categories of identity, feminist instructors need be reflective about why these topics are implemented into course curriculum, how they are inherently necessary, and what benefits they offer student writers; and armed with sound feminist ideology and pedagogy, they need to stand resolutely against the potential backlash of dashed gendered expectations. Allison (1994) writes, "Class, race, sexuality, gender—and all the other categories by which we categorize and dismiss each other—need to be excavated from the inside" (p. 35). The time for psychological reward and emotional sustenance alone has passed, and in its place, the next generation of feminist composition instructors must be willing to shirk maternal expectations and seek alternate validation in their ability to awaken and inspire culturally and socially literate excavators: writers capable of discovering, interpreting, and articulating insightful, critical, and genuine meaning from the world surrounding them.

References

Allison, D. (1994). A question of class. *Skin: Talking about sex, class & literature* (pp. 13–36). Ithaca, NY: Firebrand Books.

Corning, G. (1997). Woman[ly] teaching: Gender, pathos, and politics in the writing classroom. In D. Penrod (Ed.), *Miss Grundy doesn't teach here anymore: Popular culture and the composition classroom* (pp. 46–51). Portsmouth, NH: Heinemann.

Crabtree, R. D., & Sapp, D. A. (2003). Theoretical, political, and pedagogical challenges in the feminist classroom: Our struggles to walk the walk. *College Teaching, 51.4,* 131–40. Retrieved February 1, 2010, from the JSTOR database.

Desmet, C. (1998). Equivalent students, equitable classrooms. In S. C. Jarratt & L. Worsham (Eds.), *Feminism and composition studies: In other words* (pp. 153–71). New York: MLA.

Gmelch, S. B. (1998). *Gender on campus: Issues for college women.* Chapel Hill, NC: Rutgers University Press.

Gray-Rosendale, L. (1997). Everyday exigencies: Constructing student identity. In D. Penrod (Ed.), *Miss Grundy doesn't teach here anymore: Popular culture and the composition classroom* (pp. 147–59). Portsmouth, NH: Heinemann.

Hesford, W. S. (1998). "Ye are witnesses": Pedagogy and the politics of identity. In S. C. Jarratt & L. Worsham (Eds.), *Feminism and composition studies: In other words* (pp. 132–52). New York: MLA.

hooks, b. (2000). *Feminism is for everybody: Passionate politics*. Cambridge, MA: South End Press.

Jarratt, S. C. (1991). Feminism and composition: The case for conflict. In P. Harkin & J. Schilb (Eds.), *Contending with words: Composition and rhetoric in a postmodern age* (pp. 105–23). New York: MLA.

Jarratt, S. C. (1998). Introduction: As we were saying. In S. C. Jarratt & L. Worsham (Eds.), *Feminism and composition studies: In other words* (pp. 1–18). New York: MLA.

Lorde, A. (1999). There is no hierarchy of oppression. In E. Brandt (Ed.), *Dangerous liaisons: Blacks, gays, and the struggle for equality* (pp. 306–8). New York: New Press.

Schell, E. E. (1991). The costs of caring: 'Feminism' and contingent women workers in composition studies. In S. C. Jarratt & L. Worsham (Eds.), *Feminism and composition studies: In other words* (pp. 74–93). New York: MLA.

Stygall, G. (1991). Women and language in the collaborative writing classroom. In S. C. Jarratt & L. Worsham (Eds.), *Feminism and composition studies: In other words* (pp. 252–75). New York: MLA.

Weed, D. M. (1997). Meaning is cool: Political engagement and the student writer. In D. Penrod (Ed.), *Miss Grundy doesn't teach here anymore: Popular culture and the composition classroom* (pp. 22–29). Portsmouth, NH: Heinemann.

4

Whose Social Justice Counts? Addressing Issues of Social Justice and Equity in Schools

Christa Boske

What are the forces that shape and constrain women school leaders in promoting issues of social justice and equity in schools? The purpose of this chapter is to build an understanding of the influence of lived realities and strategies (and success stories) that transform school practices and policies toward the elimination of exclusionary practices. This work is based on personal experiences as I moved from residential treatment (i.e., special education, program director, therapist), to a PreK–12 school social worker, to inner-city school leadership positions (i.e., coordinator, director, dean, assistant principal, principal) to a tenure-track university educational leadership faculty member within predominantly white, male, English-speaking, Christian, heterosexual PreK–12 school districts and university preparation programs. This chapter uncovers the influence of cultural dominance, oppression, and silencing in an effort to address oppressive practices in both PreK–12 public schools as well as higher education.

Developing teachers and school leaders as agents of change requires a "moral vision and ethical norms . . . to account for and transform existing forms of dogmatism, oppression, and despair" (Laible, 2000, p. 686). Leading for socially just practices requires those who work in schools to listen to the lived realities of those who are underrepresented. There is a need to *look within*, to heighten awareness, and to deepen empathic responses. The possibilities for systemic school reform become imaginative possibilities when school leaders and teachers are committed to this process (Hilliard, 1991;

Stout, 1986) and internalize the knowledge and skills of reflective practice (Kottkamp, 1990; Osterman & Kottamp, 1993; Schon, 1983). However, creating deeper avenues for critical dialogue and promotion of a more just world are not often reflected in school policies or practices. Questioning oppressive school practices that perpetuate inequity and injustice for marginalized populations is still considered by teachers, school leaders, and university faculty as *questionable*, even *dangerous* (Bogotch, 2002; Boske, 2010a; Grogan, 2002; Marshall & Oliva, 2010). Those who challenge the status quo are sometimes subjected to a steady range of hostile ploys and communications, which Leymann (1990) describes as workplace mobbing. These experiences as well as others shared throughout this study illustrate the intersection of promoting issues of social justice and equity through counternarratives in schools and leadership preparation programs.

This chapter is distinct from the growing body of literature centered on leading for social justice because few descriptions of lived experiences and strategies developed are identified by school leaders, especially females who identify as queer, as vehicles to counter resistance. To sustain social justice and equity practices, school leaders need spaces to create, practice, and share their lived experiences (Boske & McEnery, 2010; Capper et al., 2006). Making a difference in the lives of those who are marginalized begins with a personal commitment—understanding how personal identities influence *how* we navigate through arenas of power (Brown, 2004; Flagg, 1998; Marshall & Gerstyl-Pepin, 2005). Reflecting on these strategies fosters new ways of talking about education, including how to address injustices due to gender, race, class, sexual identity, and language.

Conceptual Framework

Numerous scholars define what is meant by social justice (Blackmore, 2002; Bogotch, 2002; Furman & Shields, 2005; Gewirtz, 1998; Goldfarb & Grinberg, 2002; Marshall & Oliva, 2010; McMahon, 2007). For the purpose of this chapter, I assert social justice is context specific (Furman & Shields, 2005) and connect social justice-oriented work with action (Bogotch, 2002). In this study, leading for social justice and equity is defined as advocating for marginalized populations due to race, class, gender, language, sexual identity, ability (mental and physical), and other historically disenfranchised groups (Boske, 2010a, 2010b). For this chapter, I focus on the resistance or resilience of leading for social justice within public schools and higher education institutions, specifically within school leadership preparation.

Research Methodology

The purpose of this self-study is to gain a deeper understanding of how personal lived experiences as a former closeted lesbian/gay/bisexual/transgender/queer (LGBTQ) PreK–12 school leader and nontenured university faculty member influenced my ways of "doing" social justice and equity work. Reflecting on my personal journey was considered a primary task in deepening my understanding of my work as a school leader and scholar preparing school leaders for social justice and equity work in schools (also see Terrell & Randall, 2009). Although scholars who prepare school leaders encourage reflective practice (see Barnett & O'Mahony, 2006; Gray & Smith, 2007; Ketelle & Mesa, 2006; Scribner et al., 1999; Sergiovanni, 2001; Smith & Piele, 2006), exploring attitudes, childhood experiences, and cultural assumptions is pertinent to deepening empathic responses toward issues of social justice and equity in schools (Brown, 2004; Cross et. al., 1989); however, this method of inquiry is still underexplored and is in need of further investigation (Boske, 2009, 2010b; Lindsey, Robins, & Terrell, 2009).

Self-study is becoming increasingly important regarding the scrutiny between personal beliefs and school practices (Barnes, 1998; Whitehead, 1995). Self-study encourages practitioners to deepen their understanding of school practices (e.g., reflection, action research, teacher research, participant research, and practitioner research; Hamilton & Pinnegar, 1998). The methodology involves an in-depth examination, and in this case, the examination focused on my leadership development (Schein, 1989; Schon, 1983; Wheatley, 1994). The reflective process encourages intentional thoughtful examinations that seek to deepen personal awareness and critical consciousness (see Boske, 2009; Clandinin, 1995; Hamilton, 2002; Lindsey, Robins, & Terrell, 2009; van Halen-Faber, 1997). The self-examination increased my understanding of personal cultural assumptions that impacted my critical consciousness regarding structural and institutional inequities as well as white privilege. My narrative identified significant events that contoured my identity as a school leader and scholar promoting issues of social justice and equity. Examining these issues created spaces to investigate issues of privilege and power as a school leader and scholar committed to social justice oriented work (see Brown, 2004; McLaren & Kincheloe, 2007).

Primary data were drawn from personal journal entries, formal documents, and official documents (test data, letters, and other forms of data) from places of employment. I also considered responses to guiding questions throughout my lived experiences. Secondary data included (a) interactions with supervisors and (b) communication with colleagues regarding roles and responsibilities.

Findings

Two themes emerged from the study, including the use of *centered strategies* as well as *conscious, deliberate, and proactive strategies* to advance social justice and equity work in the face of resistance. Centered strategies include developing skills to look within and creating supportive networks. Conscious, deliberate, and proactive strategies include developing the knowledge, skill set, and willingness to address issues of social justice and equity.

Centered Strategies

The oversimplification of the significance of culture tends to make issues of social justice and equity seems less threatening, less political. When I entered school leadership, the notion of "tolerance" was considered "liberal" and perceived by teachers as "acting on behalf of students." I worked in a historically racially segregated city in which whites lived on the north side of the city while black and Latino/a families tended to live on the south side. Although the city was composed of predominantly black and Latino/a children and families living in poverty, the majority of teachers and department chairs were white, male, English speaking, and middle/upper class. School counselors urged white students to enroll in advanced college preparatory courses while black and Latino/a students were encouraged to attend the local community college to earn a certificate as a nail technician, beautician, firefighter, cook, or auto mechanic. School leaders participated in "contests" to see "who could suspend the most students each month." Black and Latino/a students were "locked out" of their classrooms when the bell rang to ensure "those types of students" would not be afforded the same educational opportunities as students enrolled in advanced-placement courses. At this high school, several white students identified themselves as white supremacists and some as members of the Ku Klux Klan (KKK). They paraded around the school in Nazi attire shouting praises to Adolf Hitler. After presenting the hostility to other school administrators, locker searchers were conducted and letters were found indicating the possibility of harming students of color and "shooting up the school." We also discovered white educators who allegedly encouraged these students to share their frustrations regarding racial tension in class. These beliefs allowed individuals to blame oppressed people for their "failure" in the system as well as for the "ills of society." Achieving critical consciousness was not on their radar. The cultural myth of "pulling yourself up by the bootstraps" resonated with mainstream American popular culture with a message indicating hard work equals school success. Discussions regarding teachers' and school leaders' roles in dismantling structural inequities by interrupting hegemonic school practices embedded throughout the curriculum, pedagogy, and school policies were avoided.

When speaking with white teachers as a school leader and scholar, they noted limited life experiences interacting with culturally diverse groups of people due to race, class, language, immigration status, ability (both mental and physical), and sexual identity. Several white teachers noted working specifically within inner-city schools because they "couldn't find another job anywhere else" or noting "if they could work there, they could work *anywhere*" or "their hope was to work somewhere else and buy their time." Many teachers in *these* schools blamed children and their families for the low achievement scores because "they just don't care about education." One white teacher noted during a formal teacher evaluation, "I don't know what the hell the point is to all of this anyway . . . these kids will only get as far as a mobile home." One black school leader recalled a white teacher, who was now her colleague, calling her a "dumb nigger" when she was a student in the district. Another black school leader in the same school district referred to an alleged closeted lesbian female as "carpet muncher" and "fucking dyke" during meetings concerning student discipline policies. As an assistant principal, I witnessed a middle school principal inform a young black male, who shared experiences being bullied, "If you didn't act like such a faggot and hang around girls, you wouldn't have these problems." Students who openly identified as "gay" were noted as "faggots" and "homos" by teachers, support staff, and school leaders. Resentment toward recent Mexican immigrants was noted by white school personnel who wanted "Mexicans to go back to their own country" and "take down the sign that indicates they are welcome here."

These experiences provided me with the realities of resistance. White colleagues assumed I shared similar values regarding how they understood issues of race, class, and immigration status, because I too, identified as white. Black and Latino/a peers assumed I identified as heterosexual because I "looked straight." If people assumed we shared similar attitudes and beliefs, they continued to share their "real" thoughts, which provided me with insight regarding the realities the children and families faced each day within the school district and larger community. At the end of each conversation, I clarified where I stood on issues of social justice and equity. Most of the conversations ended in silence or with people stating, "I just thought we were on the same page." Clearly, we were not. I realized the ability to move educators toward becoming more culturally proficient and changing the way in which they understood the lived experiences of those who live on the margins would be an uphill battle.

On my first day as a school leader, a white union representative informed me, "You are working with the wrong mentors." Both of my mentors were black (one male and one female), long-standing members of the community and committed to empowering black and Latino youth. I was directed by one of the union representatives to "choose another mentor or pay the consequences," which translated to, "White teachers won't work with you or support your decisions." As a woman, men questioned my ability to "make decisions" because of my desire to "bring people to the table." This was perceived as a "weakness" because, as one white male inquired, "Can't you just make a decision on your own?" I explained that "yes" I could make a decision on my own; however, I must also "live with the consequences" of not affording people an opportunity to engage in democratic methods. The possibility of changing the perceptions of the union leaders or white teachers regarding cultural diversity was daunting at best. The central purpose of my inquiry was to provide spaces for educators and school leaders to move beyond the generic idea of implementing "cultural activities" to deepen their understanding of white privilege and structural inequities. I realized the need to utilize my power and privilege as a white school leader to further develop my reflective skills and create supportive professional and school–community networks in an effort to eliminate oppressive practices. I hoped to cultivate vigorous dialogue and action to overcome the resistance toward greater acceptance and appreciation for culturally diverse groups, especially for students and families who lived on the margins.

What happened? Simply working in culturally diverse school settings was not enough to cultivate openness to diversity. Mere exposure to culturally diverse situations actually reinforced stereotypical thinking for many educators, because they were not provided spaces for deep reflection. The problem stemmed from uncritical adoptions of cultural assumptions that limited how teachers and school leaders understood their identity, institutional inequities, and, for many teachers, their white privilege. The belief that each person controls her own destiny outside of the influence of institutional barriers was the first viewpoint to be challenged. White teachers and school leaders believed students were responsible for "pulling themselves up by their bootstraps" and "they too could make it if they *just* worked a little harder." Such beliefs fostered cultural myths that allowed educators to blame groups of oppressed people for their "failure" rather than "looking within" and acknowledging what role they played in perpetuating hegemonic practices. They failed to understand how the system of failure embedded within school practices and policy disenfranchised children and their families. Many white educators came to the school district without the realization that they were beneficiaries of institutional and social systems. I realized the need to provide educators with safe spaces to consider the impact of personal beliefs and attitudes on their identity and decision-making practices. Before we could envision real change, we needed to look within and examine our generic ideals of cultural diversity and blindness toward the lived realities of oppression.

When I entered academia, I was reminded of the parallels between my work as a school leader and as an assistant professor. I assumed scholars embraced beliefs of addressing issues of social justice and equity; however, I was wrong. What was presented during the interview process as seemingly positive attitudes actually masked a lack of real understanding of cultural issues, privilege, power, entitlement, and structural inequities. Getting a pulse on attitudes toward women and lesbian/gay/bisexual/transgender/queer (LGBTQ) populations was my introduction to the university's culture and climate. I was the only female tenure-track faculty member in the department in more than ten years. As a woman, I was informed by a university supervisor he "didn't know I could actually write." Sexual comments toward female students were made openly by male colleagues as well as identifying women as "less valuable" than their male counterparts.

My university mentor invited me to meet with him off campus to discuss course objectives for the semester. During the meeting, which ended up taking place at a bar, I was informed of my "beautiful eyes" and "hmm . . . mm . . . mm" was shared with me as his eyes moved from my head to my feet. I was asked numerous times about the "meaning" behind the ring on my left hand. My mentor asked who I was dating and for his name. I informed him of *her* name. He excused himself from the table and returned advising me to "never tell anyone what you have told me because you will be fired." Although the university personnel policy protected employees according to their sexual orientation, I was informed of the "conservative nature of the university" and of my potential loss of employment if I told anyone I was a "dyke." I overheard terms such as "faggot" and "dyke" as well as phrases like "that's gay" from colleagues and university students. As a scholar interested in promoting issues of social justice and equity, I was determined to explore nuanced reasons for why and how scholars as well as aspiring school leaders advocate for or resist such issues and how attitudes and practices shift over time.

Beliefs in individualism and meritocracy also constructed a climate and culture that reinforced assumptions regarding how children achieve success in public schools. My colleagues expressed their concerns for long-standing achievement gaps, blaming oppressed people for their academic failure in schools, increased disciplinary actions, and disproportionate rates of children identified as needing special education services. Racial derogatory remarks toward undocumented workers, recent Mexican immigrants, and Spanish-speaking communities were openly shared during formal meetings. Negative comments toward students of color were made regarding their "lack of intelligence" and "inability to pass licensure exams" as well as the need to "change their accents" were also communicated by scholars. The need to deepen critical consciousness was essential to dismantling the oppressive practices demonstrated by scholars and embedded within the structural arrangements of the program.

I recognized the potential to promote greater understanding through my line of inquiry and pedagogy.

A university administrator suggested I "change my line of inquiry to *his* line of inquiry," because he focused on the "hot issues" facing educational leadership. I informed the scholar of the responsibility to interrogate dominant cultural assumptions and eliminate structural inequities that perpetuate oppression. My line of inquiry centered on the intersections of the cognitive and affective domains of school leadership with a particular focus on how school leaders transform their sense of self to lead for social justice. This line of inquiry was organized into three specific areas of interest: (a) the influence of beliefs and attitudes on school practices, (b) pedagogical practices and programmatic structures within preparation programs, and (c) the study and support of school leaders as they address social justice issues within their school communities. I was quickly reminded "nobody cares about this diversity and social justice stuff."

In the next section, I discuss the conscious, deliberate actions taken to address the unjust policies, and practices implemented in U.S. public schools. As a school leader, I spent several months collecting student discipline records (by race, recipient of free/reduced lunch, gender, native language, subject, time of day, discipline concern, and steps taken before writing a discipline referral), student achievement data, delivery of curriculum, and implications of school policy. *Whose* social justice counted? White, middle/upper-class, English-speaking, Christian, heterosexual, and advanced-placement students were the smallest number of students on campus but received the most privileged opportunities within the school. As an assistant professor, I was reminded of the lack of critical awareness and resentment toward children and families who lived on the margins. Developing intercultural relationships, encouraging multicultural experiences, and reinforcing critical reflection throughout the school leadership preparation program was essential to interrupting structural and institutional inequities.

Conscious, Deliberate, and Proactive Strategies

As a school leader and scholar working with educators to promote their critical consciousness and deeper avenues for dialogue and reflection, I became more aware of the challenges associated with the lack of complexity in understanding issues of social justice and equity in schools. As a result, I became more cognizant of conscious, deliberate, and proactive strategies to address the institutional practices that disfavor and disenfranchise marginalized groups. I recognized the need to address the heart of the issues by deepening critical consciousness, envisioning real social change, and interrupting cultural logic that reinforced the systems of inequity that exist in public schools.

As a school leader in PreK–12 schools, I diligently unpacked the question, "*Whose* social justice counts?" I addressed how school leaders, teachers, children, and families understood cultural diversity, social justice, and multiculturalism. Cultural assumptions held by my colleagues as members of the mainstream (i.e., white, middle-class, English-speaking, Christian, heterosexual, able [mental and physical]) afforded me with opportunities to be "included." After colleagues "realized" we did not tend to share similar beliefs or responses to underserved populations, many of my colleagues considered me an "outsider." Creating spaces for vigorous dialogue regarding power relations in schools was identified as "threatening" and "not something we need to discuss here."

I was aware of my racial identity and the need to discuss how I benefited from my power and privilege. As a school leader, I used my lived experiences to create spaces for teachers to openly discuss how they understood culturally responsive practices. I facilitated focus groups during team meetings, distributed anonymous surveys, and conducted face-to-face interviews. I discovered many teachers and school leaders upheld generic ideals for multicultural education and lacked critical awareness regarding structural and institutional barriers. White parents who lived in predominantly black and Latino/a neighborhoods blamed oppressed populations for the school's "failures" and "discipline problems" rather than recognizing the "system of failure" embedded in the district's policies and oppressive practices. One white family approached me and asked, "*Whose* side are you on anyway?" A white student inquired, "Are you sure you're *really* white?"

Confronting situations like this often led to stressful and challenging conversations with school–community members. Whether I was a new organizational member or served the community for several years, I was aware of possible consequences, both positive and negative, for every action taken. Although consequences for addressing the needs of children and families often led to unchartered territory, confronting oppressive hegemonic school practices and taking proactive stances were essential to making systemic change. Once I shared my beliefs regarding issues of social justice and equity, some colleagues attempted to eliminate my efforts to address issues of race and racism in schools. I responded by forming meaningful relationships with colleagues who aligned themselves with similar values and school practices. Once I subjected myself to the possibility of being socially eliminated from the educational organization, those who shared similar beliefs took notice of my actions. We met to discuss how we would form an alliance to interrupt oppressive school practices in an effort to honor students, family members, and the community at large. Allies introduced themselves as "people who believed in what I was doing" or "were trying to do the same things." Each ally worked within schools with extreme caution. They identified their anxiety as "walking on pins and needles" or "waiting for the hammer to fall." Our alliance became the foundation for grassroots movements that encouraged social justice and equity-oriented work.

Collecting both qualitative (e.g., interviews, narratives, and open-ended surveys) and quantitative data (e.g., student achievement scores, disciplinary records, and curricular activities) provided a space for teachers and school leaders to deepen their understanding of the lived realities facing students and their families. The crippling effect of recognizing the presence of discriminatory practices on PreK–12 campuses seemed to paralyze teachers. Some responded with tears, some with rage, and others with denial. Providing spaces for vigorous discussions regarding "what the data tell us" centered on detailed accounts of invalid disciplinary actions, declining graduation rates, increased student absences, and oppressive pedagogical practices.

It was imperative to address oppressive conditions as they occurred in the workplace to provide a context for teachers and school leaders to recognize how current decision-making practices perpetuated oppressive conditions. Those who serve children and families were encouraged to address the tension between hegemonic school practices, serving culturally diverse communities, and reflective practice. At the heart of this movement were opportunities to take action, interrupt oppressive practices, and work in socially just ways. Advocating for equity-oriented practices on each PreK–12 campus promoted human advocacy within each organization and was at the heart of what we did as school–community members. We took a proactive stance by forming a partnership with a university to create professional development opportunities centered on racism, structural inequities, and institutionalized oppression, which led to the creation of the Multicultural Task Force.

The Multicultural Task Force focused on reflective practice (considering dissonance between beliefs, lived experiences, and school practices), culturally proficient pedagogy, and building bridges between school and home. Teachers, support staff (i.e., security officers, police officers, secretaries, translators, social service community personnel, school counselors, social workers) and I worked collaboratively to disaggregate discipline data and student achievement scores as well as reflect on current pedagogical practices. Findings suggested school policies encouraged high rates of black/Latino/a children identified as needing special education services, a disproportionate number of black/Latino/a children receiving disciplinary actions, low student expectations, teacher preference for English-speaking students, and blaming disenfranchised children and families for "problems" facing the campus.

As an assistant principal working to raise awareness regarding culturally responsive practices and promote democratic spaces for all school members, looking at data provided a space to explore the strengths and challenges facing students, especially those from marginalized populations. We began by looking at disciplinary practices and policies. Educators found it difficult to support why 2,335 disciplinary referrals were completed within six months, which totaled an average of 140,100 minutes of classroom instruction missed by students for alleged "disruption" and "disrespect" within one middle school. In this school, black students were three times more likely to receive a discipline referral than their white counterparts. Such findings provided spaces for educators and school leaders to deepen their understanding of structural inequities as well as their role in perpetuating oppressive school practices. The process afforded educators opportunities to listen to painful stories as well as the realities faced by those served. In three years, one school decreased discipline referrals by approximately 80 percent. School personnel addressed practices that reproduced social inequities and blamed children and their families for the ills of society. The school transformed itself to a community that promoted human advocacy.

As an assistant principal and principal, I made efforts to hire teachers and support staff who lived within the community and who made visible efforts to promote issues of social justice and equity. When I was a principal, a custodian, who was originally hired from outside the community, documented unclaimed overtime as well as duties that were not performed. For example, the kindergarten bathroom smelled from urine, children did not have access to toilet paper or paper towels, and soap was not provided. The school was infested with mice, ants, and rats. During a surprise visit from the city's department of safety, the school was issued a ticket and informed we would be closed in one week if all of the issues noted on the ticket were not resolved. Upper administration expressed their "disinterest" in resolving the issues. After several phone calls to the central office with supporting documentation, as a principal, I was informed to "hire whoever you want."

At the same school, the school nurse and physical education teacher expressed interest in serving children "healthier meals" and providing families with resources for food. We started collecting data regarding the number of children who visited the nurse with complaints (e.g., constipation, vomiting, upset stomach) after school meals, the number of children who disposed of their school lunch in the trash, and the number of children who reported their only meals came from school. Data were collected during the next two months. More than 70 percent of students threw away their entire school meals because the food did not resemble meals prepared at home and complained about stomachaches and vomiting. During this process, I discovered the cafeteria staff left meat and other frozen food items "out in the sinks overnight." This was considered "common practice." After speaking with central office administration regarding the strong possibility of food contamination, I was informed to "hire a new cafeteria staff." We proposed a plan supported in brain-based research as well as field studies regarding healthier choices for students. The proposal included hiring a chef who would prepare salads, sandwiches, soup, bread, and ethnic dishes aligned with the student population. The central office team supported our proposal because "it was cheaper" to work collaboratively with the food company rather than to hire an entire cafeteria staff.

We surveyed families regarding the types of food served at home, how meals were prepared, and interest in learning additional information about nutrition and meal planning. Families expressed an interest in participating in programs on campus regarding food preparation and resources for their families. I encouraged the school nurse and physical education teacher to visit schools who engaged in alternative meal programs as well as partnerships to meet the needs of the families. Central office administrators made comments regarding my need to "collect data," "talk to people," and "survey" community members. One white male administrator asked, "Can't you just make a decision on your own? Are you that weak?" I replied, "Yes, I can make decisions by myself; however, I am not interested in serving my needs. I want to ensure we listen to the voices of those we serve."

When asked to hire new teachers at another school, I interviewed more than two hundred applicants over the phone, conducted more than fifty face-to-face interviews, met with candidates in the field, and worked with a team of teachers, families, and students to choose the best candidates for the school. The community's strengths as well as concerns raised by members of the organization were openly shared with candidates throughout the interview process (i.e., historical school community racial tension, inequitable practices, and the need for critical pedagogy). The need to find educators committed to eliminating oppressive school practices was significant to transforming the school. Within three years, the school moved from being on the "watch" list to all of the students meeting state requirements for standardized testing.

With more than eighteen years of experience in culturally diverse educational settings and ten years of school leadership experience, my professors encouraged me to enter academia. They encouraged me to share my passion and experience in leading for social justice and equity-oriented work. I accepted a position as a research assistant and worked as an adjunct on three higher education campuses preparing candidates to work in schools. Throughout my adjunct work, I discovered the need for consciousness raising, especially for preservice teachers who were members of the dominant culture (i.e., white, middle-class, English speaking, American citizens, heterosexual, attended regular-education PreK–12 classes). One white female preservice teacher noted, "I want to join the people with my shotgun so I could help fight the voluntary Texas border patrol keep out those illegal Mexican immigrants." Several of the white preservice candidates identified children who were not members of the mainstream as "those" children and blamed "these" children for societal ills (i.e., crime, drugs).

As a tenure-track scholar preparing school leaders and teachers to under-take social justice work in schools, I quickly realized the challenges in rais-ing their social consciousness and responses toward underserved populations. Candidates' comments and lived experiences centered on standardized testing and perpetuating hegemonic practices. After present-ing candidates' written narratives, assignments, e-mails, and insights, each university afforded me opportunities to create spaces for students to con-duct meaningful work by applying theory to practice. I utilized the word *pilot* within each program by collecting baseline data, surveying students, and receiving permission to conduct research. I examined how students deepened their perspectives, broadened their experiences, and drew mean-ing from their lives and work in schools. One means of proactively engag-ing students in reflecting on their ability to negotiate experiences and make meaning from complex dynamics (i.e., school organizations, society) included the incorporation of critical theory, reflective practice, and inquiry-based learning. Students were provided opportunities to learn from field-based experiences, connecting prior lived experiences and integrating their thoughts and actions taken. For example, students conducted home visits, curriculum and equity audits, and problem-based learning and facili-tated processes in which all school community members engaged in addressing issues of social justice and equity in public schools.

As a scholar preparing school leaders in Texas and Ohio, I was encour-aged to revise administrative internship courses to engage students in cul-turally diverse school contexts, increase their critical consciousness, and promote leaders for social justice and equity. Students noted the need for their experiences to be "directly tied to the realities facing twenty-first-century school leaders." However, white male faculty members at one institution noted such changes as a "burden" because "now they would have higher expectations placed on them." Discussions centered on pursuing programmatic revisions to align their vision and mission with other Research I institutions (e.g., University of Wisconsin–Madison, Uni-versity of North Carolina–Chapel Hill, Texas A & M–College Station, and University of Texas–Austin). As a tenure-track assistant professor in Ohio, I was asked to create a social justice course for an educational leadership program. The course was approved and designated as a mandatory course within the educational leadership program. Students were provided spaces to critically reflect on their school leadership identity, immerse themselves in the field, and deepen their empathic responses toward underserved populations. Students engaged in weekly audio/video reflections centered on cultural proficiency and identity embedded in a conceptual model entitled "developing a catalytic perspective" (Boske, 2009). The course also engaged students in applying critical theory to practice through conducting an equity audit, creating a research-based stance regarding social justice and equity issues, and translating their transformative work in schools to artmaking. Providing students with opportunities to lead created spaces for students to attribute their learning and professional growth to the subsequent experiences presented throughout the revised courses. A fundamental aspect of their learning and development as school leaders was their ability to engage in authentic immersion experiences, critically reflect on the influence of their school leadership identity, and participate in social justice work in schools.

Discussion

How we lead matters. Looking within shapes how school leaders understand themselves in an effort to promote humanity in schools. This self-study inspired me to reflect on the historical construction of social formation as well as my willingness to partake in the privileges associated with being white in this society. The existence of power and privilege encourages me to confront my blindness to issues centered on systemic inequities and the need to abolish privileges associated with being a member of the dominant culture. Creating a counterhegemonic narrative encouraged me to question and hold suspect proclaimed societal truths. Engaging in courageous, meaningful, reflective dialogue encouraged me to share my truth centered on what I thought, felt, and witnessed in schools. Although actions taken were considered by some as *dangerous*, articulating my values and beliefs provided a space for me to discover the power of raising critical consciousness and building alliances. Aligning with practitioners who identified as culturally proficient created a unified force within each school system. This unifying force enhanced the lives of historically disenfranchised populations by acknowledging and addressing oppressive school practices.

I consciously worked to engage in socially just practices that deepened my understanding and responses to underserved populations (Laible, 2000). My hope was to encourage dissent from mainstream conformity that maintains beliefs centered on the superiority of one group over another. This self-study encouraged me to understand how gender, race, and sexual identity permeate issues facing children and families in schools. Looking within to examine the existence of personal cultural assumptions was the first step to promoting social justice issues in schools. I realize the need to take personal risks, to become introspective, and to transform my practices. As a scholar preparing preservice school leaders, I must allow time, space, and intellectual guidance for students to analyze forces that promote hegemony and strategies to identify their authentic selves (see Cross et al., 1989).

Promoting an authentic self provides opportunities for aspiring school leaders to engage in understanding the social construction of difference (see Gergen, 1999), as well as insight regarding the influence of wider social forces influencing America's educational system (see Sleeter & Grant, 2009; Marshall & Oliva, 2006). This self-examination might encourage those who prepare school leaders to address the realities of human oppression, politics of education, and historical cultural misconceptions embedded in the fabric of our nation's wider social forces (see Marshall & Gerstl-Pepin, 2005; McLaren & Kincheloe, 2007). Opportunities such as these provide spaces to address complex struggles for power within educational arenas. These complex struggles include understanding how power and privilege shape *whose social justice counts.*

The journey of raising critical consciousness and becoming more culturally proficient urged those who prepared school leaders to provide them with intellectual guidance. Shields and Edwards (2005) propose school leaders move from managerial to dialogic leadership (p. 63). Such considerations encourage school leaders to willingly engage in conversations regarding the influence of race, class, gender, or any other interest they hold. Creating such spaces encourages school leaders to develop a strong sense of self (see Elson, 1986). It also requires faculty to provide spaces for students to question their beliefs and school practices (Shields & Edwards, 2005; Shields et al., 2002).

There is value in caring for others and addressing ways to fundamentally improve the lived experiences of those who have been ostracized, especially children within our nation's schools. As Freire (1970) reminds us, social change will occur for oppressed groups when they "create a new situation, one which makes possible the pursuit for fuller humanity"

(p. 29). These findings reinforced the need to take this charge seriously. School leaders need to deepen their understanding regarding power and privilege, as well as their role in perpetuating oppressive school practices that lead to unjust experiences. Such work requires that school leaders deepen their empathic responses and pay closer attention to the lived experiences of underserved people.

The need for those who have been marginalized to mobilize themselves is coined *identity politics*. Within such spaces, members of subordinate groups center on their lived experiences (e.g., civil rights movement, women's movement, LGBTQ movement) and validate the challenges, concerns, and achievements of these groups. Schools did not seem to serve as spaces in which the distribution of power and resources were openly discussed. There was a need to preserve cultural memory and create spaces in which underserved groups of children and their families mobilized themselves around their group identity.

Raising awareness and deepening empathic responses was a conscious movement in need of forming coalitions with people in positions of power and privilege. Leading for social justice involved conversations centered on "special interest groups" versus "promoting humanity." The divide often prevented educators from seeing beyond the lens of group identity in order to consider the needs of all children. In other words, people who were members of the dominant culture (white, heterosexual, Christian, employed, two-parent family) needed to investigate what it meant to be black, Latino, poor, single, LGBTQ, unemployed, or all of the above. Engaging in reflective work was a challenging and emotional process. The transformative work reminded us certain groups had less access to resources than others, fewer ways to make their voices heard, and forces that pushed them to live on the margins. The process encouraged people to think critically about aspects of their identity as well as the need to use power and privilege to form coalitions to interrupt oppressive practices.

Implications

Little has been written about the strategies PreK–12 U.S. school leaders use to sustain themselves as leaders of social justice and equity oriented work (Brown, 2004, 2006; Marshall & Oliva, 2010; Theoharis, 2007). While this work is based on personal experiences within the United States, there is an aspect of universality to how I overcome resistance, regardless of context. We might consider further research regarding how educators and school leaders unpack their lived experiences to interrupt hegemonic practices in schools. First, we might explore how educators and school leaders understand the impact of their childhood experiences, social interactions, and attitudes toward culturally diverse populations. How do educators and school leaders deepen their empathic responses and internalize their lived realities? To what extent, if any, are educators and school leaders immersed in spaces in which they are encouraged to investigate their role in perpetuating hegemonic practices in schools? Future research might begin by examining how individuals look within and internalize reflective practices to empower children and families who live on the margins.

Future research might also center on school leadership practices, pedagogy, and policy making that fosters cultural proficiency. Such studies may need to document educators' prior lived experiences and school practices, tracing their progress and transformations throughout their schooling and career. Furthermore, these studies might investigate processes in which educators and school leaders develop new identities that encourage social justice and equity-oriented work.

Third, studies centering on people of color in schools might uncover ways to build bridges between mainstream and disenfranchised populations. Researchers (Boske, 2010a; Delpit, 1995) have suggested people of color tend to feel isolated and ostracized by oppressive school practices that encourage the perpetuation of cultural myths. To what extent, if any, do school leadership programs provide mentoring and support for students of color?

Finally, I realize I cannot expect aspiring school leaders to take risks if I do not demonstrate courage, reflect on my school leadership identity, or transform my school practices. The key implication noted throughout this study is the significance of looking within and making conscious decisions that sustain transformative work centered on improving the lived experiences of underserved populations. This method of inquiry continues to be underexplored and is in need of further investigation (Boske, 2009; Lindsey, Robins, & Terrell, 2009).

Finding allies is critical to building a supportive network to sustain an educational agenda centered on addressing exclusionary practices.

Providing spaces for students to examine values, their commitment, and shared responsibility in promoting systemic change is significant. Acknowledging lived experiences and cultural knowledge provides school leaders with a sense of purpose. Recognizing the importance of developing meaningful familial and social relationships with people who share similar beliefs creates the emotional support necessary for school leaders and teachers to engage in dismantling hegemonic practices. Providing safe spaces to deepen empathic responses and identity is crucial to sustaining practices and policies that promote social justice and equity-oriented work. If we allow time and intellectual guidance for those who desire to engage in this type of work, they too may discover their *authentic* selves (see Cross et al., 1989; Gergen, 1999).

Conclusion

I developed and used centered strategies (see Boske, 2010b; Brown, 2004; Lindsey, Robins, & Terrell, 2010) as well as conscious, deliberate, and proactive strategies (Boske & Tooms, 2010; Dantley & Tillman, 2006; Furman & Shields, 2005) to advance social justice and equity work in the face of resistance. The experience of identifying as a white LGBTQ woman shapes what I do and encourages me to think racially and as well as sexually about the impact of heteronormativity in schools. We will need to hear more accounts of women's experiences in the field and ways in which racial and sexual identity become more comfortably visible. The tension of moving between oppression and attempts to break through boundaries established by the dominant culture may need to become more transparent. The lived experiences shared in this chapter provide spaces to reconsider how those who live on the margins undertake the transformation of society to achieve liberation through transformative work. I attribute my transformative work, which in part is due to consciousness raising, to the strategies noted in this study. These strategies urge us to deepen our empathic responses and listen respectfully to those who can see what we cannot. Raising our own consciousness is the first step to undoing the invisibility of gender, race, sexual identity, and other forms of difference. This work requires understanding and paying close attention to members of marginalized populations as social actors. The transformative work supports efforts to address the marginalization of students and their families—to create safe and intellectually stimulating places for learning as well as increasing critical consciousness, ability, and willingness to address social justice issues. What we need are women committed to working actively against privilege and interrupting hegemonic practices. Paying closer attention to people's truths is fundamental to progressive change and promoting a more just world.

References

Barnes, D. (1998). Looking forward: The concluding remarks at the Castle conference. In M. L. Hamilton (Ed.), *Reconceptualizing teaching practice: Self-study in teacher education* (pp. ix–xiv). London: Falmer Press.

Barnett, B. G., & O'Mahony, G. R. (2006). Developing a culture of reflection: Implications for school improvement. *Reflective Practice, 7*(4), 499–523.

Blackmore, J. (2002). Leadership for Socially Just Schooling: More Substance and less style in high risk, low trust times? *Journal of School Leadership, 12*(2), 198–222.

Bogotch, I. (2002). Educational leadership and social justice: Practice into theory. *Journal of School Leadership, 12*(2), 138–56.

Boske, C. (2009). It begins from within: Conceptualizing a "catalytic perspective" for school leaders. Paper presented at *The University Council for Educational Administration Annual Conference*, Anaheim, California.

Boske, C. (2010a). "I wonder if they had ever seen a black man before?" Grappling with issues of race and racism in our own backyard. *Journal of Research on Leadership Education, 5*(7), 248–75.

Boske, C. (2010b). A time to grow: Workplace mobbing and the making of a tempered radical. In A. K. Tooms & C. Boske (Eds.), *Bridge leadership: Connecting educational leadership and social justice to improve schools* (pp. 29–56). Charlotte, NC: Info Age.

Boske, C., & McEnery, L. (2010). Taking it to the streets: A new line of inquiry for school communities. *Journal of School Leadership, 20*(3), 369–98.

Boske, C., & Tooms, A. K. (2010). Social justice and doing "being ordinary." In A. K. Tooms & C. Boske (Eds.), *Bridge leadership: Connecting educational leadership and social justice to improve schools* (pp. xvii–xxviii). Charlotte, NC: Info Age.

Brown, K. M. (2004). Leadership for social justice and equity: Weaving a transformative framework and pedagogy. *Educational Administrative Quarterly, 40*(1), 79–110.

Brown, K. M. (2006). Leadership for social justice and equity: Evaluating a transformative framework and andragogy. *Educational Administrative Quarterly, 42*(5), 700–745.

Capper, C., Theoharis, G., & Sebastian, J. (2006). Toward a framework for preparing leaders for social justice. *Journal of Educational Administration, 44*(3), 209–24.

Clandinin, D. J. (1995). Still learning to teach. In T. Russell & F. Korthagen (Eds.), *Teachers who teach teachers: Reflections on teacher education* (pp. 25–31). London: Falmer Press.

Cross, T., Bazron, B., Karl, D., & Mareasa, I. (1989). *Toward a culturally competent system of care* (Vol. 1). Washington, DC: Georgetown University.

Dantley, M. E., & Tillman, L. C. (2006). Social justice and moral transformative leadership. In C. Marshall & M. Oliva (Eds.), *Leadership for social justice* (pp. 16–30). New York: Pearson.

Delpit, L. (1995). *Other people's children: Cultural conflict in the classroom.* New York: New Press.

Elson, M. (1986). *Self psychology in clinical social work.* New York, NY: W. W. Norton.

Flagg, B. J. (1998). *"Was blind, but now I see": White race consciousness and the law.* New York: New York University Press.

Freire, P. (1970). Pedagogy of the oppressed. New York, NY: Continuum.

Furman, G. C., & Shields, C. M. (2005). How can educational leaders promote and support social justice and democratic community in schools? In W. A. Firestone & C. Riehl (Eds.), *A new agenda for research in educational leadership* (pp. 119–37). New York: Teachers College Press.

Gergen, K. (1999). *An invitation to social construction.* Thousand Oaks, CA: Sage.

Gewirtz, S. (1998). Conceptualizing social justice in education: Mapping the territory. *Journal of Education Policy, 13*(4), 469–84.

Goldfarb, K. P., & Ginberg, J. (2002). Leadership for social justice: Authentic participation in the case of a community center in Caracas, Venezuela. *Journal of School Leadership, 12*(2), 157–73.

Gray, D. L., & Smith, A. (2007). *Case studies in 21st-century school administration: Addressing challenges for educational leadership.* Thousand Oaks, CA: Sage.

Grogan, M. (Ed.). (2002). Leadership for social justice [Special Issue]. *Journal of School Leadership, 12*(2), 112–15.

Hamilton, M. L. (2002). Change, social justice and re-liability: Reflections of a secret (change) agent. In J. Loughran & T. Russell (Eds.), *Improving teacher education practices through self-study* (pp. 176–89). London: RoutledgeFalmer.

Hamilton, M. L., & Pinnegar, S. (1998). Conclusion: The value and the promise of self-study. In M. L. Hamilton (Ed.), *Reconceptualizing teaching practice: Self-study in teacher education* (pp. 234–46). London: Falmer Press.

Hilliard, A. G., III. (1991). Do we have the will to educate all children? *Educational Leadership, 49*(1), 31–36.

Ketelle, D., & Mesa, R. P. (2006). Empathetic understanding and school leadership preparation. *Leadership Review, 6*, 144–54.

Kottamp, R. (1990). Means of facilitating reflection. *Education and Urban Society, 22*(2), 182–203.

Laible, J. C. (2000). A loving epistemology: What I hold critical in my life, faith, and profession. *International Journal of Qualitative Studies in Education, 13*(6), 683–92.

Leymann, H. (1990). Mobbing and psychological terror at workplaces. *Violence and Victims, 5*, 119–26.

Lindsey, R. B., Robins, K. N., & Terrell, R. D. (2009). *Cultural proficiency: A manual for school leaders.* Thousand Oaks, CA: Corwin Press.

Marshall, C., & Gerstyl-Pepin, C. (2005). *Re-framing educational politics for social justice.* Boston: Pearson.

Marshall, C., & Oliva, M. (Eds.). (2010). *Leadership for social justice.* New York: Allyn & Bacon.

McLaren, P., & Kincheloe, J. L. (2007). *Critical pedagogy: Where are we now?* New York: Peter Lang.

McMahon, B. (2007). Educational administrators' conceptions of whiteness, anti-racism and social justice. *Journal of Educational Administration, 45*(6), 684–96.

Osterman, K. F., & Kottamp, R. B. (2004). *Reflective practice for educators.* Thousand Oaks, CA: Corwin Press.

Schein, E. (1989). *Organizational culture and leadership: A dynamic view.* San Francisco: Jossey-Bass.

Schon, D. A. (1983). *The reflective practitioner.* New York: Basic Books.

Scribner, J. P., Sunday-Cockrell, K., Cockrell, D. H., & Valentine, J. W. (1999). Creating professional communities in schools through organizational learning: An evaluation of a school improvement process. *Educational Administration Quarterly, 35*(1), 130–60.

Sergiovanni, T. J. (2001). *The principalship: A reflective practice perspective* (4th ed.). Needham Heights, MA: Allyn & Bacon.

Shields, C, & Edwards, M. (2005). *Dialogue is not just talk: A new ground for educational leadership.* New York, NY: Peter Lang.

Sleeter, C. E., & Grant, C. A. (2009). *Making choices for multicultural education: Five approaches to race, class, and gender* (6th ed.). Hoboken, NJ: Wiley & Sons.

Smith, S. C., & Piele, P. K. (2006). *School leadership: Handbook for excellence in student learning.* Thousand Oaks, CA: Corwin.

Stout, R. (1986). Executive action and values. *Issues in Education, 4*(3), 198–214.

Terrell, R. D., & Randall, L. B. (2009). *Culturally proficient leadership: The personal journey begins within.* Thousand Oaks, CA: Corwin.

Theoharis, G. (2007). Social justice educational leaders and resistance: Toward a theory of social justice leadership. *Educational Administration Quarterly, 43*(2), 228–51.

van Halen-Faber, C. (1997). Encouraging critical reflection in preservice teacher education: A narrative of a personal learning journey. *Directions for Adults in Continuing Education, 74*, 51–60.

Wheatley, M. J. (1994). *Leadership and the new science*. San Francisco: Berrett-Koehler.

Whitehead, J. (1995). Educative relationships with the writings of others. In T. Russel & F. A. J. Korthagen (Eds.), *Teachers who teach teachers: Reflections on teacher education* (pp. 113–29). London: Falmer Press.

5

Teacher Leaders Working for Social Justice: Contributing to the Field

Jennifer L. Martin

... if we do not define ourselves for ourselves, we will be defined by others—for their use and to our detriment.

—Audre Lorde

... teachers who take leadership roles in their schools are successful agents and conduits in promoting cultural change. Their work as leaders—in and out of their classrooms—seems to push the school culture toward a more inclusive and collaborative one. When the work of teachers is held in the highest regard and is made visible throughout the school, the culture of the school shifts from authoritative, linear, and mechanical to open, responsive, and thoughtful. For some time, scholars and others have pushed the educational pendulum toward more collaborative and inclusive models.

—Beachum and Dentith

America's current public education system and those who work within it are subject to a polarizing public debate. Perhaps because all of us have attended school, we all have opinions about teachers, teaching, and school funding (whether or not we have training in education). To complicate this, the media have launched a large-scale assault on teachers and schools, demanding that teachers need to do more with less, at lower pay. A popular idea is that anyone can just decide to be a teacher, without any pedagogical training. To further complicate matters, there are several divides within the field of education that exacerbate negative perceptions of teachers. First, there is a natural gulf between teachers and administrators that includes a distinct division of labor and a hierarchical power dynamic. Second, there is a separation between higher education, often making policy and curricular decisions that affect K–12 education, and the practical field in which teachers work. The crux of the problem is that public school educators are not viewed as professionals. They are not looked upon as experts in their field; university professors are seen as experts, although most have spent far less time (if any) in public K–12 classrooms. Despite all of the divisive political and social commentary about education, the American public school system is seen as a lone panacea, possessing not only the ability but also the responsibility to fix all of society's ills. With the ever-increasing demands on schools, teachers are expected to take on more responsibilities, many of which include leadership roles. However, some teachers do this work for the good of the school and are not necessarily compensated monetarily for it. There are many problems within public education that require fixing, but these changes should come from within; involving teachers in these solutions by respecting and valuing their knowledge is a cost-effective and empowering place to begin.

Negative public opinions of teachers can contribute to teacher frustration and alienation, which can lead to teacher turnover and attrition. Such perceptions have contributed to an environment where teacher autonomy and academic freedom have been greatly reduced. As Steel and Craig (2006) point out:

> Researchers have pointed to uncompetitive salaries, high levels of teacher isolation, and unfavorable working conditions as among the possible causes. Surely the lack of opportunities for professional growth is a significant factor as well. In many cases, teachers are given highly structured, scripted curriculum materials for use in their classrooms, and systems of districtwide assessment and accountability procedures necessarily limit the professional autonomy of educators. (p. 677)

When teachers feel undervalued, underpaid, and unappreciated, when their work and knowledge are deemed to be meaningless, they are more hesitant to act as leaders in their schools. However, when teachers are empowered, when their knowledge is valued, they are more likely to contribute their knowledge to making schools better. As Wahlstrom and Seashore Louis (2008) state, "Pedagogical knowledge and skills provide the basic building blocks for instruction, but workplace factors also affect student learning. Among these are teachers' job satisfaction, a sense of professionalism and influence, collegial trust, and opportunities to collaborate" (p. 460). Essentially, teachers need to be empowered in order to empower others.

I will share a personal anecdote to illustrate my point of the undervaluing of public school teachers in the current social and political system. I recently attended the American Educational Research Association's Annual Meeting, where I was shocked and dismayed to hear a female scholar and leader in the field of educational leadership extol the virtues of the No Child Left Behind Act because "now teachers will be held accountable." Most teachers have always held themselves accountable for the learning that occurs in their classrooms and schools. This shocking statement speaks to the gap that exists between the university, which educates teachers, and the field in which teachers work. Although educators themselves, professors can do much to contribute to the negative perceptions of teachers. K–12 and higher education professionals must work together for social justice; they must advocate for increased academic freedom for teachers, a reduction in the negative perceptions about teachers, school improvement that utilizes teacher knowledge, and the creation of emancipatory classroom environments. As Jones, Webb, and Neumann state (2008), "In educational leadership programs, professors should require preservice and in service teachers to identify ideologies, epistemologies, or any other discourse that marginalizes and devalues teachers and PK–12 students within schools. Teachers must have the kinds of protection and freedoms to engage students in the hard work of socially-just pedagogies" (p. 11). Teachers and professors must develop and maintain a collaborative relationship, as opposed to an adversarial one.

In this chapter I explore how teacher leaders perform social justice work within their classrooms and schools and how this work can be transformative. As part of my investigation, I have examined the literature on teacher leaders, teacher researchers, feminist teachers, and social justice educators. In addition, I have used myself as a source of anecdotal information. I conducted a self-study of my own social justice work to delineate what teachers can do in their classrooms and schools in order to create more equitable educational environments. This examination and this work on the part of teachers will hopefully accomplish two things. First, it will create more equitable environments, which may play a part in closing the achievement gap. This is crucial in changing the perception that public schools today are failing. Second, it will change the negative public perception of teachers and contribute to the notion that teachers are indeed professional, capable of growth, and true contributors to the field of educational research in their own right.

Teacher leadership has many benefits including empowering teachers, creating more collaborative work environments, and sharing successful pedagogical techniques to increase student achievement. It can also contribute to reducing teacher isolation and increase their "commitment to the common good" (Wahlstrom & Seashore Louis, 2008, p. 461). It is erroneous to infer that teachers do not contribute and have not contributed to leadership within schools throughout the history of American education. As Strodl (1992) indicates, "To restrict leadership to the principal's office is to assume that teachers never deal with conflict on their own, never inspire students to higher levels of accomplishment, never respond to school-wide policy issues, or never influence the formation of collective opinions, never contribute to the configuration of school climate and culture" (p. 6). In fact, most teachers have always worked to positively impact school culture, have lent their ideas to school improvement plans, and have fought to close achievements gaps, and advocated for educational equity in their classrooms.

But teachers cannot lead alone. Teachers who work in isolation can do much within their classrooms to reduce gender inequities or racial or sexually based harassment, for example, but when their students leave the classroom, they are again faced with the potential hostile world of the school hallway. Collegiality promotes teacher leadership (Phelps, 2008), and teachers can do more for the school culture and for the school in general if they are able to work in concert with other teachers and administrators. As Phelps indicates (2008), "When teachers recognize that leading increases their overall difference-making ability, they will be more inclined to seize the chance to serve in this capacity" (p. 120). Teacher leadership can truly transform a school.

Teacher research is another area of leadership in which teachers can engage. Currently, they are often left out of the process of research in general. They are neither trained to nor given the time to conduct research. Teacher research can be emancipatory, freeing both teachers and students from regimented, irrelevant, and culturally unresponsive curricula by devising programs, interventions, and effective lessons. As Christianakis (2008) notes, "Excluding teachers from educational knowledge production and requiring them to follow curricular scripts demeans their expert knowledge and relegates it to 'craft' or 'technical work.' Including teachers in educational research honors and makes important their knowledge" (p. 107). Valuing teacher research equates to valuing teacher expertise, which is necessary in viewing teaching as a profession.

Many teachers consider themselves informal leaders: stepping outside their classrooms to assist in the creation of the school's mission, to advocate for the best interests of their students academically, and to create safer educational environments for both staff and students. As Strodl (1992) argues:

> Transformational leadership changes the lives of organizations, nations and people. Critical to the success of the informal leader is the leader's ability to empower followers. As a person who empowers others the informal leader connects with followers in terms of conflicts, problems and issues to enable followers to become successful. (p. 11)

The key to fostering maximum change is in inspiring group action.

There are many impediments to teachers being viewed as leaders in their own right. One impediment is the perceptions of administrators. There still exists a historical divide between what is viewed to be "teacher work" and what is considered "administrator work." As O'Connor (1992) indicates:

> Teacher leadership requires changes in traditional roles, attitudes, and school organization: roles which enable teachers to take on alternative responsibilities without leaving the classroom, attitudes that value teachers' work with adults as well as students, and school organization that provides time and professional support for the new roles. . . . Clearly then, teacher leadership requires a shift in authority relations in schools. (p. 20)

It is important that teachers and administrators find ways to work together to create policies at the district and state level and to improve schools from within (O'Connor, 1992). Educators need time and support to be able to negotiate these roles. Time may be the greatest obstacle to this; restructuring schools in terms of organization, teacher workload, roles, and responsibilities is necessary.

Contributing to a school's vision and risk taking are common aspects of teacher leadership, but stepping up as a social justice leader or advocate can be dangerous for teachers. Teacher leaders are often in the unique position of having to do the unpopular thing, that is, speaking out if they disagree with school policies and practices that they deem harmful for students, such as tracking students, implementing a scripted curriculum as opposed to being guided by needs of students, and focusing much instructional time on preparations for standardized testing. But this is a necessary system of checks and balances within a school organization. In order for teachers to insert themselves into these dialogues and to take on leadership roles, they must be willing to take risks, be assertive, and value their own knowledge about teaching and students in order to impact school reform (Beachum & Dentith, 2004).

Teachers and administrators must work together toward positive school reform for social justice. If this does not occur, then it is doubtful that negative perceptions of teachers will change, that our schools will improve from within, or that the achievement gap will close. Giroux (2001/1983) argues that social transformation should be the goal of public education: " . . . learning is not about processing received knowledge but actually transforming it as part of a more expansive struggle for individual rights and social justice" (p. xxvii). Much to the detriment of our children and our society, this is becoming less and less a priority. Embracing the concept of teacher leaders can lessen the demands placed on administrators and on schools in general toward a more transformative and egalitarian educational environment. "Combining the best of both [teachers and administrators] can ease increasing educational demands, reconfigure hierarchical power structures, and unite teachers and administrators in the interest of genuine renewal and true transformation" (Beachum & Dentith, 2004, p. 285). Teachers must feel empowered in order to lead and to empower others (hooks, 1994).

Social Justice Teacher Leaders: Advocating for Students, Advancing the Profession

Lieberman and Miller (2004) discuss three types of teacher leaders: advocates, innovators, and stewards. Advocates stand up and speak out for what is best for students. Innovators develop and implement creative new ideas. Stewards shape the profession of teaching in a positive manner through their work. Social justice educators do all three of these, which ultimately improves schools. Social justice education benefits both the school and the teachers. As O'Connor (1992) indicates, "Leadership experiences empowered them, increased their self-confidence and their willingness to take risks in their classrooms. We would posit that children are the direct beneficiaries when teachers 'put my teaching in perspective and provide richer classroom interactions' " (p. 21).

Teachers can do much to improve their schools from within, from creating policies to in-servicing other teachers on pedagogy, content, and technology. Teacher leaders can work with students to create positive cultural change within schools and across districts through trainings; they can conduct traditional and action research in their classrooms and schools in order to create better solutions to students' academic and behavioral challenges and solve schoolwide problems. Research based decisions assists in affirming the diversity of the student body, creating student-led incentives to succeed, and celebrating accomplishment and improvement. Phelps (2008) writes,

> Teacher leaders can change schools for the better. A willingness to assume a greater degree of responsibility allows a teacher leader to function as a school's conscience . . . Fulfilling this moral purpose, in turn, raises teachers' levels of contribution and multiplies their possible impact. (p. 120)

Again, this work benefits teachers. However, if teachers are not receiving recognition for their hard work, if this expectation falls more on one group of people (e.g., women teachers), and/or if they are not being compensated (whether monetarily or through provided flex time) for their extra work, then we are just placing undue pressure on already overworked teachers, which will exacerbate the burnout rate.

During my fifteen years in public education, I have found that the expectation of teachers has much to do with traditional gender roles. In terms of formal leadership in American public schools, traditional gender role expectations are, to a large degree, still at play. Men are still considered to be "natural choices" when determining who will run a school. This is changing with many women taking on the formal responsibilities as principals and high-level central-office administrators, but when it comes to informal leadership, having one's voice heard, participating in policy decisions or budgeting, often men's voices are more valued. As Wilson (2007) laments, "How many women have contributed their best at meetings only to find that when a man says the same thing moments later, it is hailed as genius—and his idea" (p. 34). Additionally, when it comes to the expectations of who will plan parties, activities, or provide cleanup, this expectation often falls on women—many of whom take on these additional duties without complaint.

Feminist Teacher Leadership: Working in the Margins

Working to help all students achieve is crucial, but when environments are not safe, this can be virtually impossible. Social justice work is necessary to finding solutions to these and other problems, to creating more equitable school environments, but often this work is done is isolation because it can be dangerous and frightening. Challenging the status quo of a school sometimes can mean risking one's job. It is easier to go along with how things have always been done. However, teaching can be a political act through which teachers, as Fine (2007) suggests, "can address social inequality and injustice" (p. 181). For example, teachers can advocate for the removal of sexist, racist, and homophobic language within their schools. We must not underestimate the power of "teachable moments." Teachers who are advocates for social justice do not ignore hate speech, for example. Their interventions can do much to dismantle hegemonic masculinity and the policing of heteronormativity that often dominate student discourse. Teachers who are advocates for social justice serve to protect their students even if it means they are on the line. Additionally, there is a perception that some students do not want to learn or cannot learn; nothing can be further from the truth. Teachers who advocate for social justice also work to educate the most difficult and resistant students. It is within this spirit of social justice advocacy in education that I now share some of my own teaching story involving the incorporation of feminist teaching principles and working for equity and inclusion in my own classroom and school.

In my work as a high school teacher, I have noticed much inequity in my observations of others. Although this is not the norm, I have been angered when I have seen or heard about harassment being tolerated by teachers and administrators. For example, I observed a gym class where a white male gym teacher organized a scrimmage basketball game for the boys while he allowed the girls to sit on the bleachers and talk. When a boy attempted to sit on the same bleachers, the gym teacher questioned his masculinity and his sexuality; in other words, if he did not want to play sports, not only was he gay, but he was also less of a man. This teacher's own views about gender dictated how he ran his classroom; his limited views included a dominant discourse of hegemonic masculinity that resulted in gender inequity, heteronormativity, and sexual orientation harassment.

This and other events in my personal and professional life impressed upon me the need for teachers to be allies, to go above and beyond to protect their students. This mindset led me to work in a nontraditional environment. In my third year of teaching I took a position teaching English at an alternative high school for at-risk students. Students were sent to this school for behavioral reasons. This was a small program with a soft cap of eighty students. Oftentimes, this was the students' last chance at an education and a diploma.

Immediately, I noticed a gender specific problem within the school. My female students were experiencing something that was negatively affecting them—sexual harassment. The male population of the school at that time was approximately 80 percent. Many of my female students came to me complaining of this problem. Girls came to me in tears, lamenting how boys in their classes and in the hallways taunted them, propositioned them, humiliated them, grabbed them sexually without their consent, degraded them, spread sexual rumors about them, made judgments about their sexuality, and so forth. This was done with a sense of entitlement and served to perpetuate the male-dominated culture. The girls were simultaneously upset about what was happening to them and protective of their harassers. They did not want to report what they were experiencing because they did not want to get their "friends" in trouble. Although they were conflicted, their choices not to report perpetuated this dominant discourse. The boys, on the other hand, believed that because their sexual harassment went unreported, their behavior was therefore acceptable to the girls. In other words, they felt they were doing nothing wrong.

To compound this problem, the notion of "snitches get stitches" was deeply embedded within the school culture. If students were to snitch on other students for whatever reason, there was a real fear of retaliation. Perhaps most dismaying to me as a teacher was the fact that the girls who reported these behaviors to me communicated the idea that enduring sexual harassment was just how life was for women, and there was nothing they could do about it.

Many of my female students had been victims of abuse—physical, emotional, sexual—which may have contributed to the fact that they attended the alternative school in the first place. Such abuses have detrimental effects on students and their academic performance; often students stop caring about themselves and everything around them, including school. They fail classes and act out. If their behavior is disruptive enough, they are sent to the alternative program. These students also deserved a safe, structured, and supportive environment in which to learn. However, the female students were not receiving this.

I had experienced sexual harassment as a young college student, although I did not call it that at the time. This was before Anita Hill and there was not a name for this phenomenon in popular parlance. It was the late 1980s, and I was taking a freshman math course. When comparing my test scores with a classmate, I noticed that she had been granted more points than I although we had identical answers. I went to speak to the professor during his office hours. He agreed to give me the additional points, but not without complementing me on my appearance, replete with details on certain outfits I had worn previously and explicit descriptions of my body and his opinions about it. I felt extremely uncomfortable, but I was not equipped to deal with this. I remember feeling that I just wanted to leave. I did leave, and never returned. I remained in the class but received the worst grade of my undergraduate career. As an adult, I know that I had recourse to deal with the situation, but as an eighteen-year-old, I did not. No one prepared me with the information that could have helped me in this situation. I did not want my students to experience what I did. I made it my duty to determine how best to share with them the information that would help them deal with such gender-based discrimination.

Based upon my experience with women's studies, which came late in my undergraduate studies, and my research on how such courses have helped to empower college-aged women, I knew that a women's studies program at the alternative high school could help the female students and contribute to a cultural change within the school. Their previous life experiences had taught many of these students that they were nothing more than victims. Their only defense to this was to act as if degrading treatment was "no big deal." In actuality, they were taught to be victims somewhere in their lives (most likely repeatedly); the sexual harassment they were facing was simply more of the same. For many of these girls, their defenses had taught them to become "the tough girls," "the violent girls," or those who could not be hurt.

Current research suggests that sexual harassment is a major problem in today's K–12 schools (AAUW, 2001/1993; Fineran & Bennett, 1999; Gruber & Fineran, 2008; Stein, 1999). According to the research of Gruber and Fineran (2008) on bullying and harassment in schools, 52 percent of students are bullied, 35 percent are sexually harassed, 25 percent of males and females are victims of cyberbulliying, 79 percent of LGBTQ students experience bullying, and 71 percent of LGBTQ students experience sexual harassment. However, sexual harassment has the greatest impact on self-esteem, mental and physical health, trauma symptoms, and substance abuse issues (Gruber & Fineran, 2008).

These studies suggest that students in K–12 schools are more likely to experience sexual harassment than individuals in the workplace or in higher education. Peer sexual harassment is a problem for both females and males, but females still experience the majority of it. Males often experience sexual harassment at the hands of other males (sexual orientation harassment), whereas the sexual harassment experienced by females is most often perpetrated by males. Females also experience more instances of physical harassment than do males.

Sexual harassment is a complicated phenomenon involving various interrelated factors such as gender, patriarchal norms, and issues of power. Students typically do not report incidents of sexual harassment (AAUW, 1993/2001). To compound this problem, schools often do not take action when incidents of sexual harassment are reported (Kopels & Dupper,

1999; Meyer, 2009). This failure on the part of schools causes a cadre of other problems for the victims. Ignoring claims of sexual harassment or viewing them as typical adolescent behavior or as mere bullying will not make the problems go away. In fact, to *not* deal with the issue of sexual harassment in a proactive manner only serves to create an environment that is more hostile where students do not feel safe and protected by the adults around them. When schools fail to intervene, they may be doing more than reinforcing the traditional hierarchy and devaluing the voices of girls; they may also be implicitly encouraging a pattern of male violence (Stein, 1996) and reinforcing hegemonic masculinity, which is a primary cause of homophobic harassment and sexual harassment based on gender (Meyer, 2009).

Self-esteem, gender-role orientations, locus of control, and sexist beliefs all serve to reinforce the phenomenon of sexual harassment. Research on college-age women suggests that women's studies courses have been successful in raising women's self-esteem (Stake & Gerner, 1987; Zuckerman, 1983), encouraging more egalitarian gender-role orientations in female students (Harris, Melaas, & Rodacker, 1999), altering women's loci of control toward a more internal orientation (Harris, Melaas, & Rodacker, 1999), and decreasing sexist beliefs (De Judicibus & McCabe, 2001). My goal in bringing women's studies to high school was to create a culture of empowerment where girls would find strength in their own voices, learn strategies to deal with harassing behaviors, feel they had control over their lives and bodies, and decrease sexual harassment within the school environment.

School culture is shaped by the behavior and practices of students, teachers, and the administration. If students are taught to recognize what constitutes sexual harassment and strategies to deal with harassers, then this awareness may translate into action. If students refuse to tolerate sexually harassing behavior when they experience it or witness it, then this may cause the perpetrators to alter their behavior. My objective was to determine if exposing girls to the intervention would alter their perceptions and responses to sexual harassment enough to change the school culture to one that is less tolerant of sexual harassment in general.

At this time I was asked by other teachers why I did not include boys in the women's studies course. Certainly the boys needed an intervention. All of my students benefited from learning more about gender, media literacy, and sexual harassment on a day-to-day basis in my other courses when "teachable moments" came up and in my choices of course content in English. However, the girls needed a more intensive intervention; thus the idea of an all-girls women's studies course was born. My approach represented an alternative to the victim/reactive approach; mine was a proactive approach to teaching the creation and maintenance of boundaries. Creating this intervention represented an affirmative action for the purpose of promoting gender equity within a school environment that was underserving the female student population; thus, this proposition to reduce the gender and sexual harassment occurring within the school culture was in compliance with the requirements of Title IX (see Klein, in this volume).

The female students in the alternative school did not view their experiences and voices as primary. They were accustomed to taking the back seat in classes and in hallways where the boys were louder and male privilege set the agenda. My objective was to determine if my approach would be effective in transforming student behavior. If female students were provided a place where they felt safe enough to share their experiences, learned about the nature of harassment and the power dynamics it involves, learned of the policies and procedures regarding sexual harassment in the school environment, and learned to find confidence enough with their own voices to file formal complaints when necessary, then, I surmised, sexual harassment within the school would decrease because of the activism of female students.

Prior to the course, the majority of female students had experienced sexual harassment. Most felt that sexual harassment was a problem in their school. Interestingly, although the majority of students reported experiencing some form of sexual harassment, only half of them reported it to teachers or administrators. Conversely, of the students who had not experienced it, the majority indicated that they would report incidents of sexual harassment when and if they experienced them. These findings indicate that sexual harassment has a disempowering effect on its victims. Thus, in order for me to assist in reducing sexual harassment levels within the school through the women's studies course, information about sexual harassment had to be provided as well as an emphasis on the importance of reporting incidents when they occurred. Teaching empowerment strategies for victims to use in harassing situations was also part of the course.

During the course, students learned about what behaviors constitute sexual harassment, what it feels like to be sexually harassed, what to do when experiencing it, and why victims often do not report. Students shared their own stories of facing sexual harassment and learned from one another how important it is to support victims.

> I feel as if people don't report sexual harassment because too many people get away with it and the person that it happened to is afraid that nothing is going to happen to the person who did it; and they will do it again because they got away with it the first time. I think that witnesses are scared to report it because they are afraid that that person is going to find out and do something to them. We need to start being there for these people if we know any and talk them through it.
>
> —Jenny

> I have learned lots of things about sexual harassment. It is really a crazy thing. Some people don't take it serious enough or girls just don't like to report it or they are scared. I have been through the experience and I know how it feels. It makes you feel really nasty, like someone has violated you and if you're a virgin it feels like someone has stolen something from you and you can't get it back—something so precious can't be replaced. These things haunt you 4-real.
>
> —Fran

Prior to the course, many students did not feel the things they had experienced were in fact harassment. Those who felt they had been harassed also felt they had no recourse against their harassers, assuming that the school would not do anything in terms of providing consequences for the perpetrators; this was often based on personal experience. Additionally, many students were initially resistant to the course in general. It was easier for them to blame victims than to acknowledge themselves as victims. Eventually, all of the students who took part in the class bonded over their similar experiences and realized that they could deal effectively with the issue, as would the school.

> I have experienced sexual harassment a few times, but in some cases I did not know how to deal with it. As I got older, I began to understand what it was and why I shouldn't let it continue to happen to

me. Last year [at another school] I was in my math class and a boy came up to me and humped me. That really pissed me off. I told him he needed to stop and he called me a bitch. Then I tried to hit him, but he ran so I told the principal; nothing major happened.

—Delia

People fail to report sexual harassment because they are usually or more than likely scared. They don't want to make it worse than it already is. We can change this by teaching young girls that it's okay. It's not their fault. We need to send the message out to other women that we support them in whatever they do, so they are no longer scared, and we could decrease the rates of sexual harassment.

—Cynthia

I have been harassed in school and out. What's funny is guys think they can walk on the small ones. I have been harassed in a store. Yes, it can be reported; then you have to feel like the bad one. All the girls I know have been harassed. I have seen it in school. It's in the open. I don't understand why teachers act like they don't see it. That's why some think it doesn't get taken care of, 'cause no one ever sees it.

—Susan

What I have learned in this course is that women have the same rights as men. . . . I now know the difference between flirting and sexual harassment. While we're on the subject of sexual harassment, we had plenty of people expose their personal ordeals and we all supported them to the fullest. We learned a lot about one another and this class brought us all closer. I know that everyone learned something about themselves or someone else. We revealed how vulnerable we can be and we helped one another build up nerve and self-esteem. I appreciate all of the students who have showed a sign of change even though they fought it at first. I feel that this class should continue as an after school activity every other week. I'm glad you decided to initiate a class like this even after many people claimed to hate it. I'll admit I was one of those, but I changed my mind.

—Linda

In terms of the curriculum, students examined sample sexual harassment policies and then wrote their own. They practiced filling out reporting forms.

I stressed the fact that it is crucial to keep records of specifics when experiencing sexual harassment: dates, times, behaviors, quotations from perpetrators, and the like. We practiced setting boundaries, and what to say when one is harassed. For example, students practiced, in loud strong voices, mantras such as, "No, stop it. What you are doing is harassment and that is not okay with me. If you do not stop I will report this as sexual harassment." Through this training, I found that teenage girls are not taught how to say "no," especially to boys, especially in a culture of male privilege and entitlement. We had to practice this frequently over time. I found that they were embarrassed to say the word "no" for a variety of reasons. Girls are still taught, through socialization and the mass media, to be compliant, to be nice, and to "get along." Also, in dating etiquette, girls are still taught to be "nice" when they reject. They are taught to reject through subtle nuanced responses. Boys are taught the opposite message: they are taught pursue; they are taught that girls do not really say what they mean, that "no" means the opposite of "no" (see De Becker, 1997). Because of this, I taught my students to be clear and definitive, which had an empowering effect on them. Additionally, students participated in two days of assertiveness and self-defense training to reinforce boundary setting and to learn to deal with physical intimidation.

> Before I entered this class, I knew basically nothing about feminism, equality, women's rights, and actually how much of an issue sexual harassment was before. I kind of felt overpowered by men. I still feel like a man could bring me down, but I hope to learn more and be able to stand right back up and face the situation face-to-face. I hope this class will soon become a year-long class so many girls can become more aware of the situations going on in our every day lives.
>
> —Ann

> I take sexual harassment more serious now. I think it has had an effect on the school because the girls are taking things a lot more serious. Even if a guy is just joking around, they are taking it a lot more serious because they have learned more about it. People in the school are taking it more serious because the girls don't play anymore. They don't mess around. They report something if something happens or they go talk to someone instead of keeping it to themselves.
>
> —Sherri

I believe this class should be all year round. It teaches us to stand up for ourselves and that should not have a time limit. I can't wait to have a child, to have a boy, and teach it the qualities to be a good man and support equality. I've learned a lot from this class and recognize things on a day to day basis. For instance, sexism, it still happens everywhere. But now I have the voice and tools to stick up for myself and others.

—Cassie

Eventually the students began to stand up for each other when negative comments were made in the hallways or in classes. They were careful not to use degrading language, and they would correct the language usage of others. In fact, the climate of the school changed. Girls stood up for themselves and for each other in ways that I had never seen before. This suggested to me that the girls who took part in the intervention were beginning to understand that they had a certain degree of control when faced with sexual harassment; they learned that there were things they could do about sexual harassment and that they did not have to accept such behavior as a normal fact of life. Many of the students in the class communicated that they were interested in passing on what they had learned to younger girls. This was possibly the most encouraging finding to suggest that real learning had occurred.

I am achieving so many things in life and it is because of this class. I am starting to realize about sexual harassment, and now that I do there are a lot of girls who thank me and they call for advice when they need it because I am a role model for these young girls (women). I thank this class for my achievements and I hope I can pass them down to my kids one day. I am truly loving this class because of what I will do in the future.

—Tenisha

During the semester in which the women's studies course was taught, from September to mid-January, there were a total of thirty-five office referrals for sexual harassment. More specifically, there were thirty-two office referrals for inappropriate comments of a sexual nature. There were two referrals for inappropriate sexual touching, and there was one referral for inappropriate sexual gesturing. The former two referrals were considered to be criminal sexual conduct and were committed by two different students. One of these students was expelled after a district hearing.

During the second semester, from mid-January to June, there were a total of eleven office referrals for sexual harassment. More specifically, there were ten office referrals for inappropriate comments of a sexual nature and one office referral for inappropriate sexual gesturing. Incidents of sexual harassment were reduced by more than one-third during the second semester. A combination of factors contributed to this reduction. As a result of the women's studies course, the girls spoke up when faced with harassing comments or behaviors from the boys. They voiced their discomfort to the boys when such behaviors occurred. Many girls also spoke up when they witnessed the harassment of others. As a result of their drawing attention to such conduct that otherwise may have gone unnoticed by the staff, the boys were less likely to participate in it. There are two reasons for this. First, many of the boys, unchallenged by their peers, felt such conduct was acceptable prior to the women's studies course. After, they learned that this behavior was unacceptable and ceased to engage in it. Second, the boys who knew such conduct was unacceptable in the first place were less willing to engage in such conduct because they realized there was a heightened risk of getting caught; the girls made these acts more visible by voicing their disapproval. Also, as a result of the course, many girls were more willing to report the sexual harassment they experienced and witnessed. Thus, the administration was able to identify perpetrators who previously may have gotten away with such conduct. Administrative interventions with these boys may also have contributed to the reduction of sexually harassing conduct. When the boys realized that there were administrative consequences for their actions, they were less likely to engage in sexual harassment.

More work must still be done at this school regarding sexual harassment, sexism, issues of power, and gender roles. Ideas such as female bonding, assertiveness training, and techniques to promote trust and empowerment need to be reinforced. The results found here may provide insight into how to create a curricular intervention to deal with problems such as sexual harassment in schools. Although this women's studies course included only girls, it could be expanded and tailored to include boys as well.

The teacher research that I conducted was empowering for the students and for me. I used traditional research techniques, a mixed-methods approach, to study this issue and the effectiveness of the intervention I created. I developed an instrument to measure sexual harassment and assessed the students' locus of control prior to and after the intervention. I found that students were more internally motivated after the intervention. For more information on sexual harassment, on this intervention, and on my specific research results, see Martin 2005, 2008, 2009a, and 2009b.

Consequences for Social Justice Work

As a teacher working for social justice, one expects to face a certain amount of resistance from colleagues, administrators, and students who represent and thus benefit from the status quo. For example, during the women's studies course, I faced a certain amount of resistance and even hostility from the male student population. Some did not understand what I was doing. When I explained the purpose, many were amenable to it. Some who engaged in such behaviors were angered that they would not be able to get away with it any longer. However, I never expected that I would face repercussions from a male colleague for facilitating this intervention that benefited the entire school culture in general.

In subsequent years after the first incarnation of the sexual harassment intervention, the high school women's studies course that I created and facilitated evolved into something different. After the change in culture, the specific focus on sexual harassment was no longer so prominent. Instead, the curriculum changed to suit the students' interests; male students who were interested in the material joined the course, and the curriculum incorporated service learning; students worked on projects to raise awareness on gender issues that affected people globally.

One day as I was teaching my class, there was a knock at the door. I opened it to find a former student of mine who now attended the adult education program that is housed in the same building. I could tell this student was upset. I stepped into the hallway and asked her what was wrong. She informed me that her history teacher, whom I had never met, announced that men were superior to women. She had previously taken my women's studies course and felt no qualms about standing up to him and his ideas and citing examples of why this was false. He retorted, "Name any woman who has created anything comparable to what men have achieved." She indicated that I would not be happy with his ideas. He responded that he would debate me on this issue any time, in his classroom with students present. At this point, I understood that I would have to intervene for this student. I went to the administrator of her adult education program and related the situation so that she would not be reprimanded for walking out of class without permission.

After this incident, students from this teacher's class, many of whom I had had as students previously, would say things such as, "Mr. Soandso wants to debate with you. Why won't you debate with him? Are you scared? Are you afraid you'll lose?" In fact, the teacher challenged me to the debate through these students. I was outraged by this. To me, this was not a debatable issue. I would not entertain his challenge with a response. His comments in class were tantamount to racist justifications for separate but equal. Did this teacher have no understanding of systems of privilege or historical inequities that prevented women from achieving greatness on par with men or left women's accomplishments out of the dialogue all together? After a few days, I realized that this teacher was communicating to his students that I was fearful of this debate. There was no way I would engage in such a useless dialogue or stoop to his unprofessional behavior. In the students' minds, if I were to "lose" this debate, then this teacher's opinion would be right in their eyes. This was a "lose/lose" situation.

I went to the administration and informed them of the situation and that these comments were a violation of Title IX and thus illegal. The principal was very understanding; he spoke to the teacher, who subsequently wrote letters of apology to all of his students. The teacher never said a word to me about this incident, and I never did officially meet him. I share this story because it illustrates the fact that when teachers are advocates for social justice, often they become targets. I was targeted because my views and activism were incompatible with the status quo and hegemonic masculinity.

I encountered another surprise when I attempted to take my women's studies intervention on the road. I pitched the idea of bringing it to another, more traditional, high school. I met with a high-level administrator with the hopes that she would be interested. When I explained my plan to her, she indicated to me that she could not approve. She informed me that she did not want to know the extent of the problem of sexual harassment in her school. When I asked her why, she replied, "because then we would have to do something about it." I took two things from this experience. First, my research was not valued because of my role as a classroom teacher. Second, I learned that not all administrators support teachers, teacher research, and protecting students; in other words, some are unprepared or ill equipped to do this difficult work. The goal of advancing equity for her students was not part of her agenda. This administrator did not want to put in the time and work in the short term although it would have helped her school in the long run.

Social Justice Challenges for Teacher Leaders

Bullying and harassment prevention is both a popular topic and an important issue for today's educators. However, there are some groups that are left out of this dialogue. LGBTQ harassment is a topic that is not often broached in schools. With today's increasingly conservative political agenda trickling into the public schools, as realized in abstinence-only education, for example, many educators are afraid to speak out as allies. However, as educators, we are required to protect all students and create safe educational environments for them. We are also legally obligated to protect LBGTQ students from sexual harassment as indicated by Title IX case law; many educators are unaware of this fact.

According to Williams, Connolly, Pepler, and Craig (2005), between 1 and 3 percent of adolescents report being gay or bisexual; another 10 percent are questioning. Sexual harassment has been reported to be a significant problem for these populations, as is a hostile peer environment (Williams, Connolly, Pepler, & Craig, 2005). LGBTQ youth are three times as likely as their nonminority-status peers to skip school because of safety issues and to report having been injured by or threatened with a weapon. These students are more than twice as likely to report being in a physical fight at school. LGBTQ youth are more than four times as likely to attempt suicide (Bochenek & Brown, 2001). Suicide is a leading cause of death for these youths, who report feeling greater levels of alienation, helplessness, hopelessness, loneliness, and worthlessness than their heterosexual peers. This is a problem that is still not addressed in schools as readily as it should be and thus requires social justice advocacy.

According to GLSEN (2007), 86 percent of LGBTQ students reported being harassed verbally because of their sexual orientation, 44 percent have been physically harassed, 22 percent were physically assaulted, and 75 percent hear homophobic remarks. Ninety percent of students heard the word "gay" used in a negative manner, such as "that's so gay." Tragically, 60 percent of these students failed to report these incidents to school staff members because they felt that nothing would be done about it. Thirty-one percent of students who did report their experiences with harassment indicated that nothing was done in response. Homophobic and sexist language is common in today's schools. Language is often where harassment starts. If school officials intervene when they hear harassing language used, they may prevent more serious offenses from being committed. Teachers must be encouraged to intervene when they hear this type of language and be trained how to do so effectively. Teachers should be trained to intervene with both covert and overt forms of harassment. Social justice educators must lobby for such trainings for staff and students.

There are severe consequences for students who experience harassment based on their LGBTQ status. These students generally report having more problems emotionally and behaviorally than do their sexual majority counterparts. Additionally, these youth report having less access to family and peer support than do their heterosexual peers (Williams, Connolly, Pepler, & Craig, 2005). The effects of harassment on LGBTQ youth are great and they include: avoiding certain parts of the school, having difficulty in paying attention in classes, participating less in classes, and skipping classes altogether (Sadowski, 2001).

According to Rivers and Noret (2008), students who report being harassed because of actual or perceived sexual minority status also report engaging in more health-risk behaviors, such as drug use. Unfortunately, most schools do not specifically include the category of LGBTQ status in policies and procedures prohibiting harassment and bullying. Schools with gay–straight alliances (GSAs) have been found to be more welcoming to LGBTQ students than schools without them (Sadowski, 2001).

Awareness must be raised on issues of sexual harassment based on gender and sexual orientation in teacher education programs and in professional development programs. It is also important that school districts enumerate their harassment policies to include sexual harassment based upon gender identity and sexual orientation (real and perceived) whether this is required by law or not. Teacher education programs and school districts must inform those new to the profession about the protections of Title IX. Often, teachers do not know how to deal with harassment and bullying. Training on these issues is crucial for all teachers.

On October 26, 2010, the United States Department of Education Office for Civil Rights issued ten pages of guidance to approximately 15,000 school districts and to colleges and universities receiving federal funds delineating their responsibilities to protect students from sexual and gender-based harassment and harassment based upon race, color, national origin, and disability. What will be new to many schools is that the guidelines make clear that students' sexual orientation and gender identity and expression (real or perceived) are protected under Title IX. If school districts fail to adequately protect these students, the Department can withdraw federal funds or place conditions upon them. Those districts and schools who may have failed to protect LGBTQ students in the past will now have to rectify this. This may result in harassment prevention training for staff and students and changes to enumerated policies to prohibit harassment. This is good news for social justice educators and advocates and for our students.

Advice for Social Justice Educators

There are many things that we can do to make school environments healthier and more equitable for our students. First and foremost, policy changes are necessary for equity to be possible (Darling-Hammond, 2010). Advocacy is required on the state and federal levels so that schools are adequately funded.

Some schools work together for social justice reform. However, some teachers may be working alone and in small coalitions in order to facilitate larger-scale changes in their schools and districts. Teacher leadership and teacher research can contribute to necessary reforms. For social justice principles and practices to become institutionalized, we must begin to value the knowledge of teachers and view them as experts in their field. This change requires advocacy, and it may require additional training for some. Teaching must be seen as a profession, one that does not always require outside intervention from politicians and professors. To this end, teachers must be their own advocates. As Christianakis (2008) argues,

> Teacher researchers upsets the "class" divisions operationalized in higher-ed-driven, top-down patriarchal research models. . . . teacher research situates findings in real life classrooms with real life constraints. Such positionality challenges "one size fits all" notions, such as those implemented by the Bush administration and the NCLB law. (p. 112)

If teachers desire to make changes within their classrooms and schools, they should first determine whether they have enough training. Courses and professional development in research methodology and action research can be beneficial. Current and future social justice educators should read professional journals and other literature and stay current on the legal, social, and political issues that affect education. They should involve themselves politically when education is under attack. They must speak out at board meetings and involve themselves in the current educational dialogues.

Teachers interested in social justice work and in transforming schools as places of democracy and emancipation must work in coalitions and step into leadership roles. Shared leadership is crucial in achieving and sustaining high-performing schools. Administrators must utilize teachers' strengths by creating opportunities for them to employ them. Collaboration with teachers can lessen the burden on administrators (and empower teachers), but sharing leadership requires courage and trust. Administrators who work for the goals of social justice can inspire group action. This type of leadership is risky but ultimately makes schools safer and more productive places and can reduce administrator workload.

Professional learning communities (PLCs) can assist in all of these endeavors. The main focus of PLCs is student learning; increased teacher decision making and empowerment are natural extensions of this. Teachers are to be given time to collaborate on student need, reflect on practice, and devise solutions to problems of assessment and learning. Teacher reflection is informed by theory with common goals: to raise student achievement, close the achievement gap, and advance equity. This is the true definition of praxis, which enables teachers to participate in the production of knowledge, which contributes to the notion of teachers as professionals. Collecting data by tracking and analyzing student achievement is crucial in pursuing these endeavors.

Focused professional development, in conjunction with professional learning communities, is required for school reform and teacher empowerment. Professional development should be a regular practice in the overall school reform and not the "flavor of the month."

> ... teachers judge professional development to be most valuable when it provides opportunities to do "hands-on" work that builds their knowledge of academic content and how to teach it to their students, and when it takes into account the local context (including the specifics of local school resources, curriculum guidelines, accountability systems, and so on). (Darling-Hammond, 2010, p. 227)

Often, professional development can involve teachers sharing their research, knowledge of content, process, and technology with other teachers.

Guidelines for administrators who seek to support teachers as true professionals are many. Administrators must first create a positive work/school environment, which includes ensuring adequate working conditions. They must learn to give up a certain degree of control and trust in teachers' abilities and judgment. They must listen to viewpoints that do not accord with their own, value teacher autonomy, and recognize and validate the accomplishments and contributions of teachers. Administrators must support and mentor teachers (and create, support, and value mentoring programs). It is important that they provide positive feedback (not just criticism), expect growth, and support teachers as learners. They must encourage collaboration and work to reduce teacher isolation. They must also empower teachers by encouraging leadership beyond the classroom; this is how we may begin to grow teacher leaders (adapted from Steel & Craig, 2006; Wahlstrom & Seashore Louis, 2008).

Public education has been under attack for some time. This must change because public education is the only system that must educate all students. It is truly the last bastion of democratic education in America. It is not a perfect system, but it can be improved. These improvements should come from within. Providing safe, harassment-free schools with culturally relevant curriculum is necessary in closing the achievement gap and reducing the dropout rate for many populations of students. Enlisting the assistance and expertise of teachers can assist in these reforms; teacher leadership and teacher research are necessary components. In order for us to view the teaching profession differently, we must move away from hierarchical thinking toward an empowerment model. We must cease viewing teachers as technicians and begin to view them as professionals. Educational leadership for social justice must work toward these changes in order to truly improve our schools, for they are worth saving.

References

American Association of University Women Educational Foundation. (2001/1993). *Hostile hallways: Bullying, teasing, and sexual harassment in school.* Washington DC: The American Association of University Women Educational Foundation.

Beachum, F., & Dentith, A. M. (2004, Spring). Teacher leaders creating cultures of school renewal and transformation. *Educational Forum, 68,* 276–86.

Bochenek, M., & Widney Brown, A. (2001). *Hatred in the hallways: Violence and discrimination against lesbian, gay, bisexual, and transgender students in U.S. schools.* New York: Human Rights Watch. Retrieved March 13, 2009, from www.hrw.org/reports/2001/uslgbt/toc.htm.

Christianakis, C. (2008, fall). Teacher research as a feminist act. *Teacher Education Quarterly,* 99–115.

Darling-Hammond, L. (2010). *The flat world and education: How America's commitment to equity will determine our future.* New York: Teachers College Press.

De Becker, G. (1997). *The gift of fear and other survival signals that protect us from violence.* New York: Dell.

De Judicibus, M., & McCabe, M. P. (2001). Blaming the target of sexual harassment: Impact of gender role, sexist attitudes, and work role. *Sex Roles, 44*(7/8), 401–17.

Fine, M. G. (2007). Women, collaboration, and social change: An ethics-based model of leadership. In J. L. Chin, B. Lott, J. K. Rice, &

J. Sanchez-Hucles (Eds.), *Women and leadership: Transforming visions and diverse voices* (pp. 177–91). Malden, MA: Blackwell.

Fineran, S., & Bennett, L. (1999). Gender and power issues of peer sexual harassment among teenagers. *Journal of Interpersonal Violence, 14*(6), 626–28.

Giroux, H. A. (2001/1983). *Theory and resistance in education: Towards a pedagogy for the opposition.* Westport, CT: Bergin and Garvey.

GLSEN. (2007). *The 2007 national school climate survey: Key findings on the experiences of lesbian, gay, bisexual and transgender youth in our nation's schools.* Executive Summary. Retrieved March 13, 2009, from http://www.glsen.org/cgi-bin/iowa/all/news/record/2340.html.

Gruber, J. E., & Fineran, S. (2008). Comparing the Impact of Bullying and Sexual Harassment Victimization on the Mental and Physical Health of Adolescents. *Sex Roles, 58,* 13–14.

Harris, K. L., Melaas, K., & Rodacker, E. (1999). The impact of women's studies courses on college students of the 1990s. *Journal of Research, 40*(11/12), 969–77.

hooks, b. (1994). *Teaching to transgress: Education as the practice of freedom.* New York: Routledge.

Jones, L. C., Webb, P. T., & Neumann, M. (2008). Claiming the contentious: Literacy teachers as leaders of social justice principles and practices. *Issues in Teacher Education, 17*(1), 7–15.

Kopels, S., & Dupper, D. R. (1999). School-based peer sexual harassment. *Child Welfare, 78*(4), 435–60.

Lieberman, A., & Miller, L. (2004). *Teacher leadership.* San Francisco: Jossey-Bass.

Lorde, A. (1984). *Sister outsider: Essays and speeches by Audre Lorde.* Freedom, CA: Crossing Press.

Martin, J. (2005). *Peer sexual harassment: Finding voice, changing culture.* (Doctoral dissertation, Oakland University, 2005). (ERIC Document Reproduction Service No. ED490741).

Martin, J. L. (2008). Peer sexual harassment: Finding voice, changing culture, an intervention strategy for adolescent females. *Violence Against Women, 14*(3), 100–124.

Martin, J. L. (2009a). Reclaiming feminism: A qualitative investigation of language usage by girls in a high school women's studies course. *Girlhood Studies: An Interdisciplinary Journal, 2*(1), 54–72.

Martin, J. L. (2009b). "Talk to us": A study in student generated service-learning, mentoring middle school girls. *Information for Action: A Journal for Research on Service-Learning with Children and Youth, 2*(1), 1–25.

Meyer, E. J. (2009). *Gender, bullying, and harassment: Strategies to end sexism and homophobia in schools.* New York: Teachers College Press.

O'Connor, K. (1992, April). *Assessing the needs of teacher leaders in Massachusetts.* Paper presented at the Annual Meeting of the American Educational Research Association, San Francisco, CA.

Phelps, P. H. (2008). Helping teachers become leaders. *Clearing House, 81*(3), 119–22.

Rivers, I., & Noret, N. (2008). Well-being among same-sex and opposite-sex attracted youth at school. *School Psychology Review, 37*(2), 174–87.

Sadowski, M. (2001). Sexual minority students benefit from school-based support—where it exists. *Harvard Education Letter, 17*(5), 1–5.

Stake, J. E., & Gerner, M. A. (1987). The women's studies experience: Personal and professional gains for women and men. *Psychology of Women Quarterly, 11,* 277–84.

Stein, N. (1999). *Classrooms and courtrooms: Facing sexual harassment in K–12 schools.* New York: Teachers College Press.

Steel, C., & Craig, E. (2006). Reworking industrial models, exploring contemporary ideas, and fostering teacher leadership. *Phi Delta Kappan, 87*(9), 676–80.

Strodl, P. (1992, March). *A model of teacher leadership.* Paper presented at the Eastern Educational Research Association Annual Meeting, Hilton Head, SC.

Wahlstrom, K. L., & Seashore Louis, K. (2008). How teachers experience principal leadership: The roles of professional community, trust, efficacy, and shared responsibility. *Educational Administration Quarterly, 44*(4), 458–95.

Williams, T., Connolly, J., Pepler, D., & Craig, W. (2005). Peer victimization, social support, and psychosocial adjustment of sexual minority adolescents. *Journal of Youth and Adolescents, 34*(5), 471–82.

Wilson, M. C. (2007). *Closing the leadership gap: Add women and change everything*. New York: Penguin Group.

Zuckerman, D. M. (1983). Women's studies, self-esteem, and college women's plans for the future. *Sex Roles, 9*(5), 633–42.

6

Course Guides, Equity, and Achievement: The Shaping of Student Status

Lisa P. Hallen and Elizabeth J. Allan

More girls are graduating from high school; more women are earning associate, bachelor, and graduate degrees than ever before (Aud et al., 2010). Achievements like these prompt many to ask, is gender equity really a problem in education? Progress seems obvious and, though it is widely accepted that girls and women have made many gains in terms of access and representation in education, quantity does not always equate to quality.

Data continue to point to gender-based dynamics shaping climates and experiences that are less than equitable for girls. For instance,

> while girls are ahead or equal to boys on most standardized measures of achievement in the early grades, by the time they graduate from high school or college, they have fallen behind boys on high-stakes tests such as the SAT, ACT, MCAT, LSAT, and GRE. (Sadker, Sadker, & Zittleman, 2009, p. 24)

Girls' opportunities in sport and other cocurricular activities were dramatically expanded by the passage of Title IX, but thirty-five years later, girls represent only 41 percent of high school athletes (NFHS, 2009), and discrimination against girls and women in sport continues to be a documented problem (National Women's Law Center, 2010). In terms of both quality and quantity of teacher time and attention in classrooms, girls receive less than boys (Sadker, Sadker, & Zittleman, 2009). Sexual harassment, cyberbullying, and girl fighting also contribute to school climates that can erode self-esteem and confidence for girls (AAUW, 2003; Paludi, Martin, & Paludi, Jr., 2007; Sadker, Sadker, & Zittleman, 2009).

Aggregate numbers lead some to assume that girls have achieved parity in educational achievement or even surpassed it. However, girls' and women's progress in fields traditionally thought to be male dominated have not advanced at the same rate across the educational spectrum. For example, while there are more girls than boys enrolled in advanced placement (AP) programs in sum, there are far fewer girls than boys enrolled in AP STEM- (science, technology, engineering, mathematics) related programs, namely calculus BC (the highest level of calculus offered by the College Board AP program), chemistry, computer science, and all three sections of the physics curricula; physics, electricity and magnetism, and mechanics (The College Board, 2009). STEM programs have received significant attention by the National Governors' Association and are a focal point for growth in high schools and colleges, yet fewer women are enrolled in the secondary pathways that prepare them or expose them to further study in these fields.

This trend continues in college. An analysis of associate's degree attainment reveals that while 96 percent of associate's degrees in family and human services were conferred to women in 2008, only 10 percent of the associate's engineering and engineering technology degrees were conferred to women (Aud et al., 2010). Likewise, in four-year institutions, while advancing in social sciences and other disciplines, women earned considerably fewer bachelor and graduate degrees in engineering and engineering technologies, physical science and science technologies, and computer information science and support services (Aud et al., 2010). These data indicate that parity has not been met, especially in the STEM fields, which continue to be male dominated and highly rewarded spheres. Women are also underrepresented in other educational arenas. For example, only 1 in 17 girls who played on a high school athletic team will have an opportunity to play in college (Acosta & Carpenter, 2010). Similarly, while the numbers of women in educational leadership continue to grow, it remains the case that women are clustered at lower rungs of the prestige ladder (Allan, in press).

These disparities can have far-reaching consequences. Once students graduate from high school, graduate from college, and move on to careers, economic outcomes still reflect a stubborn pattern of inequity. Referring to young adult graduates, Aud et al. (2010) found that:

> In 2008, at every educational level, the median of the earnings for young adult males was higher than the median for young adult females; for example, young adult males with a bachelor's degree earned $53,000, on average, while their female counterparts earned $42,000. (p. vi)

This one strand of evidence (higher high school completion, higher degree attainment, but in limited fields with smaller earnings regardless of degree) points to a larger picture. Though great strides have been made, there are still considerable inequities including earnings and social capital. These realities are often lost in debates that portray women's education as equal to, or perhaps even superior to, men's educational experiences in U.S. institutions.

While the past forty years of legislative progress have helped create greater equity for girls, there is danger in the notion that we are at a "mission accomplished" stage. Gender equity need not be framed as a zero-sum game, though it is often represented this way. Rather, we assert that schools can improve educational climates for all students without disadvantaging either gender. Further, when considering disparities rooted in socioeconomic status (SES) and race, it is clear gains are necessary for *both* boys and girls, particularly those from low-SES backgrounds. In referring to her studies on white working-class students, Weis (2008) writes:

> The production of class . . . must be understood as deeply nested in race and gender. By nested, I mean that race and gender lie within class and class dynamics wherein both the production and movement of class can be understood only with serious and continued attention to the ways in which other key nodes of difference both wrap class and simultaneously serve to produce it. (p. 292)

Thus, it is necessary to examine gender, race/ethnicity, and SES as linked in a complex web of production. While this analysis foregrounds gender and SES in particular, our approach was guided by understanding the social construction and interplay of multiple identity categories.

Socioeconomic Status and Student Achievement

Historical accounts of American higher education have shown SES disparities in college enrollment for centuries (Lucas, 1994; Thelin, 2004). Many
advances have been made by lower-SES students as colleges, laws, and
higher education policies have evolved over time (Lucas, 1994; Thelin,
2004). However, a more recent analysis by the National Center of Education Statistics (NCES) shows that socioeconomic differences in college
enrollment have existed and persisted since 1972 (Planty et al., 2009).
Since then, immediate college enrollment has been higher for high-
income students than for their lower-income peers (Planty et al., 2009).
For more than thirty-five years, extensive research and policy efforts have
focused on assisting lower-income students with increasing their academic
achievements in high school and continuing to postsecondary enrollment.
In spite of these efforts, a significant socioeconomic gap persists.

Lower-income students are six times more likely to drop out of high
school than their higher-income peers (Wirt et al., 2004). Students whose
parents do not have college experience are more likely to be from low-
SES backgrounds (Chen, 2005). Over the past three decades, low-SES
students' educational aspirations have been rising, but their postsecondary
enrollment statistics continue to fall behind middle- and higher-SES peers,
especially those whose parents have a postsecondary degree (Planty et al.,
2009). In addition, it has been widely established in the literature that
lower-SES students are less likely to be placed in courses that prepare them
for college-level study and less likely to go to college than peers from
higher-SES backgrounds (Chen, 2005; Gamoran & Mare, 1989; Lucas,
1999; Oakes, 1995, 2005; Rosenbaum, 1975; Sirin, 2005; Weis, 2003;
Yonezawa & Wells, 2005). These and others concur that lack of academic
preparation in high school adds to the barriers faced by many lower-SES
students, particularly when navigating the high school-to-college transition.

The analysis highlighted in this chapter emerges from our interest in
examining ways in which educational paths can be shaped and potentially
limited through curricular processes that are often thought to enhance
equity. While we consider multiple aspects of girls' identities, a feminist
analysis ensures that gender is not overlooked as is often the case when
it is assumed that gender equity has been achieved. In sum, we draw upon
feminist perspectives to analyze how high school course guides may

contribute inequity as they shape understandings and beliefs about who is/ is not capable and desirable in particular courses of study.

We write as parents, educators, and scholars who have first-hand experience with schools. Allan is a professor of graduate studies in higher education and women's studies at a public university, and Hallen is a doctoral student who currently works as a high school guidance counselor in a public secondary school. Our analysis builds from Allan's (1999, 2003, 2008) policy discourse analysis research, where she offers new ways of viewing problems and policy in educational contexts. Hallen's experience as a high school guidance counselor led us to consider how policy discourses carried by public school documents may contribute to reinscribing gender and class inequities.

Informed by her experience as a high school guidance counselor, Hallen noted how course placement and student socioeconomic status seemed to be related. In one high school, though the free/reduced lunch rate was approximately 40 percent in a given year, the school's F/R lunch enrollment in AP courses was only 9 percent. Similarly, she noticed gendered patterns based on different courses and programs, such as enrollments in higher-level STEM classes or in "at-risk" courses.

Tracking in Schools

In a modern comprehensive public high school, ability grouping is a common and thoroughly ingrained practice in both instruction (by teachers, administrators, and policy makers) and learning (by students and parents). Ability grouping has existed in public high schools for more than a century, and it follows that educators in 2010 were themselves educated in tracked classes and have taught tracked classes, particularly at the junior high and high school levels. Tracking is often accepted as a normal aspect of school organization and instructional management, rendering the process invisible and unproblematic to many educational stakeholders (Anyon, 2006; Apple, 1990; Carlson, 2006; Fine, 2003; Oakes, 2005; Weis, 2003).

In addition to the presumed common sense of this practice, there are other frequently cited reasons why tracking methods continue. Oakes (2005) provides four assumptions that undergird tracking, which include: students learn better when with their academically similar peers; *slower* students will feel more positive about themselves if they are with similarly abled students; school placement processes appropriately and equitably reflect students' past achievements and *native abilities*; and instruction is easier for teachers in similarly grouped classrooms. These four assumptions are linked with nuanced ideas of ability, meritocracy, and appropriateness and have contributed to the normalization and invisibility of tracking in schools. Hence, its long-term effects are rarely called into question (Anyon, 2006; Apple, 2006; Brantlinger, 1993; Oakes, 2005; Weis, 2003; Yonezawa & Wells, 2005; Yonezawa, Wells, & Serna, 2002).

Tracking Outcomes

The organization of high school curricula helps shape students' future economic paths and possibilities. Students' placement in high school courses has been found to have a significant impact on their preparation and readiness for college-level study. Much of the research posits that differentiated curricula produce stratification among students, with those placed in upper-level academic positions earning the greatest benefits both academically and socially (Gamoran & Mare, 1989; Gamoran et al., 1995; Hallinan, 1994; Heck & Mahoe, 2006; Kelly, 2007; Lucas, 1999; Oakes, 1995, 2005; Rosenbaum, 1975; Sirin, 2005).

Educators and sociologists have also studied how culture, race, gender, and SES impact educational placement and perceived ability (e.g., Carbonaro & Gamoran, 2002; Hallinan & Sørensen, 1987; Heck & Mahoe, 2006; Oakes, 2005; Sirin, 2005; Weis, 2003; Yonezawa & Wells, 2005). Heck and Mahoe (2006) summarize this pattern as follows:

> Students' previous academic records are used as a justification for subsequent placements, without addressing the problem of how race-ethnicity and social class can contribute to placement decisions or the consequences of those decisions for students' likelihood to integrate academically and socially to further their chances of educational success. (p. 438)

In sum, for decades, scholars have analyzed tracking outcomes and have questioned the degree to which schools, as social systems, are sorting students according to different characteristics under the dominant pedagogical strategy of ability grouping (Apple, 2006; Carbonaro & Gamoran, 2002; Fine, 2003; Oakes, 2005; Oakes & Guiton, 1995; Rosenbaum,

1975; Rumberger & Palardy, 2005). Yet the debate continues in academic circles and the practice of tracking continues in most public comprehensive high schools.

Research Design

Our analysis is framed by poststructural discourse theories shaped by Michel Foucault's configuration of power and subjectivity and feminist appropriations of these. Feminist poststructural perspectives provide new lenses with which to view "commonsense" practices, to challenge hegemonic representations, and to consider alternative strategies that promote equity and social justice. The policy discourse analysis method has been applied in research related to women's commission policy reports (Allan, 1999, 2003, 2008), diversity action plans (Iverson, 2005), and images of educational leaders and leadership (Allan, Gordon, & Iverson, 2006; Gordon, Iverson, & Allan, 2009).

More specifically, this chapter builds on insights from Hallen's research, where she employs policy discourse analysis to examine a national sample of U.S. public comprehensive high school documents and investigate questions about achievement specifically related to socioeconomic status, equity, curricula, and organization of public secondary schools. Her work addresses the following questions: What are the predominant discourses that emerge from a sample of U.S. public high school course guides? What subject positions/images of students emerge from these discourses? What realities are likely to be re/produced as a result of these subject positions and their representation across the curriculum in U.S. public high schools?

In this chapter, we add feminist theory and gender as primary lenses through which to view Hallen's data. First, we highlight some key concepts forming the basis of policy discourse analysis. We then summarize Hallen's study of U.S. public comprehensive course guides. Finally, we share our perspectives about how this research underscores the importance of considering a feminist approach to understanding and addressing school problems and policies.

Policy Discourse Analysis

More than simply a stretch of text on paper, discourse includes language, speech, text, and meaning, representations that both reflect and shape reality. Allan (2008) refers to discourses as "dynamic constellations of words and images that are actively reinforced, resisted, and reconstituted" (p. 6). Ball (1990) writes:

> . . . discourses are about what can be said, and thought, but also about who can speak, when, where and with what authority. Discourses embody meaning and social relationships, they constitute both subjectivity and power relations. . . . Thus, discourses construct certain possibilities for thought. They order and combine words in particular ways and exclude or displace other combinations. (p. 2)

Usher and Edwards (1994) explain that in a Foucauldian position, these discourses can be construed as truths. They write:

> Foucault is not claiming that a discourse is a set of true statements but rather that a discourse, in defining what can be said and thought, *provides the means for statements to be assessed as true, the reasoning which enables truth-claims to be made and validated.* (Usher & Edwards, 1994, italics added, p. 90)

Important to this investigation, discourses shape policies and practices (Allan, 1999, 2003, 2008; Bacchi, 1999; Ball, 1990; Carlson, 2006; Marshall, 1997; Pillow, 2000, 2003; Scheurich, 1994). Understanding policy as discourse allows researchers to investigate other relationships and realities at work that are created by the language and texts used to craft policies (Allan, 1999, 2003, 2008; Ball, 1990; Scheurich, 1994). In the context of a public high school, discourse influences operations, management, instruction, curriculum, and classification of students, among other functions reflected in the school environment and in a school's documents. All of these discursive influences are at work and circulating throughout policy construction (Allan, 1999, 2003, 2008; Ball, 1990; Foucault, 1995; Marshall, 1997; Scheurich, 1994).

Policy discourse analysis is a method to uncover and dismantle dominant, naturalized images by analyzing policy as discourse (Allan, 1999, 2003, 2008; Bacchi, 1999; Iverson, 2005; Marshall, 1997; Scheurich, 1994). Policy discourse analysis " . . . provides an opportunity to examine ways in which policy can both support and subvert dominant discourses that emphasize particular perspectives and obscure others" (Allan, 2008, p. 32). This method allows us to uncover images of students and examine how they are represented across curricular tracks within a larger sociopolitical landscape.

High School Course Guides as Data Source

Many schools outline the central way students access their education through annually published documents that describe high school classes or levels of study, called course guides. These documents are booklets that depict school rules, procedures, and policies. Course guides outline a school's mission and reflect a school's values and culture. These documents are a relevant data source because they also describe a school's curriculum, rules, academic policies, prerequisites, corequisites, reward systems, and, in some cases, the course placement process. In addition, course guides often (but not always) include other academic indicators that help explain course content, what is expected in each course, and for whom (which students) they are designed. Some course guides describe how a student *gets placed* in various courses/tracks, while others simply describe the different courses *available* to students.

School documents like curriculum guides are cultural *artifacts*. They *comprise* words, policies, and rules, but they also *carry* and *convey* values, images, and ideas. These images produce powerful messages about student capabilities, school priorities, mattering, difference, dominance, and other overt and discrete ideas about merit, choice, responsibility, success, and failure. These messages contribute to school culture and to the perspectives of those making decisions about student capabilities, their potential, and what they are permitted to do academically and socially. As such, these documents provide a valuable yet underutilized source for examining ways in which discourses contribute to creating particular realities in schools.

Initial Findings

At first glance, it makes sense that curriculum guides and related policies facilitate school organization and management of students and personnel. However, when examined through the lens of discourse theory, it is possible to see how these documents also draw upon and reinscribe dominant discourses that shape environments where schools and their officials are positioned as expert gatekeepers of the curriculum. In turn, students and their parents are often positioned as outsiders or supplicants petitioning to become insiders. Next, we elaborate these initial patterns, including discourses of professionalism and gender.

Discourse of Professionalism

A dominant discourse of professionalism does not stand alone in normalizing particular approaches to administering school curricula. Rather, this discourse, like others, is supported (and contested) by a web of other discourses. For example, the discourse of professionalism is supported by the broader discourse of enlightenment humanism that privileges autonomy, reason, and progress as the means of achieving human rights and freedom (Weedon, 1999). A discourse of professionalism also intersects and is closely aligned with discourses of excellence, quality, and productivity commonly invoked in academic contexts (Bensimon, 1995; Gumport, 1993; Hey & Bradford, 2004; Readings, 1996). So while we describe a dominant discourse of professionalism made evident by the curriculum guides, we also want to emphasize, as Readings (1996) does in his examination of a discourse of excellence in universities, that these guides carry "divergent . . . discourses, even if one discourse dominates over the others at certain moments" (p. 14).

A critical examination of the discourse of professionalism in education (especially teacher education) has been the focus of scholarly attention related to education reform (e.g., Bloch, 1987; Densmore, 1987; Heyning, 1997; Labaree, 1992; Larson, 1990; Popkewitz, 1994, 1995; Seddon, 1997). According to Heyning (1997), most educational reform policy reports published in the 1980s advocated for increased professionalism in teaching. "The cultural appeal of professionalism is often grounded in notions of upward mobility and it is believed that teachers will receive higher professional status if they become more like doctors and lawyers" (p. 8). Typically, the concept of professionalism is linked to ideas about quality, dependability, excellence, efficiency, and autonomy (Bensimon, 1995; Heyning, 1997; Popkewitz, 1994). Professionalism is also described as "a *state of mind* that must be earned through integrity, commitment, trust and honest hard work" [italics added] (Heyning 1997, p. 8).

Specialized knowledge or training, juried entry, and regulation of standards are traditional benchmarks of professionalism described in the literature (Argyris & Schon, 1974; Heyning, 1997; Seddon, 1997). Professions have been recognized as "gatekeeping mechanisms, making demarcations between self-regulating communities and other occupational groups that consolidated the power of the former at the expense of the latter" (Seddon, 1997, p. 232). Larson (1990) argues that professionalism as a discourse is inextricably linked to power/knowledge and serves to produce status and rewards through a system of expertise rooted in codified knowledges. Accordingly, a dominant discourse of professionalism produces a prestige hierarchy even within a "community of credentialed knowers" (like the academy). She writes:

> The unequal ability to produce or appropriate authoritative statements distinguishes the leaders from the led, the official from the unofficial spokesmen [sic], the orthodox from the marginals or the dissenters, the prestigious from the more obscure institutional roles and even, after all that, the talented from the less talented. (Seddon, 1997, p. 234)

Thus, as it is dispersed, the discourse of professionalism serves to differentiate and regulate in ways that come to appear normal. The discursive formation of subject positions and subjectivity provides that professionalism can become a "state of mind." Its dispersal guarantees that individuals learn not only to judge others but also to see themselves according to particular "standards" established through the discourse (Allan, 2008).

Policy as Discourse: Constructing Student Status

A close reading of the curriculum guides collected for this investigation reveals that a student's track and/or course placement is limited or controlled by a range of factors. There are multiple instances where a school's course selection or course change policies are incongruent with its stated mission. Generally, school mission statements reflect an ideal of working together (school, parent/s, and student) to foster maximum learning and achievement. However, some course guides send a different message. For example, one school's course guide described a three-step change process including: completing a procedural form called "parent override form" by a firm deadline; taking a standardized test by a firm deadline; and a final decision made by a department chairperson. This policy conflicts with an earlier one that touted a student's ability to *choose* classes that are "*appropriate* for their career." However, as this policy illustrates, it is ultimately a department chairperson who determines what career (and what courses) may be most appropriate for students. A dominant discourse of professionalism contributes to shaping a *troublesome outsider* subject position, where students or parents are in the position of having to petition for a change in academic program. The dominant discourse constructs the image of school officials being "in charge," "in control," and "knowing best": images of parents and students who request a change are therefore challenging the judgment of the professional expert and must undergo an extensive vetting process.

In such an environment, students and parents are typically rewarded for compliance by following the rules delineated in the curriculum guides and related policies. Those familiar with the system know how to follow the requisite rules and guidelines to gain entree/insider status. In contrast, those who are not (or choose not to be) socialized in the norms shaped by the dominant discourses will likely be at a disadvantage when seeking to gain insider status.

Some course guides list subjective requirements such as "self-motivation" and being "intellectually curious." Several course guides made note of students being "invited" to take certain classes. Kelly (2007) also found this pattern in his study of North Carolina course guides, where he made the observation that "when one is confronted with such requirements for course placement, it may feel as if gaining entry into courses was like gaining entry into an elite country club" (p. 24). Conversely, other course descriptions for middle to lower track levels frequently mentioned their suitability for "hands-on" students. Individualized assessments can also be used in exit rationale as well as entree criteria. Sadker and Sadker (1994) noted that high school guidance counselors and teachers steered girls away from advanced math and science classes if they weren't required for graduation due to their perceived ability to handle stress: " . . . they literally excuse them, a dismissal less likely to be offered to male students" (p. 125). Though perhaps unintentional, school leaders do influence students' choices, at times in gendered ways (Sadker & Sadker, 1994; Sadker, Sadker, & Zittleman, 2009). Who then is positioned to make assessments about a student's characteristics and what criteria are used for these assessments? (Kelly, 2007). How do one's own gender identity and assumptions about students' gender identity affect course placement? Individualized assessments, along with prohibitive language, helps school officials control which students are placed in which classes according to vague ideas of "appropriateness," and, at times, behavior, instead of a student's choice, ability, and interests.

Gender Discourses

Most of the academic content in the course guides is written in a gender-neutral way, as one might expect. However, the discourse of professionalism is supported by a dominant discourse of masculinity where autonomy, competition, and being in control are emphasized as natural traits for boys/men. In turn, a dominant discourse of femininity constructs the feminine subject as lacking masculine qualities and possessing those in direct contrast. Thus, it has come to be seen as "natural" for girls/women to be more collaborative, nurturing, and compliant than their male counterparts. Numerous scholars have described ways in which gender socialization is likely to influence educational outcomes (e.g., Klein et al., 2007; Sadker & Sadker, 1994; Sadker, Sadker, & Zittleman, 2009). For example, citing Walkerdine's study on teacher beliefs about learning potential (1989), Jones and Myhill (2004) note, " 'girls were felt to lack something, even if they were successful' while on the other hand it seemed that 'boys were felt to possess the very thing that girls were taken to lack' " (p. 548).

In light of these gender dynamics, when a curriculum guide describes a human anatomy class as appropriate for "the serious science student," we are left to wonder what criteria are used to determine this. How might many girls, their teachers, and even parents assess their abilities in science differently than many boys? Individually assessed criteria for course enrollment further contribute to the dominant discourse of (school) expertise and can play into naturalized images of student ability. When considered against the backdrop of dominant discourses of gender, social class, and race/ethnicity, it is possible to see how well-intended school policies and practices may unwittingly advantage some students more than others. For instance, if boys are assumed to be "naturally good" at science and girls "naturally good" in English, how might course descriptions reinscribe or potentially resist this bias? (Jones & Myhill, 2004).

What might the repercussions be for the student? How might girls, whose identities are often associated with dominant discourses that emphasize compliance and obedience (Jones & Myhill, 2004), work against a dominant discourse of professional expertise to challenge a placement decision? Further, how might girls access academic pathways that continue to be male dominated if not encouraged or approved by school personnel? Similar dynamics may operate for those students and their parents who do not see themselves as "professional" by virtue of their family background and/or academic/educational credentials.

As gender discourses shape expectations for appropriate behavior, they also construct deviancy for some girls as depicted in this policy excerpt:

> North High School [a pseudonym] encourages pregnant students to withdraw from active participation in the regular school program at the end of the semester in which their pregnancy begins and no later than such time as they can effectively perform the tasks expected of them at no risk to their health. Students who choose not to withdraw are encouraged to enroll in the Fresh Start Learning Center or North-side Learning Center [both pseudonyms].

> Pregnant students are not barred from participating in school activities. However, the student participates at her own risk. Neither the school, its employees, nor its agents are responsible for any non-negligent injuries to the mother or child. The student should use common sense and good judgment in participating in school activities.

> Pregnancy is not considered an illness as far as school attendance is concerned. Pregnant students are not given an exception to the school attendance policy and are expected to return to school as soon as possible after childbirth. Students do not qualify for any type of maternity leave.

In this example, a gendered discourse of virtue conveys images of shame, alienation, and punishment that result in a *bad girl* subject position. Reading through the lens of discourse theory, the message is that girls who are pregnant are less valuable as students as they are not encouraged to continue their learning in the same school while pregnant. This is mirrored in Pillow's studies on pregnant teens, where school policies focused on deviance, silence, and control rather than the mothers' and infants' physical/emotional needs (Pillow, 2003). Pillow writes, "teen pregnancy operates outside the norm of legitimate reproduction, marking it as a site of moral concern and state control" (2000, p. 202). This framing of teen mothers as *the* policy problem involves dominant norms about who should/should not reproduce, at what age, and how often. Citing Cusick (1989), Pillow writes, "teen pregnancy presents the paradox of young women fulfilling their reproductive responsibilities, but not in the way the state wishes them to" (2000, p. 202). The girls at the focus of this policy are also in a double bind as they are encouraged to withdraw/become invisible yet also expected to abide by the attendance policy.

Summary and Recommendations

It is important to note that these are initial findings based on several policy documents, and more extensive analysis is forthcoming. We do not claim that these patterns are representative of all schools, nor do we assume that these policy examples are created to restrict achievement. However, we assert that using policy discourse analysis on school documents like course guides can serve to extend educators' understanding of factors that may influence all students' learning opportunities.

This analysis can help promote understanding about how high school course guides contribute to constructing, re/producing, and carrying images of students with regard to ability, motivation, attitude, and merit, among other characteristics. These images are shaped in part by dominant and naturalized discourses of professionalism and gender and contribute to constructing images of what is considered "normal" and "acceptable." As such, they influence student/parent/educator beliefs about student capabilities.

A student's placement in high school courses has a significant impact on his or her preparation for college. It is therefore relevant to discuss how and for whom high school courses are often organized, described, and offered. As Oakes (2005) states, "whenever we sort students in schools and treat them differently, *we need to examine all the possible effects of these practices*" (italics added, p. 92). Though the rationale behind the origin of tracking may no longer be in place, more than a hundred years later, schools' tracked processes are still dominant and are helping to shape dominant discourses about student achievement. Oakes (2005) writes:

> The assumptions about the native abilities and appropriate future pla-
> ces of the poor and minorities that so influenced the form of the high
> school at the turn of the century may have changed considerably, but
> the mechanisms we use for sorting and selecting students for school
> programs and instructional groups have remained much the same. So
> have the results. (p. 39)

We concur and add that likewise for girls and women, even while much has changed in terms of access to education and achievement, dominant gender discourses continue to frame images and expectations about appropriate behavior for girls/boys and men/women that are often limiting. If the dominant discourses shaping curriculum guides are aligned more closely with professionalism and masculinity, it is more likely that girls and boys from lower-SES/working-class backgrounds will be disadvantaged, *even* if the policies are designed to be gender neutral and appear to maintain broad educational goals.

College enrollment patterns continue to indicate a significant socioeconomic gap spanning the past thirty-five years, and as discussed previously, college enrollment in certain majors reflects obvious gender disparities. Studies like the one described here can add to scholarly discussion and policy considerations that may help more low-SES students succeed in high school and continue in college, with the hope of advancing their professional and economic opportunities. Likewise, this method can shed light on girls' discursive representations and yield new strategies for promoting equity in a broader array of secondary courses that may help increase their enrollment in postsecondary STEM-related areas, as highlighted in this chapter's introduction.

Given that statistics about achievement in high school, particularly when analyzing SES, have reflected disparities for more than thirty-five years, it is clear that current strategies continue to fall short. Likewise, regarding gender, women's advancement in degree attainment has been extremely successful, though degree type and earnings continue to lag behind their male counterparts. We recommend that school leaders strongly consider curriculum guides, school policies, and other policy-related documents (i.e., policies and policy silences, handbooks, mission statements, norms, routines, scheduling procedures, celebrations, gatekeeping rules) as windows through which to shed new light on old problems in order to grapple with the complexities of student achievement in schools.

Educators may also benefit from deepening their understanding of how different methodologies address patterns of inequity. How can a critical awareness of dominant discourse help understand and resist status-quo tendencies? How can leaders help create alternative discourses for students that shape a more confident and capable sense of themselves?

Finally, educators must also create a broader understanding of the statistics that are available. Questions educators could ask include: How often do we analyze our students' disaggregated educational achievement statistics? What happens to our students once they graduate? Which students go to college? Which ones take remedial courses in college and why? Which students pursue which majors? What are the patterns in our school's student population? How do first-generation college students fare? How can we focus our resources on improving our educational achievement for all students? How can we make sure our policies found in handbooks and course guides accurately reflect our school mission? Analyzing dominant discourses, like those reflected in curriculum guides, will help educators become more aware of naturalized policies and practices that may contribute to socially reproductive outcomes. Such analyses can help shed light on well-intended policies and practices that may undermine the goal of promoting socially just schools and high achievement for all students.

References

Acosta, R. V., & Carpenter, L. J. (2010). Women in intercollegiate sport: A longitudinal, national study; thirty-three year update, 1977–2010. Retrieved July 28, 2010, from acostacarpenter.org.

Allan, E. J. (1999). *Constructing women's status: Policy discourses of university women's commission reports*. Unpublished doctoral dissertation, The Ohio State University.

Allan, E. J. (2003). Constructing women's status: Policy discourses of university women's commission reports. *Harvard Educational Review*, *73*(1), 44–72.

Allan, E. J. (2008). *Policy discourses, gender, and education: Constructing women's status.* New York: Routledge.

Allan, E. J. (in press). *The status of women in higher education: Beyond parity and toward equity.* San Francisco: Jossey-Bass.

Allan, E. J., Gordon, S. P., & Iverson, S. V. (2006). Re/thinking practices of power: The discursive framing of leadership in *The Chronicle of Higher Education. Review of Higher Education, 30*(1), 41–68.

American Association of University Women Educational Foundation. (2001). *Hostile hallways: Bullying, teasing, and sexual harassment in schools.* Washington, DC: Author.

Anyon, J. (2006). Social class, school knowledge, and the hidden curriculum: Retheorizing reproduction. In L. Weis, C. McCarthy, & G. Dimitriadis (Eds.), *Ideology, curriculum, and the new sociology of education: Revisiting the work of Michael Apple* (pp. 37–45). New York: Routledge.

Apple, M. W. (1990). *Ideology and curriculum* (2nd ed.). New York: Routledge.

Apple, M. W. (2006). *Educating the "right" way: Market, standards, God and inequality* (2nd ed.). New York: Routledge.

Argyris, C., & Schon, D. (1974). *Theory in practice: Increasing professional effectiveness.* San Francisco: Jossey-Bass.

Aud, S., Hussar, W., Planty, M., Snyder, T., Bianco, K., Fox, M., Frohlich, L., Kemp, J., & Drake, L. (2010). *The Condition of Education 2010* (NCES 2010–028). National Center for Education Statistics, Institute of Education Sciences, U.S. Department of Education. Washington, DC.

Bacchi, C. L. (1999). *Women, policy and politics: The construction of policy problems.* Thousand Oaks, CA: Sage.

Ball, S. J. (1990). Introducing monsieur Foucault. In S. J. Ball (Ed.), *Foucault and education: Disciplines and knowledge.* New York: Routledge.

Bensimon, E. M. (1995). Total quality management in the academy: A rebellious reading. *Harvard Educational Review, 65*(2), 593–611.

Bloch, M. N. (1987). Becoming scientific and professional: An historical perspective on the aims and effects of early education. In T.S. Popkewitz

(Ed.), *The formation of school subjects: The struggle for creating an American institution* (pp. 25–62). New York: Falmer.

Brantlinger, E. A. (1993). *The politics of social class in secondary school: Views of affluent and impoverished youth.* New York: Teachers College Press.

Carbonaro, W. J., & Gamoran, A. (2002). The production of achievement inequality in high school English. *American Educational Research Journal, 39*(4), 801–27.

Carlson, D. (2006). Are we making progress? Ideology and curriculum in the age of No Child Left Behind. In L. Weis, C. McCarthy, & G. Dimitriadis (Eds.), *Ideology, curriculum, and the new sociology of education: Revisiting the work of Michael Apple* (pp. 91–114). New York: Routledge.

Chen, X. (2005). *First generation students in postsecondary education: A look at their college transcripts* (NCES 2005-171). U.S. Department of Education, National Center for Education Statistics. Washington, DC: U.S. Government Printing Office.

Cusick, T. (1989). Sexism and early parenting: Cause and effect? *Peabody Journal of Education, 8*(4), 113–31.

Densmore, K. (1987). Professionalism, proletarianization and teacher work. In T. Popkewitz (Ed.), *Critical studies in teacher education: Its folklore, theory and practice* (pp.130–60). New York: Falmer.

Fine, M. (2003). Silencing and nurturing voice in an improbable context: Urban adolescents in public school. In M. Fine & L. Weis (Eds.), *Silenced voices and extraordinary conversations: Re-imagining schools* (pp. 13–37). New York: Teachers College Press.

Foucault, M. (1977/1995). *Discipline and punish: The birth of the prison* (2nd ed.). New York: Vintage Books. Translation by Alan Sheridan.

Gamoran, A., & Mare, R. D. (1989). Secondary school tracking and educational inequality: Compensation, reinforcement, or neutrality? *American Journal of Sociology, 94*(5), 1146–83.

Gamoran, A., Nystrand, M., Berends, M., & LePore, P. (1995). An organizational analysis of the effects of ability grouping. *American Educational Research Journal, 32*(4), 687–715.

Gordon, S., Iverson, S. V., & Allan, E. J. (2010). The discursive framing of women leaders in higher education. In E. J. Allan, S. V. Iverson, and R. Ropers-Huilman (Eds.), *Reconstructing policy in higher education: Feminist poststructural perspectives* (pp. 81–105). New York: Routledge.

Gumport, P. J. (1993). The contested terrain of academic program reduction. *Journal of Higher Education, 64*(3), 283–311.

Hallinan, M. T. (1994). School differences in tracking effects on achievement. *Social Forces, 72*(3), 799–820.

Hallinan, M. T., & Sørensen, A. B. (1987). Ability grouping and sex differences in mathematics achievement. *Sociology of Education, 60*(2), 63–72.

Heck, R. H., & Mahoe, R. (2006). Student transition to high school and persistence: Highlighting the influences of social divisions and school contingencies. *American Journal of Education, 112*(3), 418–46.

Hey, V., & Bradford, S. (2004). The return of the repressed: The gender politics of emergent forms of professionalism in education. *Journal of Education Policy, 19*(6), 691–713.

Heyning, K. E. (1997, March). *Professionalism and reform in teaching curriculum: An archaeology of postsecondary education.* Paper presented at the annual meeting of the American Educational Research Association, Chicago, IL. (ERIC Document Reproduction Service No. ED 407 110).

Iverson, S. V. (2005). *A policy discourse analysis of U.S. land-grant university diversity action plans.* Unpublished doctoral dissertation. University of Maine, Orono.

Jones, S., & Myhill, D. (2004). "Troublesome boys" and "compliant girls": Gender identity and perceptions of achievement and underachievement. *British Journal of Sociology of Education, 25*(5), 547–61.

Kelly, S. (2007). The contours of tracking in North Carolina. *High School Journal, 90,* 15–31.

Klein, S., et al. (Eds.). (2007). *Handbook for achieving gender equity through education* (2nd ed.). Mahwah, NJ: Lawrence Erlbaum.

Labaree, D. (1992). Power, knowledge and the rationalization of teaching: A genealogy of the movement to professionalize teaching. *Harvard Educational Review, 62*(2), 123–54.

Larson, M. S. (1990). In the matter of experts and professionals, or how impossible it is to leave nothing unsaid. In R. Torstendahl & M. Burrage (Eds.), *The formation of professions: Knowledge, state and strategy* (pp. 24–50). London: Sage.

Lucas, C. J. (1994). *American higher education: A history.* New York: St. Martin's.

Lucas, S. R. (1999). *Tracking inequality: Stratification and mobility in American high schools.* New York: Teachers College Press.

Marshall, C. (1997). Dismantling and reconstructing policy analysis. In C. Marshall (Ed.), *Feminist critical policy analysis: A perspective from primary and secondary schooling* (pp. 1–39). Washington, DC: Falmer.

National Federation of State High School Associations (2009). 2008–09 High school athletics participation survey. Retrieved 28 July, 2010 from: www.nfhs.org/content.aspx?id =3282&linkidentifier=id& itemid=3282

National Women's Law Center. (2010). The battle for gender equity in athletics in elementary and secondary schools. Washington, DC: Author. Retrieved July 28, 2010, from http://www.nwlc.org/resource/ battle-gender-equity-athletics-elementary-and-secondary-schools.

Oakes, J. (1995). Two cities' tracking and within-school segregation. *Teachers College Record, 96*(4), 681–90.

Oakes, J. (2005). *Keeping track: How schools structure inequality* (2nd ed.). New Haven, CT: Yale University Press.

Oakes, J., & Guiton, G. (1995). Matchmaking: The dynamics of high school tracking decisions. *American Educational Research Journal, 32*(1), 3–33.

Paludi, M., Martin, J., & C. Paludi, J. (2007). Sexual harassment: The hidden gender equity problem. In S. Klein (Ed.), *Handbook for achieving gender equity through education* (2nd ed., pp. 215–29). Mahweh, NJ: Lawrence Erlbaum.

Pillow, W. (2003). "Bodies are dangerous": Using feminist genealogy as policy studies methodology. *Journal of Education Policy, 18*(2), 145–59.

Pillow, W. S. (2000). Exposed methodology: The body as a deconstructive practice. In E. A. St. Pierre & W. S. Pillow (Eds.), *Working the ruins:*

Feminist poststructural theory and methods in education (pp. 199–219). New York: Routledge.

Planty, M., Hussar, W., Snyder, T., Kena, G., KewalRamani, A., Kemp, J., Bianco, K., & Dinkes, R. (2009). *The Condition of Education 2009* (NCES 2009-081). National Center for Education Statistics, Institute of Education Sciences, U.S. Department of Education. Washington, DC.

Popkewitz, T. S. (1994). Professionalization in teaching and teacher education: Some notes on its history, ideology, and potential. *Teaching & Teacher Education, 10*(1), 1–14.

Popkewitz, T. S. (1995). Teacher education, reform and the politics of knowledge in the United States. In M. B. Ginsburg & B. Lindsay (Eds.), *The political dimension in teacher education: Comparative perspectives on policy formation, socialization and society* (pp. 54–75). Washington, DC: Falmer.

Readings, B. (1996). *The university in ruins*. Cambridge, MA: Harvard University Press.

Rosenbaum, J. E. (1975). The stratification of socialization processes. *American Sociological Review, 40*(1), 48–54.

Rumberger, R. W., & Palardy, G. J. (2005). Does segregation still matter? The impact of student composition on academic achievement in high school. *Teachers College Record, 107*(9), 1999–2045.

Sadker, M., & Sadker, D. (1994). *Failing at fairness: How our schools cheat girls*. New York: Touchstone.

Sadker, D., Sadker, M., & Zittleman, K. (2009). *Still failing at fairness: How gender bias cheats girls and boys in school and what we can do about it*. New York: Scribner.

Scheurich, J. J. (1994). Policy archaeology: A new policy studies methodology. *Journal of Education Policy, 9*(4), 297–316.

Seddon, T. (1997). Education: Deprofessionalized? Or regulated, reorganized and reauthorized? *Australian Journal of Education, 41*(3), 33–50.

Sirin, S. R. (2005). Socioeconomic status and academic achievement: A meta-analytic review of research. *Review of Educational Research, 75*(3), 417–53.

The College Board. (2009, February). *The 5th annual AP© report to the nation*. Princeton, NJ: Author.

Thelin, J. R. (2004). *A history of American higher education*. Baltimore, MD: Johns Hopkins University Press.

Usher, R., & Edwards, R. (1994). *Postmodernism and education: Different voices, different worlds.* London: Routledge.

Walkerdine, V. (1989). *Counting girls out.* London: Virago.

Weedon, C. (1999). *Feminism, theory and the politics of difference.* Malden, MA: Blackwell.

Weis, L. (2003). Acquiring white working-class identities: Legitimate and silenced discourse within the school. In M. Fine & L. Weis (Eds.), *Silenced voices and extraordinary conversations: Re-imagining schools* (pp. 88–108). New York: Teachers College Press.

Weis, L. (2008). Toward a re-thinking of class as nested in race and gender: Tracking the white working class in the final quarter of the twentieth century. In L. Weis (Ed.), *The way class works: Readings on school, family, and the economy* (pp. 291–304). New York: Routledge.

Wirt, J., Choy, S., Rooney, P., Provasnik, S., Sen, A., Tobin, R., et al. (2004). *The condition of education 2004. NCES 2004-077*: U.S. Department of Education.

Yonezawa, S., & Wells, A. S. (2005). Reform as redesigning the spaces of schools: An examination of detracking by choice. In L. Weis & M. Fine (Eds.), *Beyond silenced voices: Class, race, and gender in United States schools* (rev. ed., pp. 47–62). Albany, NY: State University of New York Press.

Yonezawa, S., Wells, A. S., & Serna, I. (2002). Choosing tracks: "Freedom of choice" in detracking schools. *American Education Research Association, 39*(1), 38–67.

7

The Risks of Sex-Segregated Public Education for Girls, Boys, and Everyone

Susan S. Klein[1]

Many people have called Title IX the most important law passed for women since they obtained the right to vote in 1920. Title IX of the Education Amendments of 1972 is the primary U.S. civil rights law prohibiting sex discrimination in education.[2] Title IX is patterned after Title VI of the Civil Rights Act of 1964, which helped implement the 1954 *Brown v. Board of Education* Supreme Court decision prohibiting race segregation. Title VI makes discrimination on the basis of race, color, and national origin in programs and activities that receive federal financial assistance illegal.[3]

---

[1]This chapter is based in part on the April 27, 2010, presentation at the Clearinghouse on Women's Issues meeting in Washington, D.C., by Drs. Bernice Sandler, Senior Scholar at Women's Research and Education Institute, who is known as the "Godmother of Title IX," and Susan Klein, Education Equity Director, Feminist Majority Foundation and editor of the *Handbook for Achieving Gender Equity through Education* (Klein, 2007). Klein updated and expanded on the Clearinghouse presentation in developing this chapter and Sandler, along with Rosalind Barnett, Nancy Brown, Kim Gandy, Elizabeth Homer, Amy Katz, Renata Maniaci, Jennifer Martin, Dawn Pickard, and David Sadker, reviewed and suggested many improvements in the chapter.

[2]Title IX (20 U.S.C. § 1681): No person in the United States shall, on the basis of sex, be excluded from participation in, be denied the benefits of, or be subjected to discrimination under any education program or activity receiving federal financial assistance.

[3]Title VI of the Civil Rights Act of 1964 (Pub. L. 88-352, title VI, Sec. 601, July 2, 1964, 78 Stat. 252.): No person in the United States shall, on the basis of race, color, or national origin, be excluded from participation in, be denied the benefits of, or be subjected to discrimination under any program or activity receiving federal financial assistance.

Title IX prohibitions against sex discrimination are limited to education and thus not as broad in scope as Title VI, but the principles prohibiting sex segregation in education are very similar to the principles prohibiting race segregation. However, few educators and others understand the risks and problems with sex-segregated public education as well as they understand the reasons for racial integration.

In many areas, Title IX has contributed to more deliberately equal treatment of girls and boys, women and men in education. This has led to many triumphs for women's equality. For example, in 2008 to 2009, women finally earned more doctorates (50.4%) than men (Bell, 2010). Title IX has also helped men and boys by allowing them to participate in traditionally female courses of study such as home economics, nutrition, and nursing and to be protected from homophobic sexual harassment (Sandler & Stonehill, 2005; The Triumphs of Title IX, 2007).

However, the Bush administration signaled that it planned to allow single-sex classrooms and schools in 2002 when its Department of Education (ED) issued a notice to change the Title IX implementation regulation to increase schools' flexibility in using deliberate sex segregation in public education. The Bush ED issued proposed changes in Title IX regulation in 2004 and made them final in 2006 (Office for Civil Rights, 2006; Title IX Defined web page). This ED 2006 Title IX regulation allows K–12 nonvocational schools more flexibility in their use of purposeful and absolute sex segregation than the Congressionally reviewed 1975 Title IX regulation had permitted.[4] Legal experts point out that this sex segregation violates Title IX, the Equal Protection Clause of the Fourteenth Amendment to the U.S. Constitution, the Equal Educational Opportunities Act, and in some cases also state laws.

Based on the Feminist Majority Foundation (FMF) study of the "State of Public School Sex Segregation in the States" (Klein, 2011) and insights from others, it is likely that officially approved sex segregation was used in about 1,000 U.S. K–12 public schools in the 2007 to 2009 school years.

FMF and organizations participating in the National Council of Women's Organizations and the National Coalition for Women and Girls in

---

[4]Purposeful sex segregation means that males and females are separated or excluded by a rule or policy based on their biological sex (not gender roles). This segregation has been absolute, meaning that no exceptions are made to allow any boy in girls' classes or the reverse. We recommend that if sex segregation is allowed, that it no longer be absolute.

Education have requested that the Obama Administration and Secretary of Education rescind this 2006 Title IX regulation and return to the 1975 Title IX regulations used by other federal agencies. But as of November 2010, this has not happened.

This chapter provides multiple insights on why sex-segregated public education is risky for everyone while addressing six public policy reasons to rescind the Bush administration's 2006 ED Title IX regulation, which contributed to the increase in public school sex segregation. Other critically important reasons why sex-integrated education (or nonsexist coeducation) is desirable include: increasing the development of human potential by decreasing sex stereotyping and creating expanded expectations for girls and boys, helping students become better socialized for real life and work that are not sex segregated, increasing the full use of neuroplasticity in brain development, and increasing variability among the species[5] (Barnett & Rivers, 2004; Klein et al., 2007; Pickard, 2010; Sadker, Sadker, & Zittleman, 2009).

Using the 1975 Title IX regulations,[6] sex segregation in public education should only be allowed if it meets all legal requirements and if there is compelling evidence that it is more effective in achieving gender equity outcomes[7] than comparable (less risky) coeducation. Many view purposeful

---

[5]Pickard noted that inbreeding of members of groups that practice sex and other types of segregation such as Hasidic Jews has led to genetic problems and recommends diversity for human survival.

[6]We sometimes use the 1975 Title IX regulations (plural) when discussing the pre-2006 Title IX regulations because they were issued by different federal agencies. These regulations only allow sex segregation for limited exceptions, such as affirmative or remedial purposes to end sex discrimination in the desired outcomes. The ED 2006 Title IX regulation (singular) conflicts with and does not replace these federal Title IX regulations from other agencies.

[7]Gender equity outcomes: 1. Ensure that both women and men acquire, or are given equitable opportunity to acquire, the most socially valued characteristics and skills (even if they have been generally attributed to only one sex), so that fewer jobs, roles, activities, expectations, and achievements are differentiated by sex. This would be accompanied by a decrease in gender stereotyping in decision making by or about individuals and a decrease in sex segregation in education and society caused by gender stereotyping and other inappropriate discriminatory factors. 2. Ensure parity or equity between women and men in the quality of life, academic, and work outcomes valued by our society, without limitations associated with sex stereotypes, gender roles, or prejudices. Both women and men have important roles to play in attaining these outcomes.

sex-segregated public education (as it is generally practiced) as turning back the clock toward increased sex discrimination and sex stereotyping that is harmful to everyone (Stone, 2007).

The rest of this chapter will make recommendations on standards that should be used (hopefully after the rescission) when deciding if any sex segregation is allowed even for increasing gender equality in the outcomes. The following six public policy reasons to rescind the ED 2006 Title IX regulation provide a framework for our discussion of the risks of sex-segregated public education.

1. The 2006 ED Title IX regulation conflicts with stronger protections against sex discrimination in public education that are still guaranteed under the 1975 Title IX regulations used by other agencies, the U.S. Constitution, and other federal and state laws.

2. Inappropriate public school sex segregation has increased since the Bush administration signaled it would weaken the Title IX regulation in 2002.

3. Separate is rarely equal, especially in public education. Sex segregation has a negative impact on both girls and boys because it often favors one sex over the other and encourages misguided sex-stereotyped education practices.

4. Most justifications for deliberate public school sex segregation are improper because the sex-segregation strategies they actually use violate legal standards and are based on scientifically unsound educational policies and practices such as false beliefs that males and females learn in different ways.

5. There is no credible evidence that sex-segregated public education is more effective in increasing gender equality and other desirable outcomes than less risky equally well-resourced gender equitable coeducation.

6. Sex-segregated public education in the United States is more expensive than the less risky coeducation alternatives.

These reasons are intertwined. For example, good research on this topic must be conducted using a framework that addresses legal issues as well as educational, psychological, and economic measures. Thus, it is important to assess gender equality in the educational practices as well as in the outcomes that result from these activities and to compare sex segregation with coeducation and the impact on both girls and boys.

Public Policy Reasons to Rescind the 2006 Bush Title IX ED Regulation

Reason 1. The 2006 ED Title IX regulation conflicts with stronger protections against sex discrimination in public education that are guaranteed under the 1975 Title IX regulations used by other agencies, the U.S. Constitution, and other federal and state laws.

Early History of Title IX Protections against Sex Segregation

In the early 1970s, much public attention focused on adding the Equal Rights Amendment (ERA) to the U.S. Constitution and on ways girls and women were not always treated fairly in education. When Title IX passed in 1972, routine sex segregation, such as woodworking or shop for boys and home economics for girls, or career days for boys and fashion shows for girls, was no longer allowed.

The 1975 Title IX regulation used by the Department of Health, Education and Welfare's Office of Education and later the Department of Education (ED) created in 1980 provided guidance on how Title IX should be interpreted. It prohibited most sex segregation in education institutions that received federal financial assistance. For the most part, sex-segregated classes, programs, and schools have always been considered sex discrimination under Title IX. Sex stereotyping is also considered sex discrimination. Essentially, Title IX says that other than the exceptions listed in the law, it is illegal to classify (or discriminate against) people on the basis of sex, just as under other laws such as Title VI of the Civil Rights Act it is illegal to classify or assign students on the basis of race or national origin. Thus, extra benefits or opportunities cannot be given based on the sex or race or national origin of a student. Students can be sorted in many other ways, such as test scores, previous grades, and so forth, but not by sex or race.

All federal agencies except the ED still use the stricter provisions against sex segregation in the 1975 Title IX regulations rather than the

more permissive 2006 Title IX regulation. These 1975 Title IX regulations contain a few exceptions where some sex segregation is allowed.
For example, certain youth groups, such as the Boy Scouts and Girl
Scouts and fraternities and sororities, may meet in schools. Under Title
IX, some K–12 schools that were single sex before 1975 can remain
single sex.[8] Dormitories may be single sex (although coed dormitories
are increasingly popular). Additionally, sexuality education classes can
be conducted separately for boys and girls. Also, under the 1975 Title
IX regulations, some sex segregation is allowed in athletics such as in
contact sports.

But the most relevant exception for this discussion is that under the
1975 regulations, some affirmative action (to help females or males) is
allowed as long as the purpose is to reduce sex discrimination—the key
purpose of Title IX. However, few deliberate sex-segregated programs
were used for affirmative action under Title IX before the Bush
administration signaled that it was weakening the standards required to
justify sex segregation under Title IX. For example, when some science
programs were designed to attract girls, some parents of boys objected
and pointed out that their boys needed this kind of program, too, and boys
were allowed in. The same practice was followed with the programs that
were developed primarily to help women overcome math anxiety (Tobias,
1993).

Also, instead of segregating girls to provide them with remedial support
or affirmative benefits to help them receive more equitable outcomes,
many people active in the women's movement have pushed for coeducational classes and schools to become less sexist and for more gender
balance in classes such as physics. They have also encouraged the identification and use of best practices from private single-sex and coed schools.
Examples include encouraging females to speak up, using a variety of
teaching techniques including collaborative learning and competitive
activities, and encouraging teachers to consciously pay equal attention to

---

[8]However, other laws such as the Fourteenth Amendment and the PA Equal Rights
Amendment have been used to prohibit sex segregation. Women were allowed to enter
the Virginia Military Institute after the 1996 Supreme Court decision, and the 1983 PA
decision allowed girls to attend the previously all-male academic Central High School in
Philadelphia (Klein, 2007, Chapters 5 and 9).

all the students in the class, not just those who are the most vocal and active (Klein, 2007, especially Chapters 7 and 9; Sadker, Sadker, & Zittleman, 2009).

The 2006 ED Title IX Regulation Weakens Protections against Sex Discrimination

Allowing single-sex classes, programs, and schools, especially when they reinforce sex stereotypes, is the biggest threat to Title IX since the 1984 Supreme Court *Grove City College v. Bell* decision, which limited Title IX protections only to specific programs that received targeted federal funding. This meant that enforcement of Title IX was extremely limited from 1984 until Congress passed the Civil Rights Restoration Act over President Reagan's veto in 1988. For example, sex discrimination in athletics was generally allowed during these years because the federal government rarely funded athletic programs. The Civil Rights Restoration Act made it clear that Congress intended Title IX and other federal civil rights laws such as Civil Rights Act Title VI to apply to the whole institution providing education services, not just to the specific program or student receiving federal financial assistance (Nash, et al., 2007).

When the draft version of this 2006 Title IX regulation was released in 2004, only about 100 of the more than 5,000 public comments were supportive (Klein, 2005), but the Bush ED proceeded to issue the 2006 version with few changes. Many discussions of the history of this 2006 ED Title IX regulation improperly attribute it to provisions in the 2002 *No Child Left Behind* legislation. However, that legislation did not call for a change in the Title IX regulation. It did allow for single-sex education "consistent with existing law" specifically as one provision for local programs and it required guidance on single-sex education. The Bush ED of its own volition issued a notice of proposed regulation in 2002 to let advocates of single-sex education know that it planned to allow more flexibility in purposeful single-sex education. (See more details under reason #2, FMF's *Title IX Defined* web page, and Klein, 2005).

The limited safeguards in the 2006 ED Title IX regulation specifically allow single-sex classes, schools, programs, and extracurricular activities in primary and secondary nonvocational public schools as long as there is "substantial equality." This 2006 regulation also includes procedural guidance limiting some inappropriate sex segregation by requiring that:

- Enrollment in a single-sex class or school must be completely voluntary.
- A "substantially equal" coeducational class or extracurricular activity in the same subject or activity for the excluded sex must be provided.
- An "important governmental objective" "to improve educational achievement of its students," provided that the "single-sex nature of the class or extracurricular activity is substantially related to achieving that objective" must be shown. These "sex-based means used to further that objective" must be "genuine" and (must . . .) "not rely on overly broad generalizations about either sex."
- A link between an education goal and the single-sex program must be shown. The 2006 Title IX regulation requires that the "single-sex classes or extracurricular activities are based upon genuine justifications and do not rely on overly broad generalizations about the different talents, capacities, or preferences of either sex and that any single-sex classes or extracurricular activities are substantially related to the achievement of the important objective for the classes or extracurricular activities." (Office for Civil Rights (2006) Section 106.34 (b) (3)). This standard was defined in more detail in the 2010 ED and Department of Justice (DOJ) Amicus Brief in the Vermilion Parish School Board case where a dissertation by the school's principal used inaccurate information about the benefits of his "experiment" to justify sex-segregated classes to the school board.
- Evaluations are required every two years to justify the continuation of the single-sex class, program, or school and to ensure that they are based on genuine justifications that do not rely on sex stereotypes.

Although these procedural requirements in the 2006 regulation provide some restrictions on inequitable and illegal sex segregation, collectively they are rarely followed by schools implementing sex segregation. (See Klein, 2010, 2011 and the discussion under Reason 2.)

Legal experts have pointed out many flaws in the 2006 ED Title IX regulation that show weakening Title IX conflicts with the way Congress intended it to be interpreted, as well as with the U.S. Constitution's

Fourteenth Amendment Equal Protection Clause, federal laws such as the Equal Educational Opportunities Act (1974), and equal rights provisions in state constitutions (Nash et al., 2007). Proponents of adding the Equal Rights Amendment to the U.S. Constitution point out that the ERA would provide more extensive and stable legal protections against sex discrimination in all public entities. For example, ERA would also protect against sex discrimination outside of education programs and activities and in public entities even if they are not recipients of federal financial assistance.[9]

The cases against schools that have engaged in sex segregation by the American Civil Liberties Union (ACLU) and the recent briefs appealing the *Vermilion Parish* Federal District Court decision that allowed sex-segregated classes to continue provide many details on how regulations for Title IX should be interpreted so that they are consistent with the existing civil rights protections (American Civil Liberties Union, 2010; National Women's Law Center, 2010; Stone, 2007; U.S. Depts. of Justice & Education, 2010).

Reason 2. Inappropriate public school sex segregation has increased since the Bush administration signaled it would weaken the ED Title IX regulation in 2002.

The Increase in Sex Segregation in Public K–12 Education

Over the years before and two decades after the passage of Title IX in 1972, single-sex private education declined and deliberate single-sex public education was rare. Single-sex public education was so rare that it was barely mentioned in the *Handbook for Achieving Sex Equity through Education* (Klein, 1985). The 1994 classic *Failing at Fairness: How America's Schools Cheat Girls* reported that "Today, single-sex schools are an endangered species; they are [often] illegal in the public system and vanishing rapidly from the private sector" (Sadker, Sadker, & Zittleman, 2009, p. 253). From 1975 to 2002, equity advocates focused on counteracting accidental or deliberate sex discrimination in coed schools. Attention was

---

[9]While this chapter focuses on public schools, even private K–12 schools that receive some federal financial assistance are covered by Title IX prohibitions against sex discrimination, including illegal sex segregation.

on creating gender-equitable coed physical education classes as required by the 1975 Title IX regulation (Geadelmann et. al., 1985), on ensuring that previously sex-segregated vocational education schools and classes would be integrated, and on identifying and decreasing sex-discriminatory classroom interactions in coed classes (Lockheed, 1985).

During the 1990s, a few Congressional efforts to suspend Title IX to allow experiments with public school sex segregation failed. In 1996, new well-publicized single-sex schools were established in New York City and California. They were justified under the affirmative provisions in the 1975 Title IX regulation to advance gender equity. The Young Women's Leadership School of East Harlem was established in 1996. But this public school faced legal challenges because there was no evidence that it was more effective in helping its female students succeed and overcome sex discrimination than comparably well-resourced coed schools serving the same types of students with a similar commitment to gender-equitable education.[10] The evaluations of the 1996 California dual academy experiment (where the state provided extra funds to six paired girl and boy schools) found that they created more problems (especially for boys) than they solved (Datnow, Hubbard, & Woody, 2001). The Supreme Court decisions allowing girls into the Virginia Military Institute and men into the nursing program at Mississippi University for Women also helped discourage sex segregation in public education.

Despite these fairly well-funded single-sex experiments in New York and California, before 2002, the major focus was on equity in instruction, especially in creating sex equity in coeducational classroom interactions. But, concerns changed and the *Handbook for Achieving Gender Equity through Education, 2nd Edition* (Klein, 2007) devoted most of Chapter 9, "Gender Equity in Coeducational and Single-sex Educational Environments," and a good part of the summary Chapter 31 to this emerging challenge to gender equality.

The forthcoming FMF study of the "State of Public School Sex Segregation in the States" (Klein, 2010) documents more than 600 public

---

[10]As of 2010, this school is still operating along with Young Women's Leadership schools across the nation. These public schools and their affiliates also receive support from the Young Women's Leadership Network (www.ywlnetwork.org). However, none of the CA Dual Academies remain sex segregated.

schools with purposeful single-sex classes in school years 2007 to 2008 and 2008 to 2009. These totals include about eighty public single-sex schools or dual academies. This estimate does not include many more public schools that only have:

- Short-term segregated sexuality education as allowed specifically in 1975 Title IX regulation.
- Sex-segregated physical education classes. (Many of these classes do not involve contact sports and violate Title IX.)
- Sex segregation for youth in the juvenile justice system (correctional schools).
- Unintentional sex segregation in elective or special courses—especially common in vocational education and special education.

However as noted earlier, it is likely that there were even more than the 600-plus public schools that did not publicize their deliberate sex-segregated classes. Most published estimates of schools with single-sex classes are based on information in the National Association of Single Sex Public Schools (NASSPE) website maintained by single-sex education advocate Leonard Sax. The FMF researchers used multiple sources for information on public schools with sex segregation and found both overreporting and underreporting on the NASSPE website. Despite rhetoric that single-sex education is an important public school choice, it is very difficult to find information on single-sex education strategies on school websites. An examination of the Office for Civil Rights (OCR) 2006 large-sample survey results indicated that many coed public schools said they had single-sex academic classes for the 2006 to 2007 school year. This suggests that they started this sex segregation before the 2006 ED Title IX regulations became effective in November 2006.

The OCR 2006 survey results showed that 2,885 schools reported having specific types and numbers of single-sex academic classes in the 2006 school year. Klein and Sesma (2010) called some of the schools to verify the survey response that they had single-sex classes during 2006 and also found that many continued sex-segregated classes in subsequent years. Research by others, such as ACLU public information requests and the Brown and Pickard (2010) study of public charter schools in Michigan also found more sex segregation in public schools than they were able to locate using publicly shared information.

Future trends in sex-segregated public education depend in part on the leadership of the Obama administration and gender-equity advocates who support rescission of the 2006 ED Title IX regulation. Even if researchers documented 1,000 public schools with sex-segregated classes, this would be a small proportion of the 98,000 U.S. public schools in 14,000 school districts serving nearly 50 million public school students (President's Council of Advisors on Science and Technology, 2010).

Many Schools Have Used the 2006 ED Title IX Regulation as Permission to Sex Segregate—Often Inappropriately

The forthcoming FMF study on the "State of Public School Sex Segregation in the States" (Klein, 2010) and legal cases challenging sex-discriminatory sex segregation led by the American Civil Liberties Union (ACLU) have shown that the minimal protections for voluntary sex segregation, coeducational options, adequate justification of need for segregation, and evaluations that are required in the 2006 ED Title IX regulation have generally been ignored.

Schools rarely articulate their sex-segregation policy and procedures and do not provide a specific justification for sex segregation as an affirmative action to decrease sex discrimination. Except for the sexual attraction argument, which obviously fails for gay and transgender youth, it is hard to find a rationale for excluding one sex to accomplish a specific governmental objective. For example, the FMF researchers did not find anything on a school website justifying a girls' physics class because they were not performing as well as boys or because there is evidence that they will learn physics better in an all-girl class than in a coed class.[11] If the school does provide some justification language, it often repeats generalized misconceptions about the purported advantages of single-sex education, which are used by single-sex education advocates such as Leonard Sax and his National Association of Single Sex Public Education. Sax and others assert that girls and boys learn differently and thus need to be

---

[11]This is a hypothetical example. We know of no studies that show girls learn physics best in a sex-segregated class.

taught differently in sex-segregated classes (Kaufmann, 2007a, 2007b; NASSPE website).[12]

Schools may indicate that they are using the sex-segregated classes to reduce sex stereotypes, but their actions show the reverse. It was also rare to find a school or subject area where there are sex-segregated classes for only boys or only girls. Most schools had the same number of all-boy and all-girl classes in each subject area. This also points to a generalized justification based on sex stereotyping rather than a specific justification that some type of sex segregation will help improve gender-equitable outcomes for either girls or boys who need affirmative "catch-up" support.

Few, if any, schools have publicized the required evaluations of their single-sex programs to let parents and researchers know if their objectives have been met. In the rare cases where they may conduct an evaluation, they rarely ask the question, "Did the sex segregation improve gender equity in outcomes?" Ideally, each school should conduct a study to determine if sex segregation is better than coeducation for its students. FMF found few evaluation results based on systematic studies, although it was common for media reporters to describe some anecdotal information about teacher, student, or parent reactions to single-sex classes. Occasionally journalists also reported how some outcome, such as test scores for the single-sex classes, went up compared to previous years or compared to a coed class. But these articles rarely referenced evaluations or studies that could be examined for the adequacy of their methodology and credibility of their conclusions.

Few state Title IX coordinators have been able to identify and monitor the public schools with single-sex classes in their states, although many helped FMF researchers learn about sex segregation in their states. A key exception is the South Carolina Department of Education, which encourages sex-segregated classes in its public schools and maintains a website with information on South Carolina public schools that use "single-gender" education. Iowa and Washington have accountability requirements related to reporting on or evaluating single-sex schools and classes.

---

[12]Leonard Sax created the National Association of Single Sex Public Education. In recent years he has acknowledged that sex differences are not universal and that single-sex education may not be best for all girls and boys.

However, there are currently no state or federal requirements for the public sharing or the submission of justifications for, or evaluations of, single-sex schools or classes related to the Title IX requirements.[13] Thus, despite the consistent Bush administration and Congressional education legislation focus on accountability and attaining scientific evidence of effectiveness, it is difficult to find detailed justifications for, or evaluation results on, the effects of sex-segregated public education. In their efforts to verify schools with sex segregation, FMF found many websites that post comments on schools and sometimes even describe student demographics, but there was no information on these third party websites or on the official school websites about their sex segregation practices, and FMF did not find any evaluations of the school's sex-segregation practices.

Although the 2006 ED Title IX regulation stresses that the single-sex classes must be completely voluntary, it is rare to find compliance with this in coed schools with single-sex classes. Many children have been placed in single-sex classes without their permission or that of their parents. [14]

Often schools with sex-segregated classes do not have a coed option, or if they do have some coeducational classes, there is no substantial equality. For example, in the ACLU *Vermilion Parish* case, the plaintiffs were assigned to single-sex classes. When their mother objected, one was assigned to the coed special education class even when that was not appropriate for her. Dual academy schools that separate all of their students by sex for all or most classes and other school activities also do not provide a coed option for students who do not choose sex segregation. FMF even found that some of these dual-academy schools in Philadelphia are the "default" neighborhood schools, so if the parents do not want their child to be in sex-segregated classes, they must find other schools that will admit their children.

It is difficult to have substantial equity in three types of classes—boys, girls, and coeducational—and on all of the important indicators of equity. In the ACLU Breckinridge County Board of Education case (2009), a girl

---

[13]Some states have requirements for other types of school reports and accountability, but it is unlikely that many Title IX coordinators or others have the chance to review these for information related to the legality or effectiveness of single-sex education practices in these schools.

[14]This breach has been documented in the ACLU cases against illegal sex segregation in public education.

wanted to be in a coed class, but the most advanced mathematics class, where she belonged, was the all-girl class. When the school discovered the girls were doing better than the boys, the school tried to slow down the girls' class so the boys' class could catch up. In addition to the level of the class, some other indicators of equity may include assessments of curriculum, teacher quality, type and effectiveness of instruction, number of students in the class, equal resources and facilities, and, of course, absence of sex stereotyping.

In many cases, these schools not only do not have substantial equity, but they increase sex stereotyping by teaching girls and boys differently. Sometimes they even teach the girls and boys different content. Sex stereotyping is compounded by teaching teachers to believe that there are important sex differences when, in fact, sex similarities related to learning are more prevalent (Hyde & Lindberg, 2007). Teaching teachers to treat boys and girls differently and according to sex stereotypes is illustrated by a *Washington Post Education Review* article on "Separate but Equal" (Houppert, 2010).

Lack of Enforcement and Education to Discourage Illegal Sex Segregation

In addition to weakening Title IX protections, the Bush administration did little to enforce Title IX in general. The Obama administration has reversed the Bush administration's objectionable guidance related to equity in athletics, but to date, its only visible action related to sex-segregated public education has been the Department of Justice (DOJ) and ED brief filed to support the ACLU appeal in the Vermilion Parish case (2010). Many organizations supporting gender equity have requested that the Obama administration rescind the Bush ED 2006 Title IX regulation.

ED and DOJ are hiring more staff especially in regional civil rights offices and may take a more active role working with Title IX Coordinators to help them learn about the oversight needed for schools engaging in unjustified and potentially illegal sex segregation. The FMF study (2011) found that few state Title IX coordinators had much knowledge of this aspect of Title IX and even fewer included this guidance on their websites. If recommendations for an updated Women's Educational Equity Act (WEEA, 2010) are approved, the federal government should be able to provide more funding and guidance to Title IX coordinators and their gender equity partners to decrease these gender inequities related to sex segregation.

Reason 3. Separate is rarely equal, especially in public education. Sex segregation has a negative impact on both girls and boys because it often favors one sex over the other and encourages misguided sex-stereotyped education practices.

Why Many Object to Sex Segregation and Race Segregation in Education

"Separate is not equal" is a key principle articulated by the Supreme Court in the 1954 *Brown v. Board of Education* decision, which made race-segregated education illegal under the U.S. Constitution. Additionally, there are substantial research studies by Gary Orfield (2009) and many others that show advantages of racial integration. Similarly, there are powerful studies especially in some business environments that show the value of having males and females work together to increase productivity and democracy (Eisler, 2007).

Whether talking about facilities, quality of instruction, levels of expectations, treatment of students, or preference for a particular teacher, it is very difficult to provide even "substantial" equality in sex-segregated schools, classes, or activities. As in race or ethnic discrimination, the less prestigious or less valued group often receives less favorable resources.

Sex-Segregated Public Education Can Harm Girls

Throughout U.S. history, sex-segregated girls have generally received inferior resources and more sex-stereotyped limitations than boys (Tyack & Hansot, 1990). This continues to apply to current public school sex segregation. For example:

- When the Albany, New York, Brighter Choices dual academies split into two school buildings, the boys got the new school and the girls remained in the old building (Klein et al., 2007).
- The "best" teachers may be assigned to the boys' classes because boys "need" the help more. Similarly, boys are often assigned to smaller classes than the girls because the girls are supposed to be easier to manage (Sadker, Sadker, & Zittleman, 2009).

- Stereotypes about being passive, feminine, girly, or uncompetitive are often emphasized. For example, a Dayton, Ohio, second-grade public school for girls in a low-income African American neighborhood focused on instruction on etiquette such as how to eat in a fancy restaurant.

- Sex segregation of women and girls is often "justified" by views that they need to be protected from men and boys, but this often limits girls' options and fails to teach boys who may be causing problems to behave according to societal standards or to provide for safety for all students.

- Sex-segregated girls miss out on the more extensive knowledge transfer available to segregated males. This inequity was used in the litigation that resulted in allowing girls to enter the all-boys academic public high school in Philadelphia as well as the 1996 Supreme Court decision that integrated the previously all-male Virginia Military Institute (Cohen, 2010).

Sex-Segregated Public Education Can Harm Boys

Masculine stereotypes tend to be exaggerated and encouraged in sex-segregated classes. Here are some of the ways sex segregation harms boys:

- The teachers of boys are likely to emphasize machismo behaviors including competition, aggression, hiding emotions, and higher prestige for sports and fame than academic success (Barnett & Rivers, 2007; Cohen, 2010).

- Boys who do not fit these stereotypes are made to feel like outsiders even though the proponents of sex-segregated education often mention how boys who are not "masculine enough" will benefit from these classes (Cohen, 2010).

- Sexual harassment and bullying related to homophobia are often exaggerated in all-male groups.

- Expectations that boys are not good at writing and some other verbal and self-control skills may be reinforced.

- Boys will lose out on the often good academic modeling and positive encouragement of girls.

- Sex-segregating black males does not ensure better achievement or even higher teacher expectations for their success. This was a clear finding in the California study of the dual academies (Datnow, Hubbard, & Woody, 2001). Some recent data also suggest that states with the lowest numbers of public schools with sex segregation may also have the highest black male graduation rates. When comparing graduation rate information for black males in neighboring New York (25%) and New Jersey (69%) in a Schott Foundation for Public Education study (Balfanz, 2010) with information on states with sex-segregated schools, we found that New Jersey had only one sex-segregated school and New york had twenty-two (Klein, 2010, 2011). Moreover, when black males do well in sex-segregated schools, we have not seen any evidence that this should be attributed to the sex-segregated program itself or, instead, to the extra attention, resources, and better instruction than in comparable coed schools.

Sex Segregation in Public Education Is Generally Bad for Everyone

Sex segregation emphasizes sex-role stereotypes rather than individual needs and abilities. Sex-segregated classes focus on the differences between girls and boys and thus make the other sex strangers. They also contribute to potential employment discrimination, as it is common to assign male teachers to boys' classes and female teachers to the girls' classes. (Assigning teachers on the basis of their sex violates both Title IX and Civil Rights Act Title VII.) Due to the relative scarcity of men teachers, this may also lead to hiring a male teacher who is less qualified than a female teacher to instruct the boys' classes. In some highly acclaimed sex-segregated public schools, extra public and private resources are used to help the targeted population, often minority boys or girls. It is logical that these richly resourced schools may be providing their students with more benefits than less endowed coed schools, but the results do not indicate that the sex-segregated grouping is what contributes to their success. They also draw resources away from the more universal improvements to help with systematic reform to help students in coed schools (Balfanz, 2010).

As it is generally practiced, sex-segregated public education increases sex discrimination and sex stereotyping compared to sex-integrated public education. It also creates extra problems for lesbian, gay, and transgender students and staff. Although there are still inequities other than single-sex programs in our public schools, the inequities in the sex-segregated schools and classes create unnecessary harm that can be avoided by retaining or returning to coeducation.

In December 2009, CNN American Morning ran a story that supported sex-segregated classes, although it also contained a snippet from long-time teacher educator and gender equity expert Professor David Sadker discussing why sex-segregated classes were educationally unsound. The show spent most of its time with Leonard Sax, a well-known advocate of public school sex segregation and founder and head of the NASSPE, and it highlighted one of his well-publicized schools, Virginia's Woodbridge Middle School. The video showed a boys' class at this school playing an active competitive game throwing things at a board with a sexy lady among other targets. The girls' class had dim lights to help girls cooperate in a restful atmosphere (Klein, 2009).

South Carolina has a whole state education agency (SEA) office encouraging "single-gender" classes. Their teacher training focuses on sharing "good practices" on how to teach girls and boys differently according to "gender" roles or stereotypes. It is common to see news articles describing "single-gender" middle school classes that allow boys to move around a frosty cool class and toss a ball to determine whose turn it is to talk or to clap and stomp their answers while girls are told to raise their hands and to mostly talk in whispers in a toasty warm classroom that smells like flowers (Lauer, 2008; South Carolina Department of Education website).

Reason 4. Most justifications for deliberate public school sex segregation are improper because the sex-segregation strategies they actually use violate legal standards and are based on scientifically unsound educational policies and practices such as false beliefs that males and females learn in different ways.

Background on Legal Standards That Allow Limited Sex Segregation in Public Education

The initial 1975 Title IX regulation clearly limits sex segregation to very unique circumstances such as using single-sex education in public schools for affirmative purposes to decrease sex discrimination in the outcomes.

The 2006 ED Title IX regulation expanded allowable sex segregation by recipients of ED funds and helped decrease attention to gender-fair coeducation. It permitted sex segregation for broad purposes that were not tied to remedial or affirmative actions to increase gender equality.[15] As documented earlier in this chapter, when "given an inch" by this more permissive 2006 ED regulation, we found that schools went well beyond what was allowed in justifying and implementing sex segregation. As the saying goes, many single-sex education advocates have been "given an inch and taken a mile"—in this case they went in the wrong direction. Now, even when schools use the affirmative action justification allowed under the 1975 Title IX regulation, and even if they follow some of the procedural guidelines in the 2006 ED Title IX regulation, they rarely provide evidence that their risky sex segregation[16] is more effective than less risky and less costly coeducation in increasing gender equality or other desirable student outcomes.

The wide-scale abuse of increased "flexibility" in allowing sex segregation in public education can be understood by examining how existing standards are being used inappropriately to justify public school sex segregation. We believe the 1975 Title IX regulation (which allows very limited sex segregation for affirmative purposes) requires full compliance with very clear legal and research standards as discussed below. These standards can be met only if very specific sex-segregation strategies are supported by high-quality evidence that they increase gender-equity outcomes more effectively than a comparable coed option and if they do not produce inequities while they are being used for either females or males.

Recommendations for Establishing Federal Standards to End Illegal and Scientifically Unsound Sex Segregation Policies and Practices

The 2006 ED Title IX regulation must be rescinded because its goal to allow sex segregation for vague governmental objectives undermines the sole purpose of Title IX—to decrease sex discrimination. The 2006 ED

---

[15]During this time it was pointed out that schools used an affirmative action justification rather than the allowable remedial action because they didn't want to admit that they had previously been legally responsible for allowing sex discrimination. Thus, we focus on the affirmative rather than remedial purposes in this chapter.

[16]We are calling public school sex segregation "risky" because it is likely to contribute to substantial inequities and be illegal.

Title IX regulation inappropriately allows sex segregation to be justified for vague improvement purposes instead of ending sex discrimination. The vague "governmental objectives" allowing the justification of sex segregation in the 2006 ED Title IX regulation are not appropriate and they are often interpreted as allowing anything that someone might consider improvement. These "improvements" range from providing parents an option to choose sex segregation because they like it and think it will increase test scores—even if this broadens the gender gap and increases sex stereotyping and sex discrimination in the desired outcomes.

There are also other problems with this 2006 regulation, such as additional exemptions from compliance with equity standards by specific types of schools and somewhat different standards for single-sex schools and coed schools with single-sex classes.

If any sex segregation is allowed for affirmative purposes using the 1975 Title IX regulations, it must meet the following five equity standards:

(1) If sex segregation is allowed to decrease sex discrimination in desired outcomes, it must not be totally exclusionary and it must have compelling evidence to justify its proposed actions.

The school would need to provide compelling answers to questions such as: What is the specific gender-equity problem that will be ameliorated by the specific sex-segregation strategy? What is the evidence that it will be more effective than comparable coeducation? Will it be feasible and cost effective? This may mean that if there was a program for girls that had evidence that it helped them enter well-paying "nontraditional" careers better than a coeducational program with similar purposes and resources, it would be legitimate for a school to select this single-sex program primarily for girls. This sex-segregation strategy would only meet adequate criteria for continuation if the students in the single-sex class did better than similar students in the comparably well-resourced coed class and if there was ample evidence that the sex segregation was the cause of the decrease in sex-discriminatory outcomes.

If legitimate indicators, in addition to increasing gender equality such as overall increases in test scores, are measured, they could be used as a supplemental justification to either support or discourage the use of the sex-segregation strategy based on the nature of the evidence.

The current Women's Educational Equity Act (WEEA) of 2001 prohibits the exclusion of boys from programs designed for girls, and the

August 2010 gender-equity advocates' draft of a revised WEEA also prohibits the exclusion of girls in programs designed to advance gender equality for boys. This nonexclusion principle (such as allowing males in women-focused courses as feminist religion professor Mary Daly was required to do) should be applied to entities covered by Title IX. It is already being used in higher education institutions, which are almost all covered by Title IX protections. The use of policies prohibiting the total exclusion of individuals based on sex should also provide needed flexibility to accommodate transgendered students and staff.

(2) There must be a well-articulated school-specific and class-specific need for using predesignated sex-segregation strategies for affirmative action.

Until the brief by the U.S. Departments of Justice and Education (2010) supporting the ACLU appeal of the *Vermilion Parish* case, it was not clear that these agencies expected more prior evidence and a classroom-specific justification for why the sex segregation would meet "*an important governmental or educational objective.*" (p. 21). This brief says "ED's regulations thus make clear that single-sex classes are the exception rather than the rule and place the burden on recipients wishing to establish such classes to show that they have met the criteria specified in the regulations." (p. 16) and that "the recipient must meet the regulatory requirement for *each* single-sex class" (p. 17). These justifications "must be genuine"— and "must not rely on overbroad generalizations about the different talent, capacities, or preferences of males and females." (p. 17). We assume that DOJ also would use this same principle of a required classroom-specific justification for the exceptions in the 1975 Title IX regulations allowing remedial or affirmative action that are used by all non ED agencies.

Additionally, if guidance is provided on how to implement the 1975 Title IX regulation, it would help to include and strengthen three procedural requirements from the 2006 Title IX regulation: completely voluntary options, equal coeducational opportunities, and the disqualification of a justification based on overbroad stereotypes. (See previous discussions in this chapter.)

In the *Vermilion Parish* case associated with the DOJ and ED brief described in this section, the Vermilion Parish School Board actually received some school-specific justification for the proposed sex-segregated classes in a dissertation by the middle school's principal, David

Dupuis. However, the Federal District Court hearing revealed that the reported justification for needing a sex-segregated intervention was inadequate in two respects. One was that no data were presented to show that boys or girls needed sex segregation in any specific classes due to poor performance or other special considerations. The other problem was that Dupuis' dissertation presented "extremely flawed" results (*Doe v. Vermilion Parish School Board*, 2010, p. 7). An analysis of the dissertation by the ACLU expert (Halpern, 2009b) found errors in his data and statistics. For example, while the data in the dissertation showed that grades had improved during the experimental period of sex segregation, the verified grades showed the reverse to be true.

It is rare to find any detailed pilot study that is used to justify sex segregation in a specific school. In this case, the Vermilion Parish School Board members and the Parish school administrators failed to verify the dissertation research, the sole legal basis for the school board agreeing to the sex segregation. The District Court said that this failure was negligence on the part of the school board and administrators.

(3) Overbroad stereotypical generalizations or related pseudoscience understandings of sex differences must not be used to justify, select, or evaluate actual sex segregation strategies.

As discussed earlier, most of the justifications for sex-segregated public education are based on overgeneralized stereotypes, which are not allowed under the 2006 ED Title IX regulation. Additionally, these justifications rarely address needs in the school that could possibly be improved by using a sex-segregated strategy in any specific class. Often, these justifications say that one of their objectives is to decrease sex stereotypes. This could mean that they would be describing an affirmative strategy to end sex discrimination in line with the 1975 Title IX regulations. However, what they actually do in the sex-segregated classrooms is to teach boys and girls differently according to sex-stereotyped notions of what they need. (See discussion of Reason #3, separate is rarely equal.)

In addition to being based on these impermissibly "overbroad generalizations about the different talent, capacities, or preferences of males and females" (p. 17), the conclusions used in these generalizations are rarely supported by systematic research evidence from multiple studies, although they underlie the work of single-sex public education advocates such as Leonard Sax and Michael Gurian (Arms, 2007).

Our understandings of what is good for us do change. As previously mentioned, there is increasing evidence of the positive effects of race integration and sex integration. Common inaccurate justifications for sex-segregated public education that support the illegal general sex stereotypes include:

- A belief in inherent differences in abilities between the sexes.

  Actually, differences between boys and girls are negligible compared to the differences among all girls or all boys. In other words, the differences within each sex are far greater than the differences between the two sexes. Think of height as an example: we would all agree that men are generally taller than women. Yet there are many men who are shorter than some women and women who are taller than some men (Halpern, 2009a; Hyde & Lindberg, 2007).

- A belief that there are sex differences in learning.

  While there are some small physiological differences in male and female brains—just like body size—there is no evidence that these minor differences have any impact on learning. The so-called "conclusions" of brain research typically go far beyond the research and ignore how the role of culture and environment interplay with the physiological brain. There are no male and female "learning styles" (Eliot, 2009; Halpern, 2009a).

- A belief that boys and girls are so different in the way they learn that they will learn better in sex-segregated classes.

  "There is no (quality) evidence based on multiple studies by independent reviewers that shows that girls learn better than boys do in co-operative groups or boys excel when they are placed in competitive situations" (Halpern, 2009a, pp. 24–25). There are also some related misperceptions such as: a belief that boys are so distracted by girls that they cannot learn in their presence and a belief that girls won't get into "trouble" (read pregnant) if kept away from boys (Halpern, 2009a). The review by Campbell and Sanders (2002) shows how quality research fails to support related assumptions about the value of single-sex education. For example, they find no support for the assumption that "Sexual tension between girls and boys and the desire to impress each other is a distraction to learning that can be eliminated by single-sex schooling" (p. 40).

(4) Constitutional Equal Protection criteria must be used to assess the treatment of all groups. This should apply to comparisons between males and females and between the sex-segregated groups and the coed groups.

In addition to using the 1975 Title IX regulation, a public school must meet the Equal Protection requirements described in the Supreme Court Virginia Military Institute (VMI) 1996 decision and also referenced in the 2006 Title IX regulation. These Equal Protection standards (such as equal access to knowledge, quality teachers, same size classes, etc.) must be met for boys and girls and for single-sex and coed classes. Using these legal standards, sex segregation might be justified *if* there were evidence of a need to decrease sex discrimination and evidence that a sex-segregated delivery strategy worked better (to a substantial degree) to decrease sex-discriminatory outcomes than a comparable coed strategy.

A related standard of completely voluntary selection of single-sex or coed grouping by parents and students is also critically important, but it may make it harder for the school to meet this Equal Protection standard if there is a differential demand for segregated or coed classes.[17]

(5) Comparative effectiveness is an essential part of any equity evaluation standard.

Schools should be able to show evidence that the proposed sex segregation has had or will have a more positive impact on increasing gender equity than comparable coeducation and that it has no negative impact on the boys or the girls. This is a standard where both the legal equality standards and the research comparison and evidence of effectiveness standards mesh. Another comparison should determine if the initial "needs" or the initial specific objectives to justify the sex segregation are met by the recipients of sex segregation better than by the nonrecipients.

If any sex segregation is allowed using the 1975 Title IX regulations, it must meet high quality research and evaluation standards.

Quality research and evaluations are needed to provide initial justifications for acceptable and legal sex segregation as well as to justify the continuation of existing public school sex segregation.

---

[17]As part of these related completely voluntary participation standards, we recommend that the parents and students must opt in to the more risky sex-segregated class or school. Segregation shouldn't be the "default" assignment.

The 2006 Title IX regulation requires evaluations every two years, but no clear standards have been provided on the quality of these evaluations, the nature of the comparisons, the questions they should address, or who should receive them, and if they should be made publicly available. Also, since the initial need for sex segregation was rarely specified, if there was some evaluation, it was probably not focused on success in meeting the specific initial needs or goals whether these were to meet general governmental objectives or to use sex segregation as an affirmative action to decrease sex discrimination in outcomes. New federal standards are needed to address all of these concerns.

In addition to making appropriate continuation decisions at the school level, reviews of multiple high-quality evaluations are needed to gain insights into the potential value of any type of sex-segregated public education. Rigorous standards such as those used by the ED "What Works Clearinghouse" must be specified for any sex segregation that might be allowed under Title IX or other civil rights laws. However, FMF found only a few formal evaluations of sex-segregated public school classes. They had mixed or negative results about the effectiveness of the sex-segregation strategy. In some cases, evaluation results were used to justify ending some sex-segregation practices (Klein, 2010, 2011). Most public reports of sex-segregated classes in coed schools are journalistic snapshots of sex-stereotypic activities in single-sex classes, sometimes using video. Occasionally the schools will report student outcomes compared to previous years when different cohorts had coed classes. These evaluations and reports of comparisons of test scores by students in coed and single-sex classes often did not provide sufficient information to judge their credibility or validity.

There are many problems with the relatively few studies that exist of sex segregation in public education. Although most studies of public school sex segregation are not as misleading as the previously discussed Dupuis dissertation in the *Vermilion Parish* case, few studies provide adequate information on the equity process measures discussed previously or on the comparative outcomes using comparable groups and careful methodology. Some of the common methodological flaws related to studies of single-sex public education include:

1. Drawing conclusions about the value of sex-segregated education for an individual study, not a review of multiple similar education interventions

Similarly, it is common for those examining sex-segregated public education to base their conclusions on anecdotal observations or a few "critical" incidents rather than on unbiased systematic collection of data on how the treatments compare and on the relationship of the treatments to the results. For example, one male science teacher in a television interview stated that he was so happy teaching an all-boys science class because the "research showed that boys liked more hands-on teaching." There is no research on this at all, and indeed the research shows that girls, too, like hands-on activities.

2. The Hawthorn Effect

Dating back to the 1930s, a large number of research studies in different fields show that when something new is done, it is likely to have an effect simply because it is new. Thus, sex-segregated programs often are successful at the beginning because they are new. The effects often diminish substantially after a while because they did not result from the program itself but from the excitement that it was something new. Thus, short-term evaluations of sex-segregated programs may be misleading, especially since the effect is often not evaluated over multiple years.

3. The John Henry and Pygmalion Effects

The success of some or all of the sex-segregated programs is contaminated by the expectations that the children and the program will succeed. If you tell parents, staff, and students that the sex-segregated program will make it easier for the children to learn than their previous experience, that alone may be enough to make a program succeed initially. For example, research on a small group of children chosen randomly described how their teachers were told that the tests show that these children will really take off during the coming year, and indeed the children did better than other children. Expectations and motivations do matter.

4. Bias in the studies

The proponents of single-sex public education are likely to identify measures and report on results in biased and inappropriate ways—often unintentionally (Halpern, 2009a, 2009b). This bias is illustrated in the Dupuis dissertation and in other studies where teachers rate student performance higher when they expect it to be higher when given a certain treatment. (It is difficult to have a single-sex class where the evaluators do not know or are "blind" to the composition of the class.)

5. Selection bias

Often more motivated students or their parents volunteer for the new innovative class such as the all-boy or all-girl class. Similarly, the best teachers may be selected for these "showcase" classes. It is difficult to overcome this bias by random assignment when the law requires that all participation in public school sex segregation must be completely voluntary.

6. Inequitable resources for comparison groups

Teachers for the sex-segregated classes typically receive some training on how to teach the all-male and all-female classes, where the teachers of the coed classes receive no extra training such as for treating their male and female students equitably in classroom interactions. Regardless of the quality or the aim of the training, the teachers may be more enthusiastic because it is something new and they may, in turn, pay more attention to students than they had previously paid. These differences may make the students learn better. Many of the sex-segregated classes include other benefits not available to coeducational classes, such as a newly painted classroom, a small student-teacher ratio, an enriched curriculum, and so forth. It is difficult to separate the effect of single-sex classrooms from the effects of these other factors. In some instances, the single-sex classes for boys and girls may also not have the same facilities, resources, and the like, thus making them inherently unequal even if both have more resources than the coed classes.

Advice on Applying these Rigorous Standards to Justify Sex Segregation

It is important to use these standards for the deliberate decisions to allow or discontinue sex segregation in public education. When addressing questions about the legality, quality, fairness, and effectiveness of sex-segregated public education, these standards should be used for both pre- and postimplementation decisions. The preimplementation decision should be used to review evidence justifying the risky sex segregation before the sex-segregated public education policy and specific instructional strategies are approved. The second and continuing set of decisions should occur after the sex segregation is implemented to help determine if the specific sex-segregation practices that were used should be continued because they meet the equality requirements and decrease sex discrimination in desired outcomes.

In making these decisions, both process and outcome indicators should be evaluated using proper comparisons. For example, these comparisons would examine how effective classes for girls were compared to classes for boys and how each single-sex class compared to the most comparable coed classes. Evaluators would also examine the effectiveness of the sex-segregated programs in addressing the initial gender-equality needs.

Reason 5. There is no credible evidence that sex-segregated public education is more effective in increasing gender equality and other desirable outcomes than less risky equally well-resourced gender-equitable coeducation.

Much of the deliberate sex segregation that has been occurring in U.S. public schools is "justified" based on inaccurate and misleading research suggesting that sex segregation will improve educational outcomes more than comparable quality coeducation will. These misleading research claims often indicate that single-sex public education will reduce sex stereotyping and improve other student outcomes (and thus might be justified using the 1975 Title IX regulations allowing limited sex segregation for purposes of decreasing sex discrimination in outcomes). But high-quality legitimate research provides no consistent evidence that sex-segregated education contributes to the achievement of better (or more gender-equitable) outcomes for girls or boys than comparable coeducation (Arms, 2007; Salomone, 2007; U.S. Department of Education, 2005). Instead, this body of research generally indicates that sex segregation increases rather than reduces sex stereotyping (Barnett, 2007; Datnow, Hubbard, & Woody, 2001; Halpern, 2009a).

Most research on single-sex education has been on private schools, not on single-sex classes in U.S. public schools. Therefore, it is inappropriate and inaccurate to state that single-sex classes (in public schools) have been proven to be better than coed classes. Additionally, the quality research in private schools rarely shows effectiveness of their single-sex education compared to comparably resourced private school coeducation.

A widely cited meta-analysis of fairly high-quality studies of single-sex schools was sponsored by the ED. The analysis did not find conclusive results favoring either single-sex or coed schools. The authors of this important review also noted that they were not able to include any studies that provided evidence of student outcomes related to measures of increased gender equity (Arms, 2007; U.S. Department of Education, 2005).

There has been little evidence that any specific sex-segregation strategies are more effective than coed strategies with similar purposes (Halpern, 2009a; Klein & Homer, 2007). Thus, it is quite a challenge for a school to identify and justify a specific sex-segregation approach to decrease sex-discriminatory outcomes in a specific class. The only effective single-sex strategy that the ED Gender Equity Expert Panel identified was a program developed for women in women's prisons called Orientation to Non-Traditional Careers for Women (ONOW), (U.S. Department of Education, 2001). However, it was not feasible to compare this ONOW program with a similar coed program.

There are a few anecdotal and other studies designed to assess the advantages of single-sex classrooms over comparable public school coed classrooms. To date, it appears that evaluations that show the most favorable results for single-sex classes are those with the poorest methodology and the studies that show no consistent advantages are those with the best methodology. Also, it does not appear that single-sex education is more effective in increasing gender-equitable outcomes than coeducation. These findings suggest that it will be difficult to satisfy the ED 2006 Title IX regulations' requirement that sex segregation be justified.

Reason 6. Sex-segregated public education in the United States is more expensive than the less risky coeducation alternatives.

Sex segregation in public schools is more expensive than coeducational classes and schools. The separate and often duplicate operations and facilities for public single-sex education are more costly than comparable coeducation. It takes more time and money to assure that all facilities and resources are equitable for both girls and boys in segregated rather than in coeducational facilities. These challenges are apparent even in simple things like ensuring equal numbers of students in the parallel boy and girl classes. A study of "single-sex Catholic schools found that per-pupil expenditures at boys' schools were 25 percent higher than those at girls' schools, and 30 percent higher than those at coed schools" (Campbell & Sanders, 2002, p. 39). Equalization of student–teacher ratios is also a challenge because the selection of sex-segregated education is required to be completely voluntary.

After the rescission of the 2006 ED Title IX regulation, it is still important to use the previously discussed multiple standards. However, the additional costs in time and resources to meet these standards should be considered in any decision to use sex-segregated public education. For every single-sex class, the 2006 regulation requires a substantially equal coeducational class. In many cases, it also requires substantially equal single-sex classes for both girls and boys. It also requires voluntary selection and evaluations every two years. If implemented adequately, these procedural standards can be quite expensive. Additional resources are needed for staff training to address how to counteract, rather than reinforce, sex stereotypes, a particularly difficult challenge when the classes are sex segregated.

Schools that sex segregate have already faced expensive lawsuits for violations of Title IX and other federal and state nondiscrimination laws. The higher costs of single-sex classes were even noted by David Chadwell, who coordinates single-gender initiatives in South Carolina. He explained that the number of public schools in South Carolina with single-sex classes was reduced in 2009 to 2010 due to state and local budget cuts (see SC Department of Education website).

Summary and Recommendations

This chapter describes how the *Risks of Sex Segregated Public Education for Girls, Boys, and Everyone* can be reduced if the ED 2006 Title IX regulation is rescinded and if appropriate standards are used to guide the use of any sex-segregated education that is still allowed under the 1975 Title IX regulation, the 14th Amendment to the U.S. Constitution, and other applicable laws.

Many aspects of the 2006 ED Title IX regulation have been challenged on both legal and scientific bases. To remedy the damage resulting from these 2006 regulations and to prevent future inequalities, it is critically important to provide clear and comprehensive guidance on the standards needed to justify any sex segregation that would continue to be allowed under the 1975 Title IX regulation exceptions for affirmative actions to increase gender equality in desired outcomes.

Additionally, federal background information accompanying this rescission should explain how the Bush administration's weakening of Title IX regulations encouraged misguided and illegal education policies. These policies led to scientifically unsound and costly sex-segregation practices in about 1,000 public schools during the 2007 to 2008 and 2008 to 2009 school years. Sex segregation, allowed under the 2006 ED Title IX regulation, was absolute—meaning that only girls were allowed in the girls' classes or schools and vice versa for boys. This absolutism is also detrimental to transgender students. In increasing schools' flexibility in allowing sex segregation, this 2006 ED regulation did not even mention what many consider a legitimate justification for single-sex education. It omitted reiterating the affirmative purposes that were in the 1975 Title IX regulations allowing limited sex segregation to decrease sex discrimination.

When ED rescinds the 2006 ED Title IX regulation and reverts to the 1975 Title IX regulations as recommended, it is important to encourage ED and DOJ to require that any proposed sex segregation meet the recommended legal equity standards as well as the standards for high-quality research comparisons. Both agencies can provide consistent guidance on preventing illegal and scientifically unsound sex-segregation policies and practices in accordance with all the 1975 Title IX regulations, the U.S. Constitution, and other relevant federal laws.[18]

Standards they address should:

- Allow sex segregation only for affirmative purposes to decrease sex discrimination in the desired outcomes as already allowed in the 1975 Title IX regulations.
- Insist that there be an approved well-articulated specific school and class need for using a predesignated sex-segregation strategy for the above affirmative purposes.

---

[18]DOJ's Civil Rights Division has authority to coordinate regulations for all agencies responsible for Title IX implementation and issued a common rule that provides Title IX regulations for all the federal entities that do not have their own unique Title IX regulations.

- Prohibit any justifications or comparative evaluations to be based on overbroad stereotypical generalizations related to understandings of sex differences.

- Require voluntary selection of equal coed and single-sex options. This should apply to comparisons between females and males and between the sex-segregated groups and the coed groups. Exceptions should be made to allow appropriately qualified males, females, or transgendered students in female or male classes or schools if this is what they want.

- Require adequate convincing evidence of comparative effectiveness of the single-sex school or class over comparable coeducation.

- Provide guidance on how evaluation studies should use high research quality standards to learn if the single-sex treatment is better on important outcome measures of effectiveness than the coed treatment and if the sex-segregated boys do better than the sex-segregated girls.

- Require that all public school sex-segregation plans and justifications be approved by appropriate governing authorities (with adequate expertise[19]) and that all approved plans, justifications, approval notices, and annual evaluation reports be easily available from free and easily accessible websites.

Additionally, to be effective in decreasing public school sex segregation, education policy makers and the public need to understand that much of the existing or planned single-sex public school education is risky, likely to be unjust or unfair, and a waste of valuable education resources. All decision makers need to understand their roles and the roles federal, state, and local education agencies and Title IX coordinators have in implementing the rigorous standards and ending inappropriate public school sex segregation.

Researchers and evaluators also need to use the legal framework as they develop their studies. In using these standards, decisions about public school sex segregation should be informed by high-quality research on the evidence of effectiveness of these strategies. Comparative evaluation results that adequately justify any public school sex segregation for

---

[19]It was evident that the Vermilion Parish School Board lacked expertise to judge a greatly flawed evaluation report.

affirmative purposes allowed under the 1975 Title IX regulations could be used as models.

It is likely that the better the quality of the study, the less likelihood results will show that sex segregation is either equitable in its treatment of students in the compared groups or that it advances desired gender-equality outcomes. Since high-quality research is very expensive, public school sex segregation strategies should not be initiated unless there are some preliminary indicators from other related situations that the strategy will be more effective in advancing gender equity than comparable coeducational strategies are. Additionally, if the government allows even limited sex segregation for affirmative purposes to increase gender-equitable outcomes, it should make descriptions of the strategies and the justifications and evaluations of these sex-segregation experiments publicly available on easily accessible websites. Also, the governmental "authorizers" of any publicly supported sex-segregated education should collect, review, and synthesize the quality studies to learn more about the positive and negative impact of sex-segregated public education.

Finally, the 2006 weakening of Title IX by allowing increased sex-stereotyped sex segregation demonstrates the importance of maintaining and enforcing a strong and well-implemented Title IX. Title IX implementation can be increased by including a reinvigorated version of the Women's Educational Equity Act (WEEA, 2010) in the forthcoming Elementary and Secondary Education Act (ESEA). This new and improved WEEA will also be essential in helping decision makers avoid inappropriate and illegal sex segregation. An August 2010 draft of the new WEEA would establish Title IX Action Networks at the local, state, and national levels, National Gender Equity Collaboratives to conduct research, development, evaluation, and technical assistance, and an Office for Gender Equity to provide catalytic leadership to purposefully advance gender equality.

Title IX coordinators and other gender-equity advocates must become active leaders in preventing illegal and misguided sex segregation. ED can help end illegal sex segregation by rescinding its 2006 Title IX regulation and issuing standards suggested in this chapter to guide educators to meet the affirmative provisions in the 1975 Title IX regulation. Congress can make this happen by including the proposed reinvigorated WEEA in the next ESEA. We look forward to success in efforts to stop this sex-segregation backlash and continue our nation's progress in creating a society where education contributes to equal opportunities for all.

References

American Civil Liberties Union. (2009). *A.N.A. v. Breckinridge County Board of Education*, Civ. Action No. 03:08-CV-4-S (E.D. KY).

American Civil Liberties Union. (2010). Brief for plaintiffs—*Appellants v. Vermilion Parish School Board.* Appeal from the U.S. District Court for the Western District of Louisiana. Case 10-30378, Document 00511133244 Date filed 5-28-2010. Retrieved September 20, 2010, from http://educationaltruths.yolasite.com.

Arms, E. (2007). Gender equity in coeducational and single sex educational environments. In S. Klein (Ed.), *Handbook for achieving gender equity through education* (2nd ed., pp. 171–90). New York: Lawrence Erlbaum, Taylor and Francis Group.

Balfanz, R. (2010). *Yes we can: The Schott 50 state report on public education and black males 2010.* Schott Foundation for Public Education. Retrieved September 20, 2010, from http://www.blackboysreport.org/.

Barnett, R. C., & Rivers, C. (2004). *Same difference: How gender myths are hurting our relationships, our children, and our jobs.* New York: Basic Books.

Barnett, R. C., & Rivers, C. (2007, Winter). *Gender myths and the education of boys.* Independent School, National Association of Independent Schools. Retrieved September 20, 2010, from http://www.nais.org/publications/ismagazinearticle.cfm?

Bell, N. (2010). *Graduate enrollment and degrees: 1999 to 2009.* Washington, DC: Council of Graduate Schools. Retrieved October 9, 2010, from http://www.cgsnet.org/portals/0/pdf/R_ED2009.pdf.

Brown, N., & Pickard, D. (2010, October). *Single-sex schooling: A preliminary exploration into Michigan PSA's Hidden Agenda.* Research on Women and Education 36th Annual Fall Conference, Philadelphia, PA.

Campbell, P. B., & Sanders, J. (2002). Challenging the system: Assumptions and data behind the push for single-sex schooling. In A. Datnow

& L Hubbard (Eds.), *Gender in policy and practice: Perspectives on single-sex and coeducational schooling* (pp. 31–46). New York: Routledge Falmer. Retrieved September 10, 2010, from www.feminist.org/education/sexsegregation.asp or http://www.josanders.com/pdf/SingleSex.pdf.

Cohen, D. S. (2010). Keeping men "men" and women down: Sex segregation, anti-essentialism, and masculinity. *Harvard Journal of Law & Gender 33*(2), 509–53. Retrieved November 1, 2010, from: http://www.law.harvard.edu/students/orgs/jlg/vol332/509-554.pdf.

Datnow, A., Hubbard, L., & Woody, E. (2001). *Is single-gender schooling viable in the public sector? Lessons from California's pilot program.* Policy report, Ford and Spencer Foundations.

Doe v Vermilion Parish School Board, 09-civ-1565 Ruling dated (April 19, 2010) W.D.La. Retrieved August 8, 2010, from http://educationaltruths.yolasite.com.

Eisler, R. (2007). *The real wealth of nations: Creating a caring economics.* San Francisco: Berret-Koehler.

Eliot, L. (2009). *Pink brain, blue brain: How small differences grow into troublesome gaps—and what we can do about it.* New York: Houghton Mifflin Harcourt.

Equal Educational Opportunities Act of 1974. 20 U.S.C. § 1701: Congressional declaration of policy. (1974) Retrieved September 15, 2010, from http://uscode.house.gov/download/pls/20C39.txt.

Geadelmann, P., Bischoff, J., Hoferek, M., & McKnight, D. B. (1985). Sex equity in physical education and athletics. In S. Klein (Ed.), *Handbook for achieving sex equity through education* (pp. 319–37). Baltimore: Johns Hopkins University Press.

Halpern, D. F. (2009a). *Issue of single-sex education, Rene A. Rost Middle School.* Report regarding civil action No. 6:09-cv 01565. Retrieved September 20, 2010, from http://educationaltruths.yolasite.com.

Halpern, D. F. (2009b). *Supplemental review of data prepared for the plaintiffs, Dec. 14, 2009.* Report regarding civil action No. 6:09-cv 01565. Retrieved September 20, 2010, from http://educationaltruths.yolasite.com.

Houppert, K. (2010, August 8). Separate but equal: More and more schools are dividing classes by gender, but critics say it's a troubling trend. *Washington Post Magazine, The Education Review 10–21*.

Hyde, J., & Lindberg, S. M. (2007). Facts and assumptions about the nature of gender differences and the implications for gender equity. In S. Klein (Ed.), *Handbook for achieving gender equity through education,* (2nd ed., pp. 19–32). New York: Lawrence Erlbaum, Taylor and Francis Group.

Kaufmann, C. (2007a, summer). A look at single-sex classrooms. *Reader's Digest Web Site*. Retrieved August 20, 2010, from http://www. rd.com/family/a-look-at-single-sex-classrooms/.

Kaufmann, C. (2007b, summer). How boys and girls learn differently. *Reader's Digest Web Site*. Retrieved August 15, 2010, from http:// www.rd.com/make-it-matter-make-a-difference/how-boys-and-girls -learn-differently/article103575.html.

Klein, S. (Ed.). (1985). *Handbook for achieving sex equity through education.* Baltimore: Johns Hopkins University Press.

Klein, S. (2005). *Title IX and single sex education*. Feminist Majority Foundation. Retrieved August 15, 2010, from http://www.feminist.org/ education/pdfs/SingleSex.pdf.

Klein, S. (Ed.). (2007). *Handbook for achieving gender equity through education* (2nd ed.). New York: Lawrence Erlbaum, Taylor and Francis Group.

Klein, S. (2009, December 11). *Tell CNN to stop promoting sex segregation in public schools*. Feminist Majority Foundation Blogs. Retrieved September 20, 2010, from http://majorityspeaks.wordpress.com/2009/ 12/11/tell-cnn-to-stop-promoting-sex-segregation-in-public-schools/.

Klein, S. (2010, 2011). *The state of public school sex-segregation in the states*. Arlington, VA: Feminist Majority Foundation, Educational Equity Program.

Klein, S., Homer, E. A., et al. (2007). Summary and recommendations for achieving gender equity in and through education. In S. Klein (Ed.), *Handbook for achieving gender equity through education* (2nd ed., pp. 655–81). New York: Lawrence Erlbaum, Taylor and Francis Group.

Klein, S., & Sesma, E. (2010). *What are we learning from the 2006–7 Office for Civil Rights survey question about public schools with single-sex academic classes?* Preliminary report. Arlington, VA: Feminist Majority Foundation.

Lauer, C. (2008, September 19). Whittemore Park Middle/separated by sex: More learning, fewer cooties. *Myrtle Beach Sun News*, C 1.

Lockheed, M. E. (1985). Sex equity in classroom organization and climate. In S. Klein (Ed.), *Handbook for achieving sex equity through education* (pp. 189–217). Baltimore, MD: Johns Hopkins University Press.

Nash, M. A., Klein, S., Bitters, B., et al. (2007). The role of government in advancing gender equity in education. In S. Klein (Ed.), *Handbook for achieving gender equity through education* (2nd ed., pp. 63–101). New York: Lawrence Erlbaum, Taylor and Francis Group.

National Association of Single Sex Public Education (NASSPE). (2010). Retrieved September 20, 2010, from www.nasspe.org.

National Women's Law Center & Morrison & Foerster LLP. (2010). *Brief of amici curiae National Women's Law Center et al. in support of plaintiffs—appellants brief urging reversal.* Appeal from the U.S. District Court for the Western District of Louisiana. Case 10-30378, Document 00511133313. Date filed June 4, 2010.

Office for Civil Rights. (2006). *Final regulations non discrimination on the basis of sex in education programs or activities receiving federal financial assistance.* Washington, DC: U.S. Department of Education. Retrieved August 22, 2009, from www.ed.gov/legislation/FedRegister/finrule/2006-4/102506a.html.

Orfield, G. (2009). *Reviving the goal of an integrated society: A 21st century challenge.* Los Angeles, CA: The Civil Rights Project/Proyecto Derechos Civiles at UCLA.

Pickard, D. (2010, October). *The role of research in ending illegal sex segregated public education.* Research on Women and Education 36th Annual Fall Conference, Philadelphia, PA.

President's Council of Advisors on Science and Technology. (2010). *Prepare and inspire: K–12 science, technology, engineering, and math (STEM) education for America's future.* Washington, DC. Retrieved

September 20, 2010, from http://www.whitehouse.gov/sites/default/files/microsites/ostp/pcast-stemed-report.pdf.

Sadker, D., Sadker, M., & Zittleman, K. R. (2009). *Still failing at fairness: How gender bias cheats girls and boys in school and what we can do about it.* New York: Scribner.

Salomone, R. (2007). Public single-sex and coeducational schools. In B. Bank (Ed.), *Gender and education: An encyclopedia* (Vol.1, pp. 217–225). Westport, CT: Praeger.

Sandler, B., & Stonehill, H. (2005). *Student-to-student sexual harassment in K–12: Strategies and solutions for educators to use in the classroom, school, and community.* Lanham, MD: Rowman & Littlefield Education.

South Carolina Department of Education website on single gender initiatives. (n. d.). Retrieved September 10, 2010, from http://www.ed.sc.gov/agency/Innovation-and-Support/Public-School-Choice-and-Innovation/SingleGender/Index.html.

Stone, L. (2007). Turning back the clock: How the Department of Education's 2006 amendments violate the Constitution and undermine the purpose of Title IX. Arlington, VA: Feminist Majority Foundation. Retrieved September 15, 2010, from http://www.feminist.org/education/pdfs/StonePaper.pdf.

The triumphs of Title IX. (2007, fall). *Ms Magazine, 27*(4), 42–47. Retrieved March 2, 2011, from http://www.feminist.org/education/TriumphsOfTitleIX.pdf.

Title IX defined. (n.d.). Retrieved September 15, 2010, from http://www.feminist.org/education/titleix.asp.

Tobias, S. (1993). *Overcoming math anxiety.* New York: W. W. Norton.

Tyack, D., & Hansot, E. (1990). *Learning together: A history of coeducation in American public schools.* New Haven, CT: Yale University Press.

U.S. Department of Education. (2001). *Gender equity expert panel: Exemplary & promising gender equity programs 2000.* Office of Educational Research and Improvement, Washington, DC ISBN 0-16-050904-1. Retrieved September 15, 2010, from http://www2.ed.gov/pubs/genderequity/index.html.

U.S. Department of Education, Office of Planning, Evaluation and Policy Development, Policy and Program Development Studies Service. (2005). *Single-sex versus coeducational schooling: A systematic review.* Washington, DC. Retrieved September 15, 2010, from http:// find.ed.gov/search?q=Single-sex+versus+coeducational&client =default_frontend&output=xml_no_dtd&proxystylesheet=default _frontend&sa.x=27&sa.y=7&sa=submit.

U.S. Department of Justice & U.S. Department of Education. (2010). *Brief to support ACLU Vermilion Parish appeal. Case 10-30378.* Document 00511133244 Date filed June 4, 2010. Retrieved September 15, 2010, from http://educationaltruths.yolasite.com.

Women's Educational Equity Act (WEEA). (2010, August 23). *Draft language prepared for inclusion in the Elementary and Secondary Education Act of 2011.* Feminist Majority and National Organization for Women. Retrieved November 20, 2010, from www.feminist.org/education.

8

Understanding Gender-Based Leadership Learning Behaviors

Shannon R. Flumerfelt, Lindson Feun, and C. Robert Maxfield

Understandings in the field of leadership development have changed in recent times in significant ways. The purpose of this chapter is to enhance this body of knowledge by extending it to consider gender-based leadership learning schema for emerging educational leaders.

This chapter is intended to contribute on two fronts: to the business case for organizational investment in aspiring leaders and to the developing pedagogy of leadership learning so that the organizational investment in aspiring leaders is maximized. The chapter includes perspectives regarding some of the current conditions impacting leadership development, the need for improved leadership training programs, and gender differences in leadership learning behaviors. In addition, a study of emerging educational leaders is presented where differences in leadership learning behaviors by gender are described. The study uncovers that there are "two handfuls" of leadership learning behaviors that are significantly different for females. As schools desire to better develop corporate capacity through effective talent-management initiatives, these findings provide helpful insight on where learning differentiates for female and male leaders and how to incorporate those differences into leadership development programming.

Literature Review

The Strategic Significance of Leadership Development

Human Resource Strategy

Leadership development is a respected element of human resource strategy and is often a core value in talent management, training and development, and human capital management initiatives (Frauenheim & Scally, 2008). In fact, organizations are prone to focus on specifically managing the talent of aspiring and established leaders versus all generic employee groups in an organization. This means that human resource efforts are increasingly concerned with first identifying and then assisting in the learning and performance of their emerging and practicing leaders. This human resource strategy is situated in an environment where human resource operations are becoming more engrossed in talent development, performance management, and leadership succession by creating capacity with current employees (McCauley & Wakefield, 2006). Hence, out of both internal corporate needs within the organization and external forces upon the organization, it is best practice for the core mission of human resource services to be strategically linked to leadership development initiatives.

Increases to leadership development programming are evident in the education sector from national, state, and local initiatives. Arne Duncan (as cited by Johnson, 2009), Secretary of Education, states that education leadership development is linked to school improvement. The U.S. Department of Education (2009) supports many leadership development projects in states such as Massachusetts, Illinois, Ohio, Tennessee, California, and Kentucky. Local initiatives abound as well, such as the initiative presented by Joel I. Klein, Chancellor of New York City's Department of Education, where $4,229 per building is allocated for participation in leadership development training (personal communication, March 31, 2009).

Organizational Strategy

Beyond the work of human resource professionals in organizations, leadership development is also encouraged as a core organizational strategy. For example, Day (2000) proposes leadership development as one venue for organizational capacity building, and Gronn (2003) describes the "discourse of leadership as a vehicle for representing organizational practice"

(p. 267). Further, these views indicate that this approach is an essential one whereby the survival and sustainability of organizations depends on leadership development as a core overall strategy.

Embracing leadership development as organizational strategy is based on the simple case of leadership as a resource in high demand yet in low supply. The scarcity of leadership in use is a severe problem, a well-documented crisis that reinforces the need for leadership development strategies, and in public sectors, this problem is acute. There is a need for organizational strategy to develop leaders, as a lack of talent management and succession planning are creating the conditions for a major leadership crisis (Tierney, 2006). Fullan and Ballew (2001) believes that effective leadership development has been lax in spite of prolific opportunities to lead, resulting in a problematic gap in schools.

While many organizations deal daily with the problems of scarcity of leadership, there are two barriers that impede the adoption of leadership development as strategy, a lack of understanding of what leadership is and a lack of female leadership development. The first barrier, a misunderstanding as to what leadership is, has been explored as a common organizational phenomenon. Gronn (2003) provides insight into this barrier as confusion presides between what leadership is and what leaders do (navigate change, transform) versus what management is and what managers do (maintain status quo, transact). He contends that these differences must be made clear to adequately address the leadership crisis and before leadership development can become organizational strategy. As Gronn does, Peterson (2006) traces the scarcity of leadership to the root cause of the proliferation of management ill conceived as leadership. He points out that it is difficult to find sustaining and authentic organizational leadership practices, while it is easy to find management in use, further igniting the leadership shortage crisis. As Porter-O'Grady and Malloch (2007) state, the differences in the way organizations are lead are due to their ability to respond to drastic changes in the essence and nature of work as defined in the information age. This barrier of confusion between leadership and management occurs because defining leadership on a pragmatic level proves difficult (Wilmore & Cornell, 2001) because school administrators often operate under a vision of what school leaders should be like, not under their actual on-site performances in real time. This causes more confusion when leadership conceptualizations are disconnected from leadership practice. Bolman and Deal (2003) bluntly describe the results of this phenomenon, a scarcity of leadership in use, as the "curse of cluelessness" in organizations. This barrier to overcoming the leadership scarcity problem in organizations and the misunderstanding of what leadership is must be addressed to facilitate leadership development as an organizational strategy.

The second barrier to overcoming the overall scarcity of leadership and the adoption of leadership development as a core organizational strategy is the lack of female talent management. Wilson (2007) describes this problem well as she points out that while women represent 46 percent of the workforce, leadership positions are dominated by males. This disparity is alarming as she describes further that women make up "only 9.4 percent of top executives and 15.6 percent of corporate officers" and, further, "a mere 14.6 percent of board seats in five hundred of the country's largest companies" (p. xii). These percentages of female leadership positions are out of proportion to the total workforce numbers and the market presence of women. Furthermore, these percentages undermine the established case for the diversification of organizational leadership (Wolfman, 2007).

There are many disparaging situations related to the lack of female leadership in public schools. As Noel-Batiste (2009) states, "less than five percent of public school superintendents are women and less than twenty-seven percent of public secondary school principals are women (Digest of Educational Statistics, 2004). Despite the fact that teaching has remained a feminized profession, educational administration continues to be dominated by males (Glazer, 1991, making this disparity one of education's most challenging issues" (online). There is mounting moral outrage and concern for the economic impact of such discrimination (McKenna, 2007). It is indeed a strange situation that there exists a shortage of leaders with a supply of female leaders available. This is an unfortunate barrier to leadership development with poor consequences, a missed opportunity to benefit organizations and society (Penney, Brown, & Oliviera, 2007). So, as organizations understand the importance of leadership development as a core organizational strategy, they must also understand that there is a barrier to overcome in regard to female leadership development.

When leadership development is more strategically focused on current goals and benchmarks of the organization, there is also a need to increase understandings of the philosophical and contextual underpinnings of personal leadership development and practice. Under these conditions, leadership is understood as effective performance and demonstrated potential for positively impacting the organization, particularly when it comes to female leadership development and the case for leadership diversification. Wolfman (2007) advocates for urgency in advancing the case for female leaders: "What remains to be seen is whether the proponents of leadership diversity are able to build strategic coalitions that can catalyze these forces and make sure that the transformation process will be measured in years rather than decades" (p. 62). McKenna (2007) also contributes to this issue, saying, "The nation needs to maximize all human capital, in order to meet our own challenges and stay competitive in this global economy" (p. 7). So the need to advance the pedagogical issues of leadership development programming so that the deliverable of a diverse workforce at all levels can be obtained is the crux of why female leadership development matters for organizations.

Leadership Learning as Schema

Many support the organizational case for the development of leaders with renewed insights into what leadership development entails, representing breakthrough conceptualizations about leadership as a system of learning (Bennis, 1999; Blanchard & O'Connor, 1997; Goleman, 1995; Kouzes & Posner, 1995). Such evolved approaches advance leadership development beyond traditionally conceived checklists of competencies, which solely focus on what the leader does. What is being discovered is that what a leader thinks and how a leader develops and learns is intricately connected to what he or she does. These ideas reinforce understandings of leadership as a system of interconnected interactions of what a leader understands, believes, and does (Barth, 2001). In current times, practitioners of leadership find that explicitly simple leadership principles (Blanchard & O'Connor, 1997; Kouzes & Posner, 1995) are operationalized in decidedly systemic ways (Barbuto & Burbach, 2006; Goleman, 1995) involving highly complex workplace interactions (Johnson, Manyika, & Yee, 2005). Jenlink (2006) describes this as a constructivist view of leaders accessing different pools of knowledge, contexts, and routines.

Furthermore, Avolio (1999) proposes that when leadership is understood as a system, it is possible to consider ranges of performance, including leadership optimization. For instance, a recent study conducted by Hirst, Mann, Bain, Pirola-Merola, and Richver (2004) identified a constructivist development of leadership learning schema over a time period required to transform schema to skills in use in a way that impacted team performance. This means that leadership learning extends beyond formal training programs and into personalized preferences and individualized timelines for developing leadership capacity.

In turn, organizations have found that best practice for leadership development involves alignment of organizational values and goals with training initiatives and performance evaluations. Competency-based models of what organizations want leaders to know, value, and be able to do are presented with accompanying learning experiences designed to impact epistemology and practice (Flumerfelt, 2006). As aspiring leaders are identified in organizational settings, significant and increasing effort is allocated for a more targeted approach to leadership development.

Leadership Programs

Hence, while leadership development is better understood now than it was in the past, there is still much to learn about it (Bennis, 1999). In current times, while a topic of great popularity, there is not a shared understanding and enlightened application of leadership learning systems to development programming. And as it stands, in general, leadership programs struggle to keep up with the nature and pace of change in the field (Brown, 2003). In other words, as leadership becomes more complex in use, process-based theories must be developed so that leadership training programs can align accordingly. Instead of program design based on content, Murphy (2006) suggests principled program design. Peterson (1986) pointed this out as well and identified irrelevant coursework and leadership requirements as having little significance for school leadership practice, for example. In other words, there is a need for a better understanding of the processes and results of leadership learning in terms of formulating program design around the learner, not simply content outcomes. Hence, while leadership development is theoretically aligned with process-based approaches to leadership learning, training and development programs typically do not employ teaching methodology or accompanying assessment tools to measure such leadership learning processes. While such programs may present leadership practice under an enlightened paradigm of content delivery, they often fail to understand or assess leadership development processes as a part of the participant's learning in a similar manner. This becomes significant when leadership learning, organizational goals, and stakeholder needs are aligned as benchmarks for performance.

McGough's (2003) study of the learning processes of practicing school principals indicates that there are several complex elements in use during leadership improvement initiatives. Research provides evidence that process-based models are used in adult leadership learning (Argyis, 1991; Daley, 2000; Senge, 1990; Sergiovanni, 1992). These theorists understand adult learning as an interactive relationship between knowledge and practice (Kanungo, 2001; Kedro, 2004; Prabhakar, 2005).

So then, process-based approaches in identifying and understanding various systems of learning behaviors have a solid tradition in research. Therefore, precedence for conceptualizing learning as phenomena and then analyzing patterns of learning behavior into a schema or a system has been clearly established as a viable method for understanding it better. The application of systems-based analyses to learning behaviors is helpful in delineating the relational components of learning. It allows for mapping out the scope and sequence of the elements of the learning processes studied. The application of process-based thinking in regard to leadership development is important because such conceptualizations allow for enriched understandings through the examination of multiple elements at a time; consideration of how different elements interact and interrelate; and understanding what the scope and sequence of process interactions are.

As one contemplates both the simplicity and complexity of leadership and engages in "sense-making" as a leader, several types of learning behaviors are used. Hence, there is a need for research focused on the actual behaviors in use when learning about leadership. McCormick and Martinko (2004) advocate for such research in a study of leadership social cognitions as they posit that such research would amount to documentation of learning processes in use that would uncover patterns of behavior. Such a study has been attempted and is presented later in this chapter, focusing on emerging female leaders' learning schema. However, before presenting the study, some background on leadership learning related to gender is needed so that the results of the study can be better understood.

Gender and Leadership Learning

There are differences in leadership learning by gender. As these leadership differences between genders are examined, researchers have separated the complexities of gender-based social/power interactions from gender-based leadership differences. Rosenberg (2008) describes this phenomenon as gender-biased beliefs creating gender-biased interaction effects and non-gender-biased beliefs creating non-gender-biased interactions. Ridgeway (1999) also delineates leadership learning and performance from gender bias in a similar by recognizing that gender bias can be eliminated in interaction through equality in leadership development initiatives and that it is legitimate to simultaneously recognize differences in genders. In addition, Ridgeway (1999) provides evidence that bias-free workplaces are more successful.

In considering gender-based differences in leadership learning and development, then, researchers have been clear about distinguishing this area of study from gender-based leadership effectiveness. As a result of a literature review on this, Thompson (2000) states that although leadership style and expression may differ, "men and women were equally effective" (p. 969); therefore, there is a need for accepting the inherent cognitive complexity in leadership learning regardless of gender.

The separation of leadership effectiveness from leadership learning and leadership style is reinforced in the work of Rosener (1990), where differences in female leaders were noted as more personally than organizationally dependent for authority. Rosener overall describes females as more transformational and interactive than their male counterparts, more willing to share both power and information. Eagly, Karau, and Johnson's (1992) meta-analysis of school principals similarly found that while there were no differences in effectiveness, females shared power more, provided interactive venues more, and completed more tasks than males. Scott and Brown (2006) found significant differences in male and female leadership behaviors and accessibility to agentic versus communal protocols, with females accessing agentic protocols less than males. Yoder and Kahn's (2003) review of the literature concludes that given identical settings, both broad and specific societal structures do impact males and females differently.

Inherent in these findings are the implications that the interdependence between leadership development and resulting leadership learning behaviors are different based on gender, resulting in certain gender-based advantages and disadvantages (Armett-Kibell, 2007; Eagly & Carli, 2003). In fact, Fletcher (2004) acknowledges gender-based differences in leadership and proposes that only when male/female distinctions are overtly addressed in leadership development will the inadequate status quo of the underdevelopment of both social and human capital in organizations diminish.

Description of the Study

Given the value of leadership development as a human resource and organizational strategy; the scarcity of leaders, especially female leaders; and the need to understand what leadership is and how leaders develop, the following study was undertaken. The study is an effort to better understand the schema of leaders in education and to further understand if gender differences in leadership learning exist.

This study was preceded by a series of initial focus group research studies in 2004 with sixteen practicing and emerging educational leaders. This preliminary research identified initial descriptions of leadership learning activity and schema. In a subsequent study in 2007 with 182 practicing and emerging leaders (Flumerfelt, Maxfield, & Feun, 2007), the reliability of thirty leadership learning behaviors was tested in a schema of knowledge, values (dispositions), and application.

Background of the Study

The initial focus group research in 2004 revealed that emerging and practicing leaders sincerely engaged in increasing commitment and effectiveness by using certain learning behaviors that they described as schema. There were no tests of significant differences by gender in this early research. These behaviors were first classified and systemized into nine general leadership learning elements and then specifically described as thirty leadership learning behaviors. The sixteen focus group participants self-reported understanding leadership learning behaviors in use and how they connected those behaviors as elements.

Out of the initial focus study, the descriptors of leadership learning systems were identified and behavior descriptors of the learning schema elements were detailed. It was also learned through this study that self-management and self-facilitation of leadership growth was helped by identifying leadership learning systems in use. See Figure 1, which describes the identified schema elements as a system of three levels and three phases, at http://tinyurl.com/Flumerfelt.

In this leadership learning schema, each level is ranked and has distinct phases. The three levels and three phases are interdependent based on feedback from the preceding growth experiences. In other words, the learner may recycle through levels or phases, depending on the feedback received or goals set. Once a benefit has been obtained from a level or phase, that learning is carried forward to the next level or phase, or concurrent development may occur. The three levels of development are Knowledge, Dispositions, and Application. Each level has three similar phases named Self-Awareness, Group Awareness, and Others' Awareness. In total, nine elements are represented by Levels (Knowledge, Dispositions, Application) and Phases (Self, Group, Others) as Knowledge-Self, Knowledge-Group, Knowledge-Others, Dispositions-Self, Dispositions-Group, Dispositions-Others, Application-Self, Application-Group, and Application-Others.

What became evident through these initial studies was that all of the participants were able to think about their leadership understandings, values, and performances in an intelligent way and then articulate those processes as behaviors schema. In all, thirty leadership learning behaviors were identified through the focus group research listed in Table 8.1.

The results of this 2004 study provided descriptions of leadership learning behaviors useful in understanding how leader participants describe their learning processes. This study revealed that leadership learning processes are not generic or random, but rather are systemic, deliberate, specific, and individualized based on learning preferences.

For the second study in 2007 with 182 participants, the thirty leadership learning behaviors were examined demographically and tested for reliability based on desirability and frequency of use. The demographic analyses included comparisons by practicing and emerging leader groups and then by years of service, position, and gender within those groups.

TABLE 8.1

List of 30 Leadership Learning Behaviors by Level and Phase

Learning Behaviors	Level	Phase
Take notes, journal, self-talk about leadership	Knowledge	Self
Compare personal leadership knowledge with scholarly work, test for validity, evidence, robustness	Knowledge	Self
Contemplate leadership expectations/plan how to use concepts, strategies, decision-making strategies	Knowledge	Self
Examine leadership mistakes and how to improve	Knowledge	Self
Learn from a mentor	Knowledge	Group
Discuss potential results of new concepts with family, peers, allies, leaders	Knowledge	Group
Talk informally, "hallway talk," about leadership	Knowledge	Group
Talk with others about leadership ideas and seek support, criticism	Knowledge	Others
Seek to understand what others know about leadership	Knowledge	Others
Use new language, strategies, ideas to solve, mediate, manage change, or connect theory to general settings	Knowledge	Others
Read, research, talk, observe if leadership theories have personal relevance and relate to my prior knowledge	Knowledge	Others
Lead in new ways based on theory, research, or documentation	Knowledge	Others
Understand leadership constructs to influence others, share information where some are unfamiliar	Knowledge	Others
Self-direct leadership development activities	Dispositions	Self
Consider depth of personal relevance, benefits/values, costs/risks of leadership	Dispositions	Self
Self-reflect on dispositions and aligning actions of leadership	Dispositions	Self
Construct personal meaning of values by expression and quoting others	Dispositions	Others

(continued)

Table 8.1 (*continued*)

Learning Behaviors	Level	Phase
Develop original ideas and share those with stakeholders	Dispositions	Others
Establish new boundaries in professional, personal relationships by taking risks to advance leadership	Dispositions	Others
Inspire others to lead	Dispositions	Group
Talk with others on benefits of sharing about leadership problems	Dispositions	Group
Identify leadership disposition strengths/weaknesses	Dispositions	Group
Have confidence in my ability to lead	Application	Self
Self-analyze, -develop, -evaluate how/when to lead, grow/change	Application	Self
Discuss leadership with my family	Application	Group
Motivate self to pursue more leadership as others rely on me	Application	Others
Admit when wrong, share apologies	Application	Others
Lead from experience	Application	Others
Survey stakeholders assessing my leadership to set goals	Application	Others
Receive compliments, expressions of confidence by others	Application	Others

Table 8.2 below lists the reliability results of the thirty learning behaviors by the emerging leaders and practicing leaders.

Table 8.2 illustrates that the results of the reliability tests showed that each of these thirty learning behaviors was both highly desirable and frequently used for both emerging and practicing leader participants. In turn, the behaviors were also ranked for frequency and desirability, which showed that for both practicing and emerging leaders, some Application Development behaviors were the most popular, followed by some Values Development behaviors, and then followed by some Knowledge Development behaviors. The significance of this finding is the general schema preference for applications-based learning experiences, followed by values-based experiences, then knowledge experiences.

TABLE 8.2
Reliability Tests of Leadership Learning Behaviors by Emerging/Practicing Leaders

		Emerging Leaders			
Cases	Valid	N = 73	% = 91.3	Cronbach's Alpha	N of Items
	Excluded	N = 7	% = 8.8		
	Total	N = 80	% = 100.0	0.922	30
		Practicing Leaders			
Cases	Valid	N = 58	% = 92.1	Cronbach's Alpha	N of Items
	Excluded	N = 5	% = 7.9		
	Total	N = 63	% = 100.0	0.922	30

In addition, the study presented here indicates that the demographic data were useful in terms of understanding differences in learning behaviors and differences in the type of learning element preferred and used based on stage of leadership (emerging or practicing) and gender. Hence, it was helpful to analyze the data from the study to determine where significant differences by demographics occurred. For the practicing leaders, there were no significant differences by gender, years of service, position, or job type. For the emerging leaders, there were no significant differences by years of service, position, or job type. However, the results presented below examine significant differences by gender in the leadership learning behaviors of the emerging leaders. So, while leadership learning systems for practicing leaders were not significantly different by gender, for emerging leaders there were differences by gender for the emerging female leaders in the study.

Methods of the Study

A survey with thirty items and five demographic responses was designed by the researchers and mailed to 140 emerging leadership program participants in a three-county region. The leadership program was offered by a Midwestern university as a part of a multicounty consortium devoted to leadership talent development for K–12 schools. Confidentiality was maintained using double-blind procedures where consent forms were mailed separately from surveys. It was assumed the emerging leader participants would participate out of loyalty to the leadership program they had participated in. Respondents were categorized into two samples of males ($n = 21$, 22%) and females ($n = 76$, 78%) to determine any differences in leadership learning behaviors of these emerging leaders by gender.

Findings

The data from the survey of leadership learning behaviors were disaggregated to determine if there were any statistically significant differences on how various groups responded to the survey. Emerging leaders were asked to rate each learning behavior using a scale of 1 to 10, with 1 representing the lowest importance and 10 signifying the highest importance in terms of preference and frequency of use.

The Chi Square Test of Significance was used to disaggregate the data with a level of significance set at 0.05. The 102 surveys returned (56%) were disaggregated by years of service, position, job placement, and gender. With the number of missing cases, the Ns for each analysis ranged from 95 to 97 leaders.

Interestingly, the date analyses indicated gender was the only important factor in producing significant differences in the disaggregation of the thirty learning behaviors. The following 11 leadership learning behaviors that produced significant results by gender are described below.

> **Learning about leadership from a mentor**—Twenty-three females (30.3%) rated this learning behavior as highest importance, while only two males rated this behavior as highest importance (9.5%). Males were more likely to assign a value of 7 (33.3% or seven males) to this learning behavior.
>
> **Contemplating what is expected of a leader by planning how leadership concepts, decision-making processes, and strategies can be used**—A total of twenty-two females (28.9%) rated this behavior as highest importance, while no males rated this behavior as highest importance. Eight males assigned this learning behavior a value of 8 and eight assigned a value of 9 (33.1%).
>
> **Using new language, new strategies, new ideas to solve problems, mediate conflict, manage change, or connect leadership theory to**

generalized situations—Twenty-eight of the females (37.3%) rated this behavior as highest importance, while only two of the males (9.5%) rated this behavior as highest importance. Nine males selected 8 (42.9%) for this behavior.

Performing self-directed leadership development activities—A total of twenty-five females (32.9%) rated this as highest importance, while only two males (9.5%) gave a similar rating. Male ratings were distributed across the scale with no dominant choice.

Talking with confidants and noting the benefits of sharing about personal leadership dispositions, considerations, and common solutions to leadership dilemmas—Females (twenty-six or 35.1%) were more likely to rate this behavior as highest importance than males (two and 9.5%, respectively). Males were more likely to assign a rating of 7 (38.1% or eight males).

Inspiring peers to get involved in leadership—A total of nineteen females or 25.0 percent marked this behavior as highest importance, whereas no males assigned this rating. Males were more likely to select 7 or 8, which represented 33.3 percent and 28.6 percent (seven and six males, respectively).

Discussing leadership with my family—Fifteen females (20.0%) marked this behavior as highest importance, with no males assigning this rating. Male responses were fairly evenly distributed across the scale from lowest importance (19.0%) to 4 through 8 (14.3% to 19.0%).

Having confidence in my ability to lead—Forty-two females (55.3%) gave this behavior a rating of highest importance, while eight males (38.1%) gave a similar rating. Males were more likely to assign a value of 8 (33.3% or seven males). The predominant second choice for females was 9 (26.3% or twenty females).

Self-analyzing, developing self-awareness, self-evaluating how and when to lead, how to grow/change/improve as a leader, and impact a system—A total of forty-seven females (61.8%) gave this behavior a rating of highest importance and six males (28.6%) gave a similar rating. Six additional males assigned a value of 8 and five marked 9 (23.8%) for this behavior.

Receiving compliments and expressions of confidence in me as a leader by colleagues/administrators, staff, subordinates—Twenty-four females (31.6%) gave this behavior a rating of highest importance and only one male (4.8%) did likewise. Males were more likely to assign a rating of 8 (28.6% or six males) to this behavior.

Motivating myself to pursue greater endeavors when I realize others rely on me—A total of forty-four females (57.9%) rated this behavior as highest importance, while six males (28.6%) gave a similar rating. Seven males (33.3%) gave a rating of 9.

With all eleven analyses, females were more likely to rate each learning behavior higher than their counterparts. The predominant rating for females was highest importance. Males were more inclined to assign a value of 7 to 9 for each learning behavior.

Placing these behaviors into a matrix as outlined in Table 8.3 below based on the nine general leadership learning elements described previously in Table 8.1 indicated that female leadership behavior differences include eight of the nine elements of the leadership learning schema, excluding Values-Others.

In general, Table 8.3 illustrates a wide range of in-use gender-distinctive highly ranked leadership learning elements by emerging female leaders. More specifically, it highlights gender differences based on importance for eleven out of thirty possible behaviors. In other words, these eleven leadership learning behaviors were more significantly important to emerging female leaders than to emerging male leaders.

Discussion

The gender differences in leadership approaches and learning provide some insight into these results. The work of authors reviewed above, specifically Rosener; Eagly, Karau, and Johnson; and Scott and Brown, provide some concepts for understanding these results of highly used and highly preferred female leadership learning behaviors. While all thirty of the leadership learning behaviors under study were ranked as highly desirable and frequently used by both genders, the eleven behaviors with significantly higher rankings for desirability and frequency of use can be aligned with gender-based leadership learning theories. Because the study highlights

TABLE 8.3
Significant Emerging Leader Female Differences in Leadership Learning Behaviors

Level	Phase	Leadership Learning Behavior
Knowledge	Self	Contemplating what is expected of a leader by planning how leadership concepts, decision-making processes, and strategies can be used
	Group	Learning about leadership from a mentor
	Group	Talking with confidants and noting benefits of sharing about personal leadership dispositions, considerations, and common solutions to leadership dilemmas
	Others	Using new language, new strategies, new ideas to solve problems, mediate conflict, change, or connect leadership theory to generalized situations
Values	Self	Performing self-directed leadership development activities
	Group	Inspiring peers to get involved in leadership
Application	Self	Having confidence in my ability to lead
	Self	Self-analyzing, developing self-awareness, self-evaluating how and when to lead, how to grow/change/improve as a leader and impact a system
	Group	Discussing leadership with my family
	Others	Receiving compliments and expressions of confidence in me as a leader by colleagues, administrators, staff, subordinates
	Others	Motivating myself to pursue greater endeavors when I realize others rely on me

the distinction between male and female leadership learning schema, these differences may prove helpful in the leadership program design, implementation, and assessment of the participants.

First, Rosener's (1990) work identifying personally developed (versus organizationally developed) sources of power for females provides an explanation for selection of three behaviors: (1) performing self-directed leadership development activities; (2) having confidence in my ability to lead; and (3) receiving compliments and expressions of confidence in me as a leader by colleagues/administrators, staff, subordinates. These behaviors reflect an effort in self-direction and direction from interactive processes. This is a different approach of the use and application of power than from deriving it from formally designated organizational structure and policy. Hence, female preferences for personally developed power are reflected in the responses of the female participants for these three leadership learning behaviors.

Second, Rosener's (1990) work identifying transformational tendencies for females provides an explanation of three more behaviors: (1) contemplating what is expected of a leader by planning how leadership concepts, decision-making processes, and strategies can be used; (2) using new language, new strategies, new ideas to solve problems, mediate conflict, manage change, or connect leadership theory to generalized situations; and (3) inspiring peers to get involved in leadership. These behaviors are indicative of female leadership tendencies to focus on organizational learning, leadership succession, change management, and strategic work. This is a different approach to organizational development than from transactional emphases, which focus on tactical and current demands of the day. Female preferences in the study for transformational leadership development are represented by these three leadership learning behaviors.

Third, Eagly, Karau, and Johnson's (1992) study of female leadership tendencies to share power and information more than males do provides an explanation of these two behaviors: (1) learning about leadership from a mentor and (2) discussing leadership with my family. These selections are indicative of a view of power and information as more effective via collaboration and partnering. This is a different approach than more competitive and protective views of power and information and the risks of collaborative approaches. Female preferences in the study to distribute power and information organizationally are represented in these two leadership learning behaviors.

Fourth, Scott and Brown's (2006) analysis of communal approaches to leadership provides insight into these two behaviors: (1) talking with confidants and noting the benefits of sharing about personal leadership dispositions, considerations, and common solutions to leadership dilemmas and (2) motivating myself to pursue greater endeavors when I realize others rely on me. These two behaviors reinforce the finding that females are more communal than agentic in leadership, hence a preference for sharing problems and solutions within a community of nurturing and embracing the needs of the organization on a personal level. In contrast, an agentic approach is less focused on the personalized views of leadership improvement and the direct impact of the leader's effectiveness on others. Female preferences in the study for communal methods are represented in these two leadership learning behaviors.

In summary, past research studies on gender-based differences in leadership improvement and development are helpful in understanding why emerging female leaders studied selected these eleven leadership learning behaviors more than males did. This study points out the tendency of female leaders to prefer and rely more frequently on these eleven different behaviors than males do in terms of how to use power to benefit leadership practice, to share information to develop enriched problem identification and solution strategies, to nurture others for leadership, to strategically develop the organization itself, and to utilize communal means of interacting for professional enhancement.

Conclusion

In conclusion, the study is important to the work of leadership development initiatives when they are associated with an organizational strategy for success. It provides useful data regarding the ability of emerging educational leaders surveyed to pursue leadership development based on the generalized patterns of leadership learning. Furthermore, it provides helpful information in terms of distinguishing developmentally appropriate program design these for emerging and practicing leaders and, furthermore, for gender-based learning preferences.

In general, this study provides information on the overall learning process of leadership development, regardless of gender, as an interchange between three areas of development—Knowledge, Dispositions, and Applications—and three levels of development—Self, Group, and Others. This study provides evidence that for the participants, leadership development is a complex process of interrelated elements and is clearly not pursued in a linear manner, but rather systemically. Hence, this leadership development initiative should consider program design that matches process-based learning in terms of selection of learning objectives and goals, design of learning tools and activities, and assessment options.

More specifically, when considering the popularity of preferences for Applications Development opportunities selected by the participants, the importance of experiential learning for leadership development emerges. Experiential learning does challenge traditional leadership program design, which tends to lead with and emphasize content delivery. While an important and a highly reliable learning behavior for all participants, knowledge development was least highly ranked as preferred. Instead, participants indicated a most highly ranked preference for simulation, mentorship, internship, and field-based work regardless of gender. Hence, program owners should provide such learning experiences frequently, even as leading program activities.

Most specifically, the study highlights the distinct differences by emerging female leaders for eleven leadership learning behaviors. These behaviors represent gender-based preferences and can be helpful in program redesign in terms of facilitating female leadership development. They also help program owners to understand that there are gender-based preferences in use for leadership development. So it is recommended that individualized program design, independent study options, or differentiated instruction based on gender preferences be examined to meet the needs of these emerging leaders.

As organizations seek to meet the need for leaders and seek to understand what leaders do, the more informed the pursuit of leadership development is, the sooner this goal will be realized. Hence, developing an understanding of leadership learning behaviors and gender differences for emerging leaders adds to this body of knowledge. The distinctions between the male and female emerging leaders in this study on eleven leadership learning behaviors were significant. Recommendations for future study include replication with participants from other leadership programs and, if possible, increasing the degree of randomization. It is hoped that this initial work will serve those interested in leadership development in schools and enable them to tap into the pool of talent represented by aspiring female leaders.

References

Armett-Kibell, C. (2007). Future promise of women in science. *New England Journal of Public Policy, 22*(1), 135–50.

Arygis, C. (1991). Teaching smart people how to learn [Electronic version]. *Harvard Business Review, 3*(69), 99–109.

Avolio, B. J. (1999). *Full leadership development: Building the vital forces in organizations.* Thousand Oaks, CA: Sage.

Barbuto, J. E., & Burbach, M. E. (2006). The emotional intelligence of transformational leaders: A field study of elected officials [Electronic version]. *Journal of Social Psychology, 146*(1), 51–64.

Barth, R. S. (2001). *Learning by heart.* San Francisco: Jossey-Bass.

Bennis, W. (1999). The leadership advantage. *Leader to Leader, 12.* Retrieved March 1, 2006, from http://www.pfdf.org/knowledgecenter/journal.aspx?ArticleID=53.

Blanchard, K., & O'Connor, M. (1997). *Managing by values.* San Francisco: Berrett-Koehler.

Bolman, L. G., & Deal, T. E. (2003). *Reframing organizations: Artistry, choice, and leadership* (3rd ed.). San Francisco: Jossey-Bass.

Brown, D. (2003). Fast-trackers can lack ethics, vision [Electronic version]. *Canadian HR Reporter, 16*(8), 1–2.

Daley, B. J. (2000). Learning in professional practice. [Electronic version]. *New Directions for Adult and Continuing Education, 86,* 33–42.

Day, D. V. (2000). Leadership development: A review in context. *Leadership Quarterly, 11*(4), 581–613.

Eagly, A. H., & Carli, L. L. (2003). The female leadership advantage: An evaluation of the evidence. *Leadership Quarterly, 14*(6), 807–34.

Eagly, A. H., Karau, S. J., & Johnson, B. T. (1992). Gender and leadership style among school principals: A meta-analysis. *Educational Administration Quarterly, 28*, 76–102.

Fletcher, J. K. (2004). The paradox of postheroic leadership: An essay on gender, power and transformational change. *Leadership Quarterly, 15*(5), 646–61.

Flumerfelt, S. (2006, March). Editorial for weLead Online Magazine: Defining leadership as a process. *WeLead in Learning*. Retrieved March 2, 2011 from http://www.leadingtoday.org/Onmag/2006% 20Archives/march06/sf-march06.html.

Flumerfelt, S., Maxfield, R., & Feun, L. (2007). Leadership learning systems. *International Journal of Knowledge, Culture & Change Management, 7*, www.management-journal.com.

Frauenheim, E., & Scally, R. (2008, June 2). News in brief: IHRIM conference highlights the influence of social networking and talent management technology on HR. *Workforce.com*. Crain Communications Inc. Retrieved June 2008 from http://www.workforce.com/section/00/ article/25/56/91.html.

Fullan, M., & Ballew A. C. (2001). *Leading in a culture of change*. San Francisco: Jossey-Bass.

Goleman, D. (1995). *Emotional intelligence: Why it can matter more than IQ*. New York: Bantam Books.

Gronn, P. (2003). Leadership: Who needs it? *School and Leadership Management 23*(3), 267–90.

Hirst, G., Mann, L., Bain, P., Pirola-Merlo, A., & Richver, A. (2004). Learning to lead: The development and testing of a model of leadership learning. *Leadership Quarterly, 15*(3), 311–27.

Jenlink, P. M. (2006). The school leader as bricoleur: Developing scholarly practitioners for our schools. *NCPEA Education Leadership Review, 7*(2), 54–69.

Johnson, B. C., Manyika, J. M., & Yee, L. A. (2005). The next revolution in interactions. *McKinsey Quarterly: The Online Journal of McKinsey & Co., 4*. Retrieved November 4, 2006, from http://www.mckinseyquarterly .com/article_page.aspx?ar= 1690 &L2 =18&L3=30&srid=6&gp=1.

Johnson, J. (2009, December 11). Secretary Duncan participates in national launch of school leadership project [Tiffany Taber, Office of Communication and Outreach, Ed.gov blog/US Department of Education]. Retrieved March 1, 2010 from http://www.ed.gov/blog/2009/12/secretary-duncan -participates-in-national-launch-of-school-leadership-project/.

Kanungo, R. N. (2001). Ethical values of transactional and transformational leaders [Electronic version]. *Canadian Journal of Administrative Sciences, 18*(4), 257–65.

Kedro, M. J. (2004). Leading schools to higher plateaus—part 2. *weLead Online Magazine.* Retrieved February 17, 2006, from http://www .leadingtoday.org/Onmag/2004%20Archives/feb04/mk-feb04.html.

Kouzes, J. M., & Posner, B. Z. (1995). *The leadership challenge: How to keep getting extraordinary things done in organizations.* San Francisco: Jossey-Bass.

McCauley, C. & Wakefield, M. (2006). Talent management in the 21st century: Help your company find, develop, and keep its strongest workers. *The Journal for Quality and Participation, 29*(4), 4–7, 39. Retrieved March 3, 2011, from ABI/INFORM Global. (Document ID: 1214836601).

McCormick, M. J., & Martinko, M. J. (2004). Identifying leader social cognitions: Integrating the causal reasoning perspective into social cognitive theory. *Journal of Leadership & Organizational Studies, 10*(4), 2–10.

McGough, D. J. (2003). Leaders of learners: An inquiry into the formation and transformation of principals' professional perspectives. *Educational Evaluation and Policy Analysis, 25*(4), 449–71.

McKenna, M. (2007). Women in power. *New England Journal of Public Policy, 22*(1), 7–16.

Murphy, J. (2006). Some thoughts on rethinking the pre-service education of school leaders. [Electronic version.] *Journal of Educational Change 1*(1), p. 1–3. Retrieved July 28, 2008, from http://www.ucea.org/JRLE/ issue_vo1.php.

Noel-Batiste, L. (2009, February 19). The perceptions of female school leaders of the obstacles and enablers that affected their career paths to educational administration. [Online.] *Academic Leadership: The*

Online Journal 7(1). Retrieved May 6, 2010, from http://www
.academicleadership.org/emprical_research/574.shtml.

Penney, S. H., Brown, J., & Oliviera, L. M. (2007). Numbers are not
enough: Women in higher education in the 21st century. *New England
Journal of Public Policy, 22*(1), 167–82.

Peterson, E. (2006, March). *Scanning the future.* Webcast presentation
sponsored by *The New York Times,* American Association of State
Colleges and Universities, Society for College and University Planning. Service delivery provided by KRM Information Services, Inc.

Peterson, K. D. (1986). Principals' work, socialization, and training: Developing more effective leaders. *Theory into Practice, 25*(3), 151–55.

Porter-O'Grady, T., & Malloch, K. (2007). *Quantum leadership: A resource for healthcare innovation* (2nd ed., p. 2). Sudbury, MA: Jones &
Bartlett Publishers.

Prabhakar, G. P. (2005). An empirical study reflecting the importance of
transformational leadership on project success across twenty-eight
nations [Electronic version]. *Project Management Journal, 36*(4) 53–60.

Ridgeway, C. L. (1999). The gender system and interaction. *Annual
Review of Sociology, 25,* 191–216.

Rosenberg, S. Z. (2008). Uncommon women: Moving past tokenism and
box checking opens doors to more diversity [online]. *Directorship:
Boardroom Intelligence.* Retrieved January 20, 2009 from http://www
.directorship.com/uncommon-women/.

Rosener, J. B. (1990). Ways women lead [online]. *Harvard Business
Review, 68*(6). Retrieved May, 2008, from Business Source Premier
http://web.ebscohost.com.huaryu.kl.oakland.edu/ehost/detail?vid=5&
hid=7&sid=2562cc14-9a55-4c82-8660-86449 91bb151%40session
mgr9&bdata=JnNpdGU9ZWhvc3 QtbGl2ZQ%3d%3d#db=buh&
AN=9012241294.

Scott, K. A., & Brown, D. J. (2006). Female first, leader second? Gender
bias in the encoding of leadership behavior. *Leadership Behavior and
Human Decision Processes, 101*(2), 230–42.

Senge, P. M. (1990). *The fifth discipline: The art and practice of the learning organization.* New York: Doubleday.

Sergiovanni, T. J. (1992). *Moral leadership: Getting to the heart of school improvement.* San Francisco: Jossey-Bass.

Thompson, M. D. (2000). Gender, leadership orientation and effectiveness: Testing the theoretical models of Bolman & Deal and Quinn. *Sex Roles, 42*(11/12), 969–92.

Tierney, T. (2006). *The nonprofit sector's leadership deficit: Executive summary.* Bridgespan Group. Retrieved January 3, 2010, from http://www.onthemovebayarea.org/files/BridgeSpan%20Group%20-%20Leadership%20Deficit.pdf.

U.S. Department of Education. (2009). *Innovations in education: Innovative pathways to school leadership.* Retrieved January 20, 2010 from http://www2.ed.gov/admins/recruit/prep/alternative/index.html.

Wilmore, E., & Cornell, T. (2001). The new century: Is it too late for transformational leadership? [Electronic version]. *Educational Horizons, 79*(3), 115–23.

Wilson, M. C. (2007). *Closing the leadership gap: Add women, change everything.* New York: Penguin Books.

Wolfman, T. G. (2007). The face of corporate leadership: Finally poised for change? *New England Journal of Public Policy, 22*(1), 37–72.

Yoder, J. D., & Kahn, A. S. (2003). Making gender comparisons more meaningful: A call for more attention to social context. *Psychology of Women Quarterly, 27*(4), 281–90.

9

Women in Administration: Differences in Equity

Marjorie Ringler, Cheryl McFadden, and Valjeaner Ford

Introduction

Discriminations based on gender, ethnicity, and sex-role stereotypes in education are common within bureaucratic school governance (Benjamin, 2004). In the early 1900s, women were kept out of administrative roles because the belief in male dominance made it easy to accept that men were leaders and women were natural followers. A look at the number of women in school administration since 1905 illustrates consistent male dominance in all positions except for in the elementary school (Shakeshaft, 1989). According to Shakeshaft, "by 1928, women held 55 percent of the elementary principalships, 25 percent of the county superintendencies, nearly 8 percent of the secondary school principalships, and 1.6 percent of the district superintendencies" (p. 34). Although at first glance, these statistics seem significant, the jobs were lower paying, lower status, and lower power positions than the ones held by men.

Compounding gender inequities are the racial inequities among males and females and the larger population of adults in the job market. There are many issues that affect the educational attainment among ethnic minorities that will impact their attainment in school leadership. This chapter will discuss gender, ethnic, and salary differences in school administration. In addition, this chapter will discuss how principal preparation programs affect the inequities present among school administrators. To do so, this chapter discusses a study of faculty in principal preparation programs that disaggregated data based on gender and ethnicity. The data analysis draws comparisons to national trends and the findings reveal compelling results that indicate that even though there has been progress in increasing the number of women in positions of academia, there is still much work to be done in equalizing salaries for women and in diversifying the faculty ethnicity.

Women in School Administration

While studies of women and their leadership in schools continue to be limited in comparison to studies of men, information does exist about women who have broken through the "glass ceiling" of school administration, and these facts and figures reveal modest representation of women in leadership roles (Restine, 1993). Sustained increases seem promising due to progressively increasing percentages of women making up the ranks of future administrators seeking graduate degrees in leadership preparation programs (Hill & Ragland, 1995). According to Gupton and Slick (1996), "women received 11 percent of the doctoral degrees in educational administration in 1972, 20 percent in 1980, 39 percent in 1982, and 51 percent in 1990" (p. 136). As a result, the numbers and percentages of women in administrative positions have increased, beginning slowly in the 1970s and accelerating in the 1980s (McFadden & Smith, 2004).

Myths about women's leadership abilities continue to be significant aspects in the selection of school administrators (Restine, 1993). Women often are encumbered by distorted images and stereotypes such as "icy virgins, fiery temptresses, and silent martyrs" (Hill & Ragland, 1995, p. 7). In addition, negative connotations are associated with the prefix *woman*. Witmer (2006) describes "woman's work" as housekeeping and "women's intuition" as guessing rather than knowing. The need for competent educational leaders demands that these stereotypical images be discarded and leaders sought from all segments of society (Hill & Ragland).

Another important barrier to women in administration is gender-role or cultural stereotyping (Harris, Ballenger, Hicks-Townes, Carr, & Alford, 2004; Hill & Ragland, 1995; Regan & Brooks, 1995; Restine, 1993; Shakeshaft, 1989). It tends to place women in nonleadership roles that limit their goal orientation and inhibit their ability to recognize their ability to lead (Harris et al., 2004). Another explanation is that women aspire to achieve in the career they choose initially—teaching, and do not want to become principals (Shakeshaft, 1989). They do not seek administrative positions because they do not view themselves in positions of leadership (Gupton & Slick, 1996). According to Gupton and Slick, "administration in public education is male dominated and generally accepted as such by both males and females" (p. 147).

A study by Thompson (2000) directly contrasted the stereotypical assertions in earlier research by revealing no differences in the perceived effectiveness of leaders regarding gender. His accumulated findings demonstrate that "the broad differences in leadership styles in relation to gender and leadership effectiveness have clear implications for our understanding of how effective managers behave" (Thompson, p. 985). A new appreciation, new understanding, and greater empathy for this group will be gained by reexamining the experiences of women and acknowledging the importance of their leadership abilities (Schwartz, 1997).

Another study by Papa-Lewis (1987) focused on respondents' perceptions of selected intrinsic and extrinsic variables and access differences on these variables by gender. Intrinsic factors are psychological in nature and are aspects of the personality, values, and attitudes of the individual (aspiration level, sex-role stereotyping, lack of confidence and initiative, family or self-imposed constraints, low self-image, and negative perception of advancement opportunities). Extrinsic factors are those environmental factors that may mediate entrance into the administrative hierarchy (informal socialization and selection systems, sex-role stereotyping, sex/race/age discrimination, lack of role models/sponsors, lack of networks, lack of support for opposition to sex-equity policies, and lack of enforcement of Title IX mandates). The study used a fifty-six-item questionnaire to obtain results of trends. The results indicated that there were no significant differences between women and men and black and white. The study found very little evidence proving that there are intrinsic factors that keep minorities and women from entering education administration. So it is believed that extrinsic factors are playing a role in the lack of women and minorities in those positions.

In order to understand the differences in gender in school administration, it is important to understand the trends that exist in the demographics present in the United States and how they impact public schools.

Changing Diversity in the United States

The U.S. population consisted of a Caucasian majority from the 1900s to 1960s with the significant minority population of African Americans at 12 percent and all other minorities amounting to 4 percent of the remaining minority population (Tienda & Mitchell, 2006). Since the 1960s, due to immigration and fertility patterns, the U.S. population has exhibited drastic changes in diversity, with the Caucasian majority decreasing, the African American minority remaining stable in numbers, and the Hispanic minority increasing in fast increments. Between the years 2000 and 2007, the percent change of Caucasians (2.1%) and African American (8.7%) has not been as drastic as 50.4 percent of Hispanics both born in the United States (31%) and immigrant to the United States (19.4%; Fry, 2007). According to the Pew Hispanic Center, the number of Hispanics is expected to continue its rapid growth. The projected number of immigrants' children will increase from 12.3 million in 2005 to 17.9 million in 2020 (Fry, 2008). This projected growth is the overall expected enrollment growth in public schools.

The education pipeline that develops minority children into school administrators has many breaks in its path. It is important to discuss the reasons why many minorities are not graduating from high school qualified to continue their education at universities. Reasons for educational attainment are many that can be traced to challenges present before entering public schools and that are present throughout K–12 education. The many reasons are described in the next section.

Ethnic Diversity in Public Schools

The change in ethnic demographics in the United States is also reflected in the public schools. The average rate of growth of the Hispanic population enrolled in public schools between the years 1993 and 2006 has increased by more than 55 percent, comprising 19.8 percent of students, up 12.7 percent (Fry, 2007). The growing number of Hispanics in schools has increased the number of students who are likely to be English language learners (ELLs). In 1990, 32 million people in the United States over the age of five spoke a language other than English in their homes, comprising 14 percent of the total U.S. population. By 2000, that number had risen by 47 percent to nearly 47 million, comprising nearly 18 percent of the total U.S. population (U.S. Census Bureau, 2006). Nationally, the number of ELLs in public schools increased from approximately 2 million students in 1993 to 1994 to 3 million students in 1999 to 2000 (Meyer, Madden, & McGrath, 2005). The fact that these students have limited English proficiency poses a learning challenge for students in that not only are they learning a second language but they also need to learn their academics in this second language (Short & Echevarria, 2005; Tienda, 2009).

Gaps in Education

The educational trends among ethnic groups indicate an increasing gap between educational attainment levels of Caucasians, African Americans, Asians, and Hispanics as determined by graduation rates. From 1970 to 2006, the high school and college graduation rates among the four ethnic groups have steadily increased (U.S. Census Bureau, 2006). However, the percentages are daunting among college graduates. By 2006, only 17 percent of African Americans age twenty-five and above completed college degrees, yet with the steady rate of population growth of this ethnic group, the number is not as impacting as is the fact that only 12 percent of similarly aged Hispanics graduated from college (U.S. Census Bureau, 2006). Asians of age twenty-five or above had the highest number of college graduates at 49 percent, but Asians represent a low percentage of the U.S. population, in contrast to Caucasians with 30 percent graduating from college.

Socially, many of the Hispanic families who are moving into the United States come from low-socioeconomic backgrounds and work earnestly in the United States performing unskilled labor. This could be one reason for the educational gap; however, many of the Hispanic immigrants have children who are United States born and have attended school since kindergarten. Several reasons for the lack of educational attainment could be attributed to the parents' literacy levels, parents' educational attainment, and parental value of education, among many others. Many of these factors are beyond the scope and influence of public school systems. It is important, however, to discuss the ethnic diversity among school teachers and principals as they serve as role models to children in schools.

Lack of Role Models

Having a teaching force reflective of the diversity among the student population has the benefit of providing minority students opportunities to be exposed to a diversity of successful role models. According to the National Center for Education Statistics (2007), the percentage of teachers who are Caucasian is 84.4 percent, while the percentage of students is 60.3 percent. The percentage of African American teachers is 8.3 percent in comparison to 16.8 percent of the student population. Hispanics represent only 5.7 percent of our teachers but make up 17.7 percent of students. Asians comprise 1.3 percent of teachers and 3.9 percent of students. American Indians represent only .4 percent of teachers and 1.3 percent of students. Teachers of diverse backgrounds also benefit students' education attainment with their awareness of their students' cultures and the ability to build on their students' background experiences to bridge the gap between the school, the home, and the community and learning academics.

Principals are role models as well. Similar to teachers, principals have a great influence in the schooling of the changing diverse student population. The diversity trend among principals in the U.S. reflects the lack of diversity and the need to increase minorities in positions of school leadership. In 2003 to 2004, 82 percent of all school principals were Caucasian, 11 percent were African American, 5 percent Hispanic, and 1 percent American Indian/Alaska Native. The overwhelming majority of principals are Caucasians serving in schools with diverse student populations. Salaries among principals may also be enticing for those adults that qualify for the principalship. The average annual salary for public school principals in 2003 to 2004 was $75,500, with high school principals making a higher salary ($79,400) than elementary school principals ($75,400; NCES, 2007).

Adults who become principals typically come from the teaching ranks and thus to increase the number of women and the diversity of principals we need to increase the number of female teachers who chose to continue their education to become principals. To add to this, it is important to encourage diverse teaching staff to choose the school administration path. The next section discusses the role of academia in preparing female school administrators by analyzing the equity issues that permeate academia in terms of access and salary differences.

Women in Principal Preparation Programs

Women comprise well over half of the teaching force in the United States, and administrators are drawn from the teaching force. Why, then, is there such a discrepancy in the numbers of male and female administrators? Some reasons parallel those for minorities—the vicious cycle that depresses aspirations, the lack of access to "old boy networks," and the denial of opportunity for support, mentoring, and coaching, but more importantly, a large and persistent gender wage gap. The gender wage gap is even larger in principal preparation programs for the female faculty who prepare teachers to enter the world of school administration (Benjamin, 2004).

The subject of gender equity is a topic that has been discussed among numerous studies in the past that date back to the 1970s and 1980s. Administrators in public schools as well as the university level have had to establish guidelines to monitor affirmative action laws to ensure equal pay among minority faculty (women and nonwhites). Other areas of concern are women in lower senior ranks as well as tenure and non-tenure-track positions. Several studies have produced evidence of salary discrimination in favor of men faculty members. Numerous studies indicate that there has been and still exists today a gender salary difference among male and female faculty members across university campuses (Benjamin, 2004).

Gender Salary Differences

As time progressed (Ashraf, 1996), several studies indicated that evidence of salary discrimination against women in academia still exists and is very prevalent today across university campuses. Yes, progress has been made in some respects; however, in some cases, complaints and investigations led to corrective measures as an endeavor to remedy pay inequities in administration and the university level. Progress has been made, but at an unacceptable rate toward the equalization of male and female salaries. There have been numerous national studies conducted to bring light to the salary discrepancies of male and female faculty. A national survey conducted by the National Center for Education Statistics (NCES) indicated (Barbezat & Hughes, 2001) that male faculty had a disadvantage over female faculty, a salary gap of 27.7 percent attributed to discrimination.

Estimated results from numerous studies (Ashraf, 1996; Barbezat, 2002; Ransom & Megdal, 1993) all indicate that in the late 1980s, female faculty received more of a disadvantage than their comparable male colleagues. These findings were very disappointing, debatable, and even alarming. All of the findings, however, were not totally bleak or distressing. There was a small decline in percentage points that was characteristic of a small decline in the salary gap. These findings, however, were not true across the board; they varied according to the type of institution as well as other variables: experience, age, academic rank, marital status, and publications.

The gender salary gap is quite complex and has no simple answer due to the many factors involved. Results of numerous studies propose that differences in salary among female and male faculty vary depending on the types of institutions such as comprehensive colleges and universities, liberal arts colleges and universities, doctoral universities and research universities (Maurer-Fazio & Hughes, 2002). Results have determined that women employed at research universities experience the gender gap in a larger capacity than women at the other three types of universities. This does not mean, however, that female or male faculty at other types of universities at comprehensive universities, doctoral universities, or liberal arts universities are advancing better in terms of faculty salary, race, and ethnicity.

More than forty years of concentration have been given to the study of sex and ethnic differences in employment status. Analyses results of the Integrated Postsecondary Education Data System (Brown, 1997) results show that women represented only 28 percent of full-time tenured faculty but 44 percent of full-time faculty who were on a tenure track and as high as 45 percent of full-time faculty who were not on a tenure track. Startling statistics also indicate that only 20 percent of full-time professors were women, 34 percent were associate professors, 45 percent were assistant professors, and a high 51 percent were full-time instructors. The results for African Americans were also very low, representing a smaller proportion of full-time tenured than full-time tenure-track and non-tenure-track faculty. Even a smaller percentage of African American faculty was full-time professors than full-time assistant professors. Furthermore, Hispanics and other minority faculty represented only 3 percent of full-time tenured faculty (Perna, 2001).

Studies over the years have shown that women faculty and women faculty of various ethnicities hold lower ranks than male faculty when taking into account other variables such as educational achievement, experience, and institutional characteristics as well as one's academic discipline (Toutkoushian, 1999). It has thus been determined that women full-time faculty were less likely than men to advance to tenured positions at the rank of full professor, but at the same time it has also been determined that women were as likely as men to advance to associate professor. Research further suggests that different criteria are often applied in promotion and tenure decisions for women than for men and that African Americans were less likely than whites to hold tenured positions (Perna, 2001). A common thread that runs through most of the studies of gender and other ethnicities is evidence of wage discrimination against women in higher education at the college and university level.

Ethnicity among Higher Education Faculty

Faculty at higher education institutions are not representative of the diversity present in the U.S. populations. According to the NCES (2009), in fall 2007, minority faculty composed 17 percent of the higher education faculty in the United States. Of these 17 percent, 7 percent were African American, 6 percent were Asian/Pacific Islander, 4 percent were Hispanic, and 1 percent was American Indian/Alaska Native. The remaining 83 percent of faculty were Caucasian. Thus, the majority of college campuses are predominately Caucasian, sending a message to students entering postsecondary education that jobs in higher education are more attainable for those who are Caucasian.

Salaries in higher education may be an enticing factor to increase recruitment of minorities as instructional faculty at higher education institutions. Based on nine-month average salaries at Title IV degree-granting institutions, the NCES (2009) reports that assistant professors earn an average of $59,283, associate professors earn an average of $70,744, and professors earn an average of $98,020. These are enticing salaries for qualified adults. The issue is that many minorities are not graduating from high school qualified to continue their education at universities (Tienda, 2009). Reasons for educational attainment are many that can be traced to socioeconomic challenges present before entering public schools and were explained earlier in this chapter.

The analysis of gender inequities in higher education and administration provides valuable insight to differences in salaries and roles of women. Salaries in academia and school administration are enticing to women and minorities; however, as described in this chapter, there are many socioeconomic factors that play a role in selecting administration and academia as careers. The next section presents a major study conducted in the

University of North Carolina (UNC) system that analyzed current faculty salaries in educational leadership programs to determine whether there are salary inequities by gender and ethnicity.

Study Design and Methodology

The purpose of this study was to compare differences in equity among faculty in educational leadership programs in the University of North Carolina (UNC) system. This study examined several demographic variables among the faculty: gender, ethnicity, tenure, rank (assistant, associate, and professor) and salary. Our research hypotheses included:

1. There will be a greater percentage of male faculty than female faculty in educational leadership programs.
2. Female faculty will have lower salaries than male faculty in educational leadership programs.
3. Female faculty will have lower salaries than male faculty at all three levels of rank in educational leadership programs.
4. Minority faculty will have lower salaries than Caucasian faculty in educational leadership programs.

Data Collection

After obtaining Institutional Review Board approval, we contacted the University of North Carolina General Administration and requested a copy of all the 2008 to 2009 salaries in the UNC system. It should be noted that these salaries are for nine months of employment. We contacted the chairs of departments of educational leadership and/or office personnel at the eleven institutions and obtained the gender, ethnicity, rank, and tenure status.

Participants

Data for one hundred twenty-five faculty from eleven institutions within the University of North Carolina System were analyzed in this study. The institutions that participated included: East Carolina University (ECU), Fayetteville State University (FSU), North Carolina State University (NCSU), University of North Carolina–Chapel Hill (UNC–CH),

University of North Carolina–Charlotte (UNC–C), University of North Carolina–Wilmington (UNC–W), Western Carolina University (WCU), the University of North Carolina–Greensboro (UNC–G), North Carolina A&T (NC A&T), Appalachian State (App State), and University of North Carolina–Pembroke (UNC–P).

Results

Demographics

Overall out of 125 faculty, 38.4 percent of the faculty are females and 61.6 percent are males. The ethnicity of 122 faculty is as follows: 75.4 percent of the faculty are Caucasian, 19.7 percent African American, 4 percent Asian, and 0.8 percent Hispanic. Out of 122 faculty, 53.3 percent of the faculty are tenured and 46.7 percent are tenure track. Rank of 124 faculty is as follows: 41.1 percent are assistant professors, 24.2 percent are associate professors, and 34.7 percent are professors (see Table 9.1).

Demographic information is presented for each institution in Table 9.2. Only the UNC–CH and the WCU have more women than men faculty. Only FSU (a historically African American university) has more minority than Caucasian faculty, although it has no female faculty in the education leadership department. The institution with the greatest disparity in salary between females and males is the NC A&T (153%), then UNC–C (31%), followed by the UNC–CH (29.9%), UNC–W (27.6%), NCSU (22.8%), App State (22%), ECU (14.5%), WCU (7.1%), and UNC–G (6.7%), where the average male salary is larger than the female salary. UNC–P is the only institution where as an average females make more than males by 13 percent, and this is due to one faculty member who is also an associate dean.

Data Analysis

It was important to analyze the salary data according to gender, ethnicity, tenure status, and rank for all eleven institutions. The average salary for females is $74,586 and for males, $85,840, a difference of 15 percent. The average salary for minority faculty is $78,156 while for Caucasian faculty is $82,502. The average salary for female tenured faculty is $85,267 and for male tenured faculty, $98,902, a difference of 15.9 percent. The difference between female ($66,675) and male ($65,121)

TABLE 9.1
Demographics of Department of Educational Leadership Faculty for all Institutions

Gender n = 125		Ethnicity n = 125				Tenure Status n = 125			Rank n = 125		
Female	Male	Caucasian	AA	Hispanic	Asian	Tenured	Tenured Track		Asst	Assoc	Prof
38.4%	61.6%	76%	19.2%	0.008%	0.04%	52.8%	47.2%		41.6%	24%	34.4%
(48)	(77)	(95)	(24)	(1)	(5)	(66)	(59)		(52)	(30)	(43)

Note. AA = African American.

TABLE 9.2
Demographics of Department of Educational Leadership Faculty by Institution

Institution	Rank							Average Salary		
	% Female	% Male	%	Rank	% Minority	% Tenured	% Tenured Track	F	M
ECU	38	61	22	Asst	27	66	33	$81,694	$93,574
n = 18			50	Assoc					
			27	Prof					
FSU	0	100	50	Asst	66	33	66	—	$80,138
n = 6			16	Assoc					
			33	Prof					
NCSU	25	75	50	Asst	12	50	50	$76,861	$94,454
n = 8			37	Assoc					
			12	Prof					
UNC–CH	60	40	0	Asst	40	80	20	$110,059	$143,046
n = 5			20	Assoc					
			80	Prof					

(continued)

Table 9.2 (continued)

Institution	Rank				% Minority	% Tenured	% Tenured Track	Average Salary	
	% Female	% Male		%				F	M
UNC–C	42	55	Asst	47	26	47	52	$66,387	$86,970
n = 19			Assoc	10					
			Prof	10					
UNC–W	27	72	Asst	72	18	18	81	$60,369	$77,113
n = 11			Assoc	9					
			Prof	18					
WCU	60	40	Asst	40	0	30	70	$70,360	$75,417
n = 10			Assoc	30					
			Prof	30					
UNC–G	40	60	Asst	40	20	60	40	$82,443	$88,005
n = 10			Assoc	20					
			Prof	40					
NC A&T	67	33	Asst	33	100	67	33	$63,809	$161,715
n = 3			Assoc	33					
			Prof	33					

234

App St. n = 28	36	64	36	Asst	4	64	36	$68,722	$84,103
			18	Assoc					
			46	Prof					
UNC–P n = 7	43	57	57	Asst	43	57	43	$78,209	$65,829
			28	Assoc					
			14	Prof					

tenure-track faculty is 2.3 percent, with females having the higher average salary. The average salary for female minority tenured faculty is $71,838 and for male minority tenured faculty, $108,288, a difference of 50.7 percent. Female Caucasian tenured faculty have an average salary of $89,743, with male Caucasian faculty being paid $96,911, a difference of 7.9 percent. Interestingly, female minority tenure-track faculty have an average salary of $65,933, with male minority tenure-track salary being $61,486, a difference of 7.2 percent. There is a 1 percent difference between female and male Caucasian tenure-track faculty, with female faculty earning slightly more than male faculty.

Female faculty have lower average salaries than male faculty at all three levels of rank, with the greatest difference being at the professor level (see Table 9.3). The difference at the assistant professor level between female ($63,588) and male ($65,425) is less than 3 percent. Female associate professors have a 2.7 percent lower average salary than males of similar rank. The difference between the female ($100,427) and male faculty ($102,778) at the professor level is 2.3 percent. However, there is a 6.6 percent difference between female minority assistant professors and male minority assistant professors, with females having the higher average salary. There is a significant difference (22%) in average salary between female minority professors ($98,531) and male minority professors ($120,339).

Findings

The purpose of this study was to compare differences in equity among faculty in educational leadership programs in the UNC System. We have presented our findings for each hypothesis.

There will be a Greater Percentage of Male Faculty than Female Faculty in Educational Leadership Programs

There are 60.4 percent more male than female faculty in educational leadership programs in the eleven institutions within the UNC System. Although women receive 50 percent of the graduate degrees in the United States and specifically 51 percent are in educational administration, this trend is clearly not evident in the UNC system (Gupton & Slick, 1996; Mason, 2009). What is interesting to note is that although the number of females

TABLE 9.3
Salaries of Department of Educational Leadership Faculty for all Institutions

Gender	Overall	Tenured	Tenure Track	Minority Tenured	Minority Tenure Track	Caucasian Tenured	Caucasian Tenure Track	Overall Rank		Minority Rank	
Female	$74,586	$85,267	$66,675	$71,838	$65,933	$89,743	$67,046	Asst	$63,588	Asst	$65,855
								Assoc	$78,643	Assoc	—
								Prof	$100,427	Prof	$98,531
Male	$85,840	$98,902	$65,121	$108,288	$61,486	$96,911	$66,069	Asst	$65,425	Asst	$61,486
								Assoc	$80,783	Assoc	$72,408
								Prof	$102,778	Prof	$120,339

in K–12 administrative positions is on the rise, this trend is not crossing over to educational leadership programs at the college and university level. Is this due to the "glass ceiling" effect or are there other possible explanations?

Female Faculty Will Have Lower Salaries Than Male Faculty in Educational Leadership Programs

Female faculty earned 15 percent lower salaries than male faculty in educational leadership programs within the eleven institutions in the UNC System. In fact, female faculty in eight of the eleven institutions earned less than male faculty. One institution (FSU) does not have any female tenured or tenure-track faculty. The disparity between institutions ranges from the lowest, 6.7 percent (UNC–G), to the highest, 31 percent (UNC–C). This disparity clearly indicates the need for institutions to correct the inequity and create workplaces that attract, retain, develop, and encourage advancement of women in educational institutions (Harrington & Ladge, 2009).

This disparity continues when one examines female tenured faculty, who have 15.9 percent lower salaries than male tenured faculty. What is interesting to note is that this disparity does not continue when one examines tenure-track faculty. Apparently the disparity occurs after a female faculty member is tenured. Male faculty salaries increase at a faster pace than salaries of female faculty.

Female Faculty Will Have Lower Salaries Than Male Faculty at all Three Levels of Rank

It is therefore not surprising that female faculty have lower salaries than male faculty at all three levels of rank. Again, the disparity does not occur at the assistant tenure-track level but at the associate tenured level. Amazingly, this disparity is relatively low (2.1%) at the professor level. What will be interesting to see is if this disparity will continue when these females at the associate level reach the professor level.

Minority Faculty Will Have Lower Salaries Than Caucasian Faculty in Educational Leadership Programs

When we analyzed the data on minority faculty, we were not surprised to discover that minority faculty earn less (5.5%) than Caucasian faculty. We were however, surprised at several other findings. First, while female minority faculty earn 29 percent lower salaries than male minority faculty, overall this disparity discontinues at the tenure track level. Female minority faculty at the tenure-track level earn 7.2 percent greater salaries than male minority faculty at the same level. Second, female minority faculty have 7.1 percent higher salaries than male minority faculty at the assistant professor level. However, this difference is reversed at the professor level, where male minority faculty have 22.1 percent higher salaries than female minority professors. Why do female minority assistant professors earn more than male minority assistant professors and why is this disparity reversed at the professor level? One possible explanation could be that in order to recruit minority faculty, schools need to offer competitive salaries, and female minority faculty command higher salaries. Once in the system, female minority faculty do not progress through the ranks at the level of male minority faculty due to similar reasons (glass ceiling effect) their Caucasian counterparts do not.

Implications for Women in School Administration

Need to Increase Women in School Administration

Even though the number of female graduates from principal preparation programs is steadily increasing, the trend is not evident in the number of women who are faculty in principal preparation programs. It is important to have role models for school administrators that are similar to the student body. Therefore, university systems should develop strategic plans in collaboration with school districts to institute programs that promote teacher leadership, resulting in teachers entering school administration. A long-range plan for this partnership should include the increase of number of women that enter academia as professors of educational leadership.

Need to Decrease Salary Differentials

The salary gap between men and women in administration and academia persists. In addition, this gap widens when analyzing the gaps by gender and ethnicity. Even though school districts typically have a salary system based on years of experience, it is important to modify the salary system to allow for additional factors that impact women more than men such as sex-role stereotyping, constraints imposed by self and family, lack of confidence, and lack of sponsors/mentors. A strategic and effective approach is to institute a mentoring plan upon entering the teaching profession that focuses on more than just becoming a better teacher. The mentoring should also focus on building leadership skills, enhancing confidence, and flexibility to accommodate family commitments. The salary system should allow for the factors of the mentoring process and treat both men and women equitably.

Decrease Ethnic Differentials

The ethnicity gap is perhaps larger than the gender gap in terms of representation and salary. It is important to institute a systemic approach that encourages minority children to not only graduate but also graduate with aspirations to return to the school system as teachers and school administrators. To do so, the profession of education needs a salary overhaul. By increasing the salaries earned as educators, the profession will be able to compete with other professions that make higher salaries and therefore recruit top-quality teachers and leaders that will make a significant impact in schools. The same argument applies to principal preparation programs. It is the responsibility of higher education programs to diversify their faculty from one that is predominantly male to add more females and ethnic minority females. Therefore, universities of higher education must consider changing salary structures to offer equal opportunities for women.

Conclusion

With the changing diverse population in the United States, it is important to continue to recruit and retain teachers and principals reflective of the population changes. These two job roles are the basis for recruitment for educational leadership programs not only for program enrollment but also for faculty recruitment. Salaries commensurate with the field and the cost of living are enticing factors in recruiting faculty to teach in higher education institutions. This study reflects many inequities that still exist along gender and ethnic lines. It is therefore important to equitably recruit and pay qualified educators into the professoriate to model and educate the future of public school students in America.

References

Ashraf, J. (1996). The influence of gender on faculty salaries in the United States, 1969–1989. *Applied Economics, 28*, 857–64.

Barbezat, D. (2002). History of pay equity studies In R. Toutkoushian (Ed.), *Conducting salary-equity studies: Alternative approaches to research* (pp. 9–40). San Francisco: Jossey-Bass.

Barbezat, D. & Hughes, J. (2001). The effect of job mobility on academic salaries. *Contemporary Economic Policy 19*(4), 409–23.

Benjamin, E. (2004). *Disparities in the salaries and appointments of academic women and men: An update of a 1988 report of the Committee on the Status of Women in the Academic Profession.* Washington, DC: American Association of University Professors.

Brown, P. Q. (1997). *Salaries of Full-Time Instructional Faculty on 9- and 10-month and 11- and 12-month contracts 1995-96.* (NCES 97416). Washington, DC: National Center for Educational Statistics.

Fry, R. (2007). *The changing racial and ethnic composition of U.S. public schools.* Washington, DC: Pew Hispanic Center. Retrieved May 26, 2009, from http://pewhispanic.org /reports/79.pdf.

Fry, R. (2008). *The role of schools in the English language learner achievement gap.* Washington, DC: Pew Hispanic Center. Retrieved May 26, 2009, at http://pewhispanic.org/files/reports/89.pdf.

Gupton, S. L., & Slick, G. A. (1996). *Highly successful women administrators.* Thousand Oaks, CA: Corwin.

Harrington, B., & Ladge, J. J. (2009). Got talent? It isn't hard to find: Recognizing and rewarding the value women create in the work place. In H. Boushey & A. O'Leary (Eds.), *The Shriver report. A women's nation changes everything* (pp. 198–231). Washington, DC: Center for American Progress. Retrieved from http://www.americanprogress.org/issues/2009/10/pdf/awn/a_womans_nation.pdf.

Harris, S., Ballenger, J., Hicks-Townes, F., Carr, C., & Alford, B. (2004). *Winning women: Stories of award-winning educators.* Lantham, MD: Scarecrow Education.

Hill, M. S., & Ragland, J. C. (1995). *Women as educational leaders: Opening windows, pushing ceilings.* Thousand Oaks, CA: Corwin.

Mason, M. A. (2009). Better educating our new breadwinners: Creating opportunities for all women to succeed in the workforce. In H. Boushey & A. O'Leary (Eds.), *The Shriver report. A women's nation changes everything* (pp. 198–231). Washington, DC: Center for American Progress. Retrieved from http://www.americanprogress.org/issues/2009/10/pdf/awn/a_womans_nation.pdf.

Maurer-Fazio M. and Hughes, J. (2002). The effects of market liberalization on the relative earnings of Chinese women. *Journal of Comparative Economics, 30,* 709–31.

McFadden, A. H., & Smith, P. (2004). *The social construction of educational leadership.* New York: Peter Lang.

Meyer, D., Madden, D., & McGrath, D. J. (2005). English language learner students in U.S. public schools: 1994 and 2000. *Education Statistics Quarterly* 6(3). Retrieved September 28, 2006, from http://nces.ed.gov/programs/quarterly/vol_6/6_3/3_4.asp.

National Center for Education Statistics. (2007). *A brief profile of America's public schools* (NCES 2007-379). Washington, DC: U.S. Department of Education.

National Center for Education Statistics. (2009). *Employees in postsecondary institutions, fall 2007, and salaries of full-time instructional faculty, 2007–08* (NCES 2009-154). Washington, DC: U.S. Department of Education.

Papa-Lewis, R., & Leonard, P. Y. (1987). *Factors and perceptions of equal access for women and minorities in educational administration.* Paper presented at the meeting of the American Educational Research Association, Washington, D.C. (ERIC Document and Reproduction Service No. ED 283282).

Perna, L. (2001). Sex and race differences in faculty tenure and promotion. *Research in Higher Education, 42*(5), 541–67.

Ransom, M., & Megdal, S. (1993). Sex differences in the academic labor market in the affirmative action era. *Economics of Education Review, 12,* 2143.

Regan, H. B., & Brooks, G. H. (1995). *Out of women's experience: Creating relational leadership.* Thousand Oaks, CA: Corwin.

Restine, L. N. (1993). *Women in administration: Facilitators for change.* Newbury Park, CA: Corwin.

Schwartz, R. A. (1997). Reconceptualizing the leadership roles of women in higher education. *Journal of Higher Education, 68*(5), 502–22.

Shakeshaft, C. (1989). *Women in educational administration.* Newbury Park, CA: Sage.

Short, D., &. Echevarria, J. (2005). Teacher skills to support English language learners. *Educational Leadership, 62*(4), 8–13.

Tienda, M. (2009, March). *Hispanicity and educational inequality: Risks, opportunities and the nation's future.* The 25th Tomas Rivera Lecture presented at the American Association of Hispanics in Higher Education (AAHHEE). San Antonio, Texas: Educational Testing Service Evaluation and Research Center.

Tienda, M., & Mitchell F. (2006). *Multiple origins, uncertain destinies: Hispanics and the American future.* Washington, DC: National Academy Press, U.S. Government Printing Office.

Thompson, M. D. (2000). Gender, leadership orientations, and effectiveness: Testing the theoretical models of Bolman and Deal and Quinn. *Sex Roles, 42*(11, 12), 969–92.

Toutkoushian, R. (1999). The status of academic women in the 1990s: No longer outsiders, but not yet equals. *Quarterly Review of Economics and Finance, 39* (Special Issue, 679–98).

U.S. Census Bureau. (2006). *Statistical abstract of the United States, 2006.* Washington DC: U.S. Government Printing Office.

Witmer, J. T. (2006). *Moving up! A guidebook for women in educational administration.* Lanham, MD: Rowman Littlefield Education.

10

Women Leaders as Superintendents: Stories of Courage and Character

Deb Clarke

Knowing the limitations present in educational leadership and having fully recognized the inherent challenges to be faced in making the decision to pursue administration in the early 80s, part of my positive self-talk was the mantra, *"If I become a high school principal by age 50, I will buy a Mercedes."* The statement served as much-needed levity in my struggle to break through the glass ceiling to the secondary principalship because at that time, owning a Mercedes was as foreign to me as the notion of becoming a female secondary principal. Even though I pursued an education as a means to move out of an impoverished environment, the only acceptable career options for women in the early 70s were nursing, teaching, or becoming a secretary.

Raised by a mother who quit high school at age sixteen and a father who was an auto factory worker and held an evening job as a meat cutter at Kroger, I was raised to believe that attaining an education was the only means possible to change one's life. My mother's dream was for her children to attend college; thus, she made sure our career paths and choices ensured access.

This chapter tells the story of my career advances to positions of leadership that culminate in the superintendency. This story is supported by the research literature and highlights the barriers and themes that intersected my path, as well as the paths of other women leaders. Grogan (as cited in Brunner, 1999) indicated the need for women to tell their stories as superintendents, knowing they often portray a candid representation of the difficulties and rewards in the rise to positions of leadership. Brunner (1998) noted the importance of women in the profession serving as role models to other women aspiring to leadership in education.

I began my career as a teacher in the mid 70s, and over the next decade as a master's student, I learned that the path to leadership positions and the superintendency was filled with challenges for women. Hackett's research (1998), published in Van Tuyle and Watkins (2009), noted that barriers women faced included the following: (a) sexual stereotyping by board members and in the work force and (b) men threatened by competence. Shakeshaft's early research (1980), noted in Van Tuyle and Watkins (2009), compiled a review of research from 1973 through 1978 and found sex favoritism, gender bias, marginalization, and discrimination as barriers for continued study. Additional barriers included by Van Tuyle and Watkins (2009) were gender discrimination in employment opportunities and the demands of family responsibilities. Van Tuyle and Watkins (2009) indicated the reality that women were often seen as less capable than men and, as a result, were relegated to less superior roles. Van Tuyle and Watkins (2009) recognized that a significant personal barrier that women faced was self-confidence. Noting that networking and mentoring opportunities were most often related to male athletic activities or coaching, women sometimes missed valuable connections.

Gender bias, marginalization, and discrimination in the realm of education have been some of the most prominent and troubling barriers for women. Researcher Skrla (2003) page 248 . . . cited Bjork's (1999) study by the U.S. Department of Labor, which indicated that the CEO position most populated by Caucasian males in the 90s was the superintendency. Skrla (2003) goes on to cite Banks, who indicates that men have a 1 in 40 chance of becoming a superintendent, whereas women have a 1 in 900 chance in assuming the position.

Statistics have continued to verify the minimal representation of women leaders, a fact daunting in itself. In a later publication, Shakeshaft was cited by Van Tuyle and Watkins (2009) for research that highlighted a series of changes required for women to gain access to the role of superintendent, knowing that the rigidity of the current system was not favorable for women. However, despite these attempts, Skrla (2003) noted discouragement that the current data available have shown that little has changed.

Research documents the reality that gender discrimination significantly minimizes access to higher positions. Brunner (1998) indicates that women served as 70 percent of the teaching population but represented only 7 percent of the superintendents. In the 100 years, statistics have shown that women have filled only 5 to 7 percent of all superintendent positions nationwide.

Recent data published in a companion study by Van Tuyle and Watkins (2009) recognized Glass and Franceschini's America Association of School Administrators (AASA) study (2007) showing that only 6.7 percent of women in 1950 served as superintendents compared with 21.7 percent in 2006. They also found the average age to be 54.6 years and that over half held doctorates. In fact, the women held a higher percentage of advanced degrees than did the men. The study also found that nearly 93.8 percent were white whereas only 6.2 percent represented other ethnicities. On average, fewer women were married than men; 93 percent of men were married compared to 75 percent women.

This research demonstrates women had more experience, a greater percentage of advanced degrees, and knowledge of the barriers to advancement shared by female and male mentors. The reality was understood; women had to work harder as leaders to be recognized.

After graduating from college, I entered my career in the mid-1970s as an elementary special education teacher. My first five years were filled with actualizing my role in the profession, working on requirements for continuing certification, and getting involved in curriculum work with both the school and district school improvement teams (SIT). Realizing early on that I eventually wanted to seek administration, I also knew that finding the mentorship of a female leader was as critical to my progress, as was district involvement. Knowing I would have to work harder as a woman to be noticed was an implicit reality that prepared me to go above and beyond in every initiative.

The 1960s through the late 1970s represented decades of change. There was a belief that change would open up options in our society for minorities and women. Desegregation mandates were a reality, and though many cities were literally burning busses, others responded with positive, systematic change initiatives. Ron Edmonds, a Michigan State University professor, heralded the School Improvement Process in the 1970s in response to the Coleman Report that found schools could do little to impact the education of impoverished children. Instead, Dr. Edmonds began a national initiative citing schools found to be effectively developing young minds. The initiative also urged school teams to come together and utilize their talents to find ways to ensure that "All means all" when pursuing student capabilities.

In essence, this was an era in education that represented hope, when people saw possibilities, and options became available as previously closed doors opened up to new opportunities. This was the time when Congress passed the Elementary and Secondary Education Act in 1964 and the playing field began leveling for both the "haves" and the "have nots." It was a time when the hand of friendship and brotherhood/sisterhood meant helping those less fortunate move forward.

I worked with the SIT toward desegregation efforts at central and site locations in Ypsilanti, Michigan, with the support of the University of Michigan Program for Educational Opportunity (PEO). Those first years provided significant amounts of experience, knowledge, and leadership. After a year of training and implementation initiatives, the district desegregated well in advance of court-ordered busing, without incident; meanwhile, in my hometown of Pontiac, Michigan, people were burning buses and marching on Washington, D.C.

Those years did a great deal toward establishing my leadership style as a collaborative, communicative, and consensus-building leader. They also provided me with a significant understanding of the importance of involving all stakeholders in an effective strategic plan and cemented the critical nature of interpersonal skills at play in any initiative. Continued practice helped to develop political acuity and learning occurred through watching mentors and talking with them about the strategies they utilized to advance their initiatives.

Women leading school systems noted that women often use consensus building and collaboration to accomplish the goals of the organization. Women are known for the emphasis they place on empowerment as opposed to the hierarchical power more often related to men. The use of these behavior styles implicitly builds more robust accountability. In urban districts where I worked, circumstances required that schools significantly increase student achievement and simultaneously address budget shortfalls. There was a need to align revenue with expenses and eliminate deficits to ensure financial accountability. Using a collaborative leadership style served to advance my career, and teamwork was a recurring theme evident in my background. Perhaps the strongest effect of teamwork was the ownership faculty and staff assumed when their involvement was known to be critical to the success of the organization.

Early administrative training happened in Ypsilanti, where I worked from 1974 to 1990. At the time, elementary and secondary summer school principal positions were known training grounds for administrative applicants, but being limited in number, they were difficult to attain. It was fortunate for me to be granted an elementary principalship for 350 K–6 students, along with all of the incumbent responsibilities. I held this position for a number of years despite the fact that a tornado touched down in the first year, thus closing the building for two weeks and requiring us to move to a new location. That was only one of the early shows of flexibility in my career.

After five years at the elementary level, I applied to teach reading and language programs at the middle school. I was hired by a principal who was aware of my reputation as being effective with all students. This principal later became the high school principal. His move became a critical factor in my transition. I also coordinated community education post-day programs and the high school WALTEC summer youth work program.

As a master's degree student who wanted to create change, I remember considering the possibility of a secondary principalship. As a high school student, I once witnessed my black classmates herded onto police buses for conducting a sit-down protest to force their high school principal to meet with the human relations committee, while white students were simply sent back to class. Raised during decades focused on civil rights, I was deeply affected by the inequities present in both society and the education profession. Witnessing experiences such as this and others spoke volumes to the intrinsic values of equity and fairness. This event was the most graphic but, combined with lessons I learned as an educator, made it more obvious that the potential to become a role model for young women, as well as to influence organizational, long-term change, clearly existed in the role of secondary principal.

I also remember that administrators and teachers with whom I worked sometimes questioned my career goal. An assistant superintendent once commented, "We will let you be an elementary principal, but you'll never become a high school principal." Another superintendent remarked at "happy hour" (staff socialization being a large part of those early years) that the only way I'd move beyond the elementary level was if I would sleep with him. This type of sexual harassment happened more than once; it was the norm for many males in the profession. Years later when I returned for a retirement dinner of a colleague, it gave me great satisfaction to point out my success as a secondary principal in a large urban district to these same individuals, a position acquired only by demonstrating competence in my role.

Skrla (2003) referred to the silence of women who fail to question such societal and cultural norms. She noted that if we are to challenge the small proportion of females who rise to this position, that silence has to end. Right or wrong, we kept quiet during those years, knowing that speaking out would place our careers and possible advancement at risk. If anything, being victimized by sexual harassment increased my belief in the need for female role models in the profession

Armed with numerous experiences as a leader, I began the search process for an assistant principal or principal position outside of my district. Leaving my district was a reality of advancement because there was only one high school, and I knew that the principal planned to stay another twenty years. Although I was willing to relocate, the search process lasted for four years. I was passed over continuously despite the fact that gatekeepers often told me that I was the best prepared and most articulate candidate and that I had ample experience with leadership, professional development, and curriculum development. The bitter taste of failing to be interviewed, let alone be a finalist, grew. The failure of gatekeeping practices and search firms to yield more female leaders has been known to be a cultural problem when the profession is largely staffed by retired male superintendents.

In the late 80s, Pavan (1988) studied the job search strategies of 622 aspiring leaders seeking principal, assistant superintendent, and superintendent positions. She found that women submitted more applications and had more interviews and searched longer than most men. She also found that women used nearly twice as many job search strategies as men, thirteen versus seven, and demonstrated greater efforts to overcome barriers. Thus, she found that a lack of equal representation was not due to a lack of effort. In addition, Brunner's (1989) research cited that it usually takes women five years longer than men to acquire new positions.

How to access to these higher positions was a challenging notion. According to Van Tuyle and Watkins (2009), another barrier women faced was in being seen as equally competent as men. Women have often felt that carrying a larger workload was part of establishing credibility. As a result, women have often felt the need to increase their individual capabilities. Other barriers they cited in relation to gender bias were in the areas of networking and acceptance by their peers in established pathways and communication systems.

Despite the challenges, a number of factors converged to provide me with my first secondary leadership role that included the following: (a) mentorship of the superintendent, who did not listen to naysayer comments regarding my proficiency in discipline and curriculum, (b) support of the principal who had hired me at the middle school, and (c) mentoring by a female with strong curriculum experience. Each of these individuals knew I would be an effective student advocate.

In 1985, I became an assistant (class) principal at Ypsilanti High School in Ypsilanti, Michigan. At the time, the mindset was that one had to have some type of coaching experience to be successful in a secondary administrative position. This was to increase the probability one could "handle the kids" should they become unruly or confrontational. Kim and Brunner (2009) highlighted those who had had coaching positions as having greater access to secondary openings, which lead to more rapid advancement to leadership positions. The fact that I did not have that experience caused some to question if I could handle the kids.

As a new assistant principal, I had to deal with several challenges. First, the district placed me in the position a month after school had started. Second, I was given the most challenging areas to supervise, including being the ninth-grade principal. Becoming an administrator during the decade that crack cocaine entered schools, I saw many youth literally become different people under the influence of this drug, and violence became their manner of handling conflict. Once again, feeling I had been given additional challenges, I was determined to hit the ground running and exceed expectations. Resolving my first fight was no small matter in a high school with 1,850 kids. I remember seeing the male teachers on lunch duty lined up against the wall with their arms crossed, leaving me to handle the fray with security. Once they knew that I would not shy away from my duty, they got involved.

As advocates for children and as administrative leaders, our role was to ensure, faculty created support systems and interventions in curriculum standards that made it possible for all children to achieve. Young and Skrla (2003) cited work by Blount (1998), Chase (1995), Grogan (1996), Shakeshaft (1997), and Skrla (1998) that advanced the importance of women in administration staying focused on the essential role of the profession: teaching and learning. Young and Skrla (2003) found that women known to administrate effective schools and had greater concerns about teaching and learning.

After nearly five years of successful experience, mentors were again critical in helping me gain an interview for the position of principal in a large high school in Farmington, Michigan. The male superintendent in that district sought a candidate who was successful in dealing with diversity, accomplished in curriculum, and able to think outside the box. Sadly enough, though it was 1990, I could count the number of female principals in the state on one hand. The odds were not in my favor.

Having been one of fifty-one applicants for the position, many being accomplished principals in their own right, I did not even expect to get an interview. This superintendent took a chance, however, and offered me the position despite the fact that the "good ol' boys" were so sure the other finalist was going to get the job that they had started moving him into the office.

My rise to the role of superintendent began by becoming a high school principal, but it was the mentorship of key individuals that most helped my ascent. That a woman should be hired for the position left many aghast despite my strong background in curriculum and instruction and a demonstrated track record of effectiveness with diverse cultures. To give some context, the district was moving toward a heterogeneous culture, and this was causing unnecessary upheaval and no small amount of community violence. In a large community having three high schools primarily attended by a Caucasian population, the city became home to more than sixty-nine ethnic and religious groups within a few short years. That shift caused problems, and youth became very territorial, forgetting their similarities and instead identifying their differences. Some of the major changes put into place included the following: (a) offering diversity training for staff and students, (b) establishing a police liaison program, (c) putting in place equitable procedures for discipline, and

(d) updating curriculum to require that teachers help all children. It even became necessary to take steps to ensure that faculty did not check records and throw struggling kids out of new classes, telling them they were too dumb to handle classroom demands and that they should go to counseling to find another class. Some faculty members believed ethnicity impacted intelligence, and the practice was challenged by administration.

Not only did principals stop card playing during conference hours, but we also empowered a robust leadership team to engage the staff to hold higher expectations. By aligning the curriculum and eliminating class leveling, we increased academic standards. Each year faculty raised the number of students who attended advanced placement classes, took more elective academics, and raised their grades to allow for being accepted at Ivy League colleges. As a result of our students' continuous gains in achievement, the school program was we were recognized in magazines like *Newsweek* as one of the top ten high schools in the state and top 100 high schools in the United States.

In my first formal evaluation, I received high marks for performance but faced verbal criticism for wearing red fingernail polish and something other than black or blue suits. Van Tuyle and Watkins (2009) indicate that gender sometimes enters into the area of evaluation for women leaders. Years later, a new superintendent required that my evaluation include nine rather than three goals. Though he had created a number of new "hoops" for me to jump through in an effort to intimidate me, once again, all were completed flawlessly.

At district and county meetings and athletic events, I was usually the only female administrator present. I was often kept out of the good ol' boys network but seldom missed information, as I had devised alternate ways of gaining access to information. At one juncture when I was involved in hiring someone for a critical coaching position, I clearly remember hearing that the athletic director informed his peers that "should the bitch fail to get in line" with his recommendations, he and his group would "take the bitch down." He frequently positioned himself as a leader of the good ol' boys, but it was not necessary because I stayed involved with programs and always chose to champion coaches who promoted kids' growth. I acquired a reputation for building programs known to develop students' qualities and for increasing athletic participation. Our school produced multiple district and state championships and tripled the participation of females in my term as a principal and superintendent.

During my nearly ten-year tenure in that school, both parents and students expressed their appreciation for my presence in the role of principal. Sometimes a parent would say something like, "My daughter never used to believe anything was possible. Seeing you in a leadership role has opened her eyes to many new possibilities." At graduation, a senior wrote me a note thanking me for my support, using the example of her being summoned to the office as a freshman for the first time. Sensing her fear at the time, I placed a comforting hand on her knee and told her she most likely had been called down because of an unexcused absence. I told her not to be afraid but to serve her punishment and move on. The student involved wrote me a thank-you note as a senior stating, "As a ninth grader, knowing you took the time to help me that day always made me feel like I had an advocate in the school, and I was never afraid again."

Though this was one of the toughest positions I have ever held, it was a great school because the staff worked collaboratively, had high expectations for success, and made it student focused as they continued to grow professionally in their weekly delayed-start staff development block. To this day, the superintendent declares that hiring me was the smartest thing he ever did, though it was a risk on his part because I was a woman. After I had been on the job for about three years, a cochair on the SIT asked me, "Why are you still here? We thought you'd turn tail and run after the way you were treated the first couple of years. You just don't scare like the other administrators we've managed to run out of here." This comment, made in jest, was candid in its representation of how difficult secondary leadership can be for females.

Regarding race and ethnic relations, faculty was successful in guiding students as they transitioned to a school that visibly appreciated diversity. Faculty brought about this change by working with individual students and bringing groups together to recognize their similarities and learn to appreciate their differences. For example, initially, our school was a place where students remained in cliques defined by ethnicity, race, or religion, and those cliques often broke out into violence. We frequently had to postpone games because of fights. We previously never had pep assemblies because staff declared students to be unmanageable in large groups. I discovered students were not initially used to seeing a principal as a visible, daily presence in the school. They thought I was spying on them because many of them had never seen my predecessor before graduation. Once they learned my presence was an indicator of my interest, things changed as they grew to trust me. For example, when a Middle East conflict broke out, the Jewish, Chaldean, and Arabic students were respectful to each other and recognized the conflict was in another nation and not one that automatically involved their peers. Faculty knew many of them had relatives overseas whom they were worried about and as a total school community everyone involved in the school tried to help others throughout the struggle.

We were the only high school in the greater tricounty area willing to participate in a racial study by an alumnus who attended the University of Michigan. Knowing that their interests were protected first at the front office, students sent a loud message that this was a school where parents and community could "Expect the Best," which was their school motto and was worn on faculty t-shirts. Students learned that they all mattered to us, be they Arab, African American, Jewish, Chaldean, or Caucasian. Students were united in knowing that it was their school, a message we sent out continuously as we worked to increase our understanding of our similarities and differences. One time five of our students sat with five students from another area high school in an attempt to resolve a conflict that continued to threaten violence in the community if unresolved. One of our Chaldean students declared, "You may have trouble at your school, but here we all hang together, Jews, jocks, African Americans, and Arabs, and we'll kick your butts if you cause us trouble!" Minus the threat of violence, I knew when I heard that statement that our school community had succeeded in creating a place where everyone felt valued.

We also did a number of other things to increase student participation in school programs and to boost our academic achievement. Teachers increased our advanced placement (AP) classes from six to seventeen, increased participation in music from sixty to 400 kids, having two instrumental music staff. We integrated votech classes into all schedules and built a technology-based presentation mini-theater in addition to the CAD auto design and fashion design studio. During my tenure we tripled athletic participation, built two new weight and cardiovascular fitness areas, and significantly doubled required course enrollment. Students were required to declare their postgrad plans so that they left us having a destination.

Students became more involved when staff significantly increased organization memberships and meetings were held monthly with organizational leaders to stimulate awareness. We also implemented a policy of supporting each other; for example, since the band showed up for football, we had the football players go to the band concerts. We increased musicals, holding one a year for community members to audition. The first year we performed *Oklahoma*, and the grandma was played by a grandma from the community. The last year I was there, we had 200 kids try out for twelve roles in the musical *Oliver*. To help ensure that we had adequate space to have classes and activities for all, we later passed a bond and engaged a design team to completely rebuild the high school to meet the needs of staff, students, and community that was heralded by the superintendent and others as a showplace for instructional excellence. We actually tore the building down to the studs and rebuilt it according to designs that the teachers found most appropriate for their departments. For example, the band room had concert areas, practice rooms, instrument lockers of various sizes, and uniform storage areas. And classrooms had learning and presentation areas.

Though a principal deals with all sorts of challenges ranging from racism to rebuilding, the road from principal to superintendent has its own share of challenges. In a recent study, Kim and Brunner (2009) examined career paths taken to the superintendency to better understand the variance in the numbers of women and minorities in the position. The three paths that emerged were as follows: (a) a path with rapid mobility through vertical staff line movement, (b) a path with horizontal movement with positions held most often as a directors or assistant superintendents, and (c) a path having both vertical and horizontal movement. As a rule, women have had fewer opportunities to fill staff line positions, especially, secondary principalship positions, because fewer women have held secondary jobs. Kim and Brunner (2009) found that having had a secondary principalship plays a critical role in creating access to the superintendency. Kim and Brunner (2009) found that 80 percent of male superintendents held secondary positions and nearly 63 percent of those individuals were coaches. Their research further indicated nearly 65 percent of secondary principalships were held by men, a role that increased opportunity for more rapid advancement toward the superintendency. Conversely, Kim and Brunner (2009) found that only 35 percent of female superintendents held secondary principalships.

Overall, women have consistently maintained a more horizontal pattern with regard to advancement in this field. Kim and Brunner's (2009) findings showed that significantly fewer women held an administrative role; only 35.2 percent were principals at either level, and far more often they took a horizontal path. For example, according to Kim and Brunner (2009), 54.7 percent of aspiring women first held director-coordinator positions. Kim and Brunner (2009) identified that the career paths taken by the highest percentage of female superintendents were as follows:

1. Teacher, principal, central office, and superintendent   50%
2. Teacher, central office, and superintendent   17%
3. Teacher, principal, and superintendent   16.3%

Kim and Brunner's relatively recent study indicates that women have less access to staff line positions and are typically placed in central office director or coordinator positions, thereby following a horizontal path. One has to wonder whether current placement processes even address issues of equity. Are placement services even bringing forward all candidates capable of having a robust experience in the superintendent role?

My experience as a high school principal was followed by two different positions as assistant superintendent of curriculum and instruction. One district had five high schools, twenty-nine elementary schools, and four middle schools. I worked with nine directors and I had responsibility for an $88 million budget, and the overall deficit in the district was $6.5 million. Working in partnership with the county intermediate school district (ISD), Teachers aligned the curriculum to ensure all students mastered required standards and updated special education services, vocational education, and guidance and counseling programs the first year. The tremendous amount of work accomplished was a credit to teachers for getting involved, and administrators ensured the importance of their voices when presentations were made to the board of education.

Regardless of the fact that I was responsible for the coordination a budget of $88 million, I have still had to contend with the commonly held stereotype that female leaders tend to be poor money managers. My experience has simply not supported this stereotype. In every one of my positions, all deficits were eliminated within the first year, most often without hurting the program. Typically, we placed the greatest possible amount of resources behind student achievement. This was not always the strongest political action, but it became hard to argue against because not doing so would most likely stir up calls of complaint from community members. The fact that this never occurred was a testimony to strong communication and planning.

Effectively managing a mega-budget was one reason I gained the trust and cooperation of my staff, but being an alumna from Pontiac did not hurt, either. The staff used to tell me that they "had my back," as they phrased it, every step of the way. This speaks to the culture because the district is known to favor and appreciate its own. Together we developed a monitored strategic plan that had implementation guidelines and put us on the path to increasing achievement. We also eliminated a $6.5 million deficit without harming the program. One of the happiest memories I have from my time there was when I got to watch the staff open boxes of new language arts materials. The district had not made such an investment in more than ten years. It required the sale of a vacant elementary school to raise the $1,000,000 to purchase the textbooks, but we did it.

In the second district, as an assistant superintendent for instruction at a program only a quarter of the size, faculty achieved the status of Adequate Yearly Progress from the Michigan Department of Education (MDE) and were removed from the "watch" list. The focus was on creating school/community systems focused on using collaborative skills. It was common knowledge that classroom instruction had to be improved, and consequently twenty-five teachers engaged in brain-focused instructional training and used grant money to build the staff a $50,000 library of instructional materials. Faculty worked with their instructional coaches and created pacing guides and benchmark tests and adopted a new assessment program using technology. The collaborative approach was critical to the success of updating the program.

One of the big differences between those two positions was my experience with the superintendent. In the first district, staff laughed about the fact that he acted like Napoleon, often micromanaging his subordinates. In the second district, the superintendent was a valuable mentor. He presented the strongest example of outstanding people skills I have ever encountered. In an effort to "pay it forward," I made it a point to help other leaders. As an assistant superintendent, I mentored four teacher leaders or assistant principals who became either assistant principals or principals, three of whom were female.

There was a common theme in every district I entered. Each one was in crisis, having experienced significant problems with racial or ethnic tensions and low academic achievement. They needed to change quickly to experience success through celebrating diversity and raising achievement. To assume a new direction required the implementation of systemic plans. Effective mentorships and robust networking practices were also pivotal to my success in handling the increased responsibility.

The first superintendency I held was in a very challenged district. We had to do the following: (a) "right size" the district, (b) close a school, (c) balance a budget to remove a looming deficit, and (d) significantly raise achievement—all of which had to occur within the first year. Since I had developed a reputation for fixing problems, others were not surprised to find me here. As one mentor said, "They need you, and I know you can do what it takes." They knew that if it could be fixed, I was the person to do it.

By gathering the leadership and school improvement teams, the following was achieved: (a) faculty developed the educational rationale and recommendations for those schools that remained open, (b) found ways to cut the budget without hurting programs, (c) increased grants, (d) reopened early childhood programs, and (e) achieved the status of Adequate Yearly Progress (AYP) from MDE by the second year. The latter was done in concert with the teachers and three coaches hired to increase their instructional proficiency and develop benchmark tests via computer that aligned with the state standards. A team also wrote and implemented a "Gear Up" grant with Saginaw Valley and Delta College so that students were able to earn college scholarships. By the third year, every student enrolled in college with one exception. During the final week at school, a basketball player toting a gun in the neighborhood was shot in the hand, thus eliminating his college scholarship. I use this example to highlight that while in school, these same students were state champions, but they lived very tumultuous lives in the neighborhood.

Watching staff in this district make AYP two years in a row for the first time in more than a decade was an experience not soon to be forgotten. The second time it happened, an elementary principal who was known not to show emotion broke down and cried for joy. The children's excitement was exceeded only by their pride in doing well. Watching staff present at state and national conferences and receive standing ovations about what they had learned as a result of their work with the instructional and assessment coaches assigned to the buildings. End sentence here made them very proud. Faculty and community held the knowledge that what they did made all the difference to kids. A pillar of the community once commented on our actions: "You know, we're beginning to think we might have hope once again for the future." Those words spoke volumes.

A constant theme in my administrative work was my willingness to collaborate with others to move the district forward. Grogan (as cited in Brunner, 1999) identified three themes characteristic of female leaders: (a) concepts of power, (b) beliefs about decision making, and (c) notions of leadership. All three were connected by collaboration, most of which never occurred without the involvement of others. Women leaders are known for the emphasis they place on empowerment as opposed to hierarchical power, a mindset more often related to males.

In order to elicit other common experiences of women leaders in education, I interviewed seven women leaders. These women served in leadership positions ranging from high school assistant principal to superintendent and included individuals from both minority and majority cultures. They each had at least ten years of experience in leadership positions and came from large, small, urban, and rural environments. Each participant was asked to highlight the path of her career and provide me with her successes and areas of focus in her position. Following our conversations about that, I asked for clarification as needed. They were asked to highlight their challenges and share the emotional reactions to them as they were comfortable. Following their stories, I asked them to speak to challenges they faced with barriers to advancement and discriminatory practices that are highlighted in the chapter.

A common theme evident in the research and from the administrators that I interviewed was how women in leadership positions view their primary responsibilities. Brunner and Grogan (2007) noted that female leaders focus their work on the primary purpose of the organization, teaching and learning, and raising student achievement, whereas male leaders tend to focus their work on gaining power and achieving political agendas. Frequently found in large, diverse settings, female leaders also display an unspoken appreciation for diversity and seeing things from perspectives other than their own. A third critical factor cited among successful female leaders is self-reflection regarding their role and performance; this has been found to be the strongest method of improvement.

Themes evident in my background in leadership are reinforced by the background of other female leaders, who each told a story of the difference her position made in the growth of her school district. Knowing that other women leaders had diverse experiences provides inspiration for aspiring leaders. However, in the stories of their careers, the women interviewed as part of this chapter were assured that their identities would be kept secret to minimize any possibility of recognition. It is interesting that in one case, the superintendent broke down and cried because retelling the experiences proved too painful, causing her to initially back out, and another swore me to secrecy even though her former superintendent is now deceased. The threat of discovery continues to stifle women, keeping them quiet, which threatens the candor their stories can provide to instruct younger generations.

A woman whom I will call Jennifer found her path to a central-level curriculum director's position from serving as a union chairperson. Jennifer was hired primarily because of her role as union president but also as for her knowledge in the instructional core. Knowing that women did not serve in CO positions at the time, she strongly believed this to be a viable path.

Her first cabinet meeting was interesting. She spoke comfortably, feeling a part of the discussion, but was gestured to enter the superintendent's office at the end of the meeting. The superintendent made her aware that she had been placed in a CO position merely as a means to remove her from the union level and as a token of equity. Further, if her opinion were needed, the superintendent would inform her as to what to say in the future. Needless to say, Jennifer served quietly at the central level and performed numerous roles for staff.

Knowing her future depended on finding another district, she quietly began looking for other opportunities. Jennifer wanted to improve services but soon learned that her current district did not value her role as a change agent, nor did her efforts endear her to the decision makers in many districts. Eventually, Jennifer moved on to become a successful assistant superintendent for instruction in a large, urban district that was seeking an instructional leader able to transform the program for the twenty-first century. A few key factors in Jennifer's advancement were her success in working with male mentors, a robust knowledge base, and the fact that she never deviated from her goal.

Other factors contributed to Jennifer's success as well, including her strong work ethic. Jennifer knew that more would be required of her as a female, and that proved to be true. Having faced discrimination both from her superintendent in the initial conference and later in many situations, she was also left out of his communication network. Only by building an even greater base of support in the field did she succeed. Others became dependent on her office for additional resources, and Jennifer was generous in building others' capacity as leaders.

Throughout the next twenty years, she continued to build a collaborative knowledge base while working for a new superintendent who supported and respected her knowledge. Intent on building a legacy of opportunity for others, she created one of the strongest districts in the state in her role as assistant superintendent. Common to themes mentioned earlier, Jennifer focused on the primary work of instruction and was a collaborative leader.

Even when women like Jennifer have a dedicated work ethic and do everything right, stepping up into higher-level positions can challenge them at the deepest levels. Seeking a chance to prove themselves, some women travel a treacherous path to district leadership roles and the superintendency. In another interview, the journey of a black female to superintendency was an incredible undertaking. Monica's first administrative position was as an assistant principal. When considering Monica's candidacy, the principal at the high school commented that hiring her would mean that three out of four of the assistant principals would be minorities. Knowing the ideal was to have the assistant principal team parallel their student population, hiring Monica would entail having an unequal balance in terms of ethnicity. Challenged by wanting Monica and respecting the need to have a diverse team of leaders, he commented, "When you talk to Monica, you don't know she's black!" Without intent, the principal provided a common example of how Monica was marginalized and discriminated against by others who denied her race and culture. She dismissed his poor behavior lest she offend her superior, but everyone else ignored it or made light of it, too. Indeed, it was just seen as part of the struggle that comes with an administrative position.

Having been a special education teacher, Monica was seen as effective at helping at-risk kids; therefore, the superintendent called upon her to assume an elementary principalship for a very challenged school. Monica became known for her emphasis on student performance and teacher engagement. Her primary challenge, however, was the board president's wife, who served as her temporary secretary. Monica gave her three poor evaluations and finally refused to recommend the woman for permanent employment. In response to this, Monica was called before two union presidents and two board members to face three grueling hours of inquiry, none of which was focused on the employee. Monica also received threatening phone calls to her house, but she stood fast in her conviction not to hire the person in question.

Later, Monica took a leave of absence due to illness. When she returned, she was told that she had been moved to a high school as an assistant principal. Monica saw this as being demoted, or "punished," for having stood her ground. She accepted the transfer, only to find that the autocratic principal often kept her out of his network. When Monica asked to be involved, she was told no and reminded of her role. Not being informed of daily events kept Monica out of the communication loop, clearly impacting her ability to do her job effectively.

When she requested a transfer to another school, Monica faced recriminations from the staff. When tasks loomed, the principal's secretary often said, "She has the doctorate. Let her do it." A parent commented that the principal was overheard to say he would "Shut down her office!" The principal's threats didn't hold much weight, however, because Monica was responsible for the master schedule and curriculum, had support from staff, and got rave reviews from kids who felt the significance of her advocacy on their behalf. Facing such obvious discrimination makes one wonder if being a woman of color contributed to her marginalization. Though she never aspired to the superintendency, she desired to work in positions in which the role(s) she undertook had an impact on the academic performance of the student body. She also wanted to be in positions that minimized further discrimination.

Perseverance and determination were as essential to her success as was the ability to tune out naysayers. As Monica said:

> My naïveté held me in good stead during those first years. It required me to keep my integrity intact and do what's right for the kids. In some ways, this put me at odds with district leaders and caused them

to push back in ways designed to get the best of an individual or destroy their credibility.

In another interview, Linda was an administrator who broke into secondary administration on her path to the superintendent role. Having a background in instruction, Linda was known as a change agent and forward-thinking individual and was mentored by male administrators who saw her ability and helped to move her forward. Indeed, she felt that their networking opened doors for her. Hired in 1990 by an affluent district, she became involved in bonds and the planning work required for building a new high school. A proponent of professional learning communities (PLCs) and a collaborative leader, she was also a pioneer in establishing alternative block schedules, thereby giving students a chance to take more classes and expose themselves to a greater range of subjects. Able to work effectively with staff, she never allowed staff reticence to delay positive changes for kids. As a result, she made some enemies during those years from the teacher's union and the athletic staff, both powerful oppositions to her advancement. After serving for another decade as an assistant superintendent for instruction, she moved into the superintendent selection process. Becoming a finalist, she quickly learned, on more than one occasion, that the teacher's union had been successful in blocking her from attaining the desired position.

Linda was known as a "lighthouse educator," an individual known to take divergent paths to improving achievement. She was both revered and respected for her work. However, she also recognized that, fairly or not, she would finish her career as an assistant superintendent. She eventually retired from education and established a business outside the field of education.

Greta had another story to tell. She became principal at the request of mentor leaders. Known to be effective as a classroom teacher, she was often called upon to provide professional development sessions for staff because of her knowledge. Greta sought to continuously grow as an educator in her craft and widen her sphere of influence. Successful at creating a sense of community and shared purpose in any role, she was able to grow with a district as it transitioned to an urban city from a farming community. She was equally as masterful at building personal relationships and empowering leadership in others.

With respected skill in her profession, Greta was asked to be a principal of a new elementary school. Able to work effectively in this role, within a few years she was again recruited by the assistant superintendent to apply as the then current assistant superintendent was retiring. Able to expand her influence, Greta continues to build upon her strengths and extend her learning in this role. She reports no problems dealing with her rise other than some occasional challenges to her credibility raised by secondary administrators. Greta reports having learned a great deal about sports, scheduling, and high school instructional issues. Greta believes having gained the respect of her peers has made it easier to orchestrate change. She is known for her persistence, and others recognize her desire to help kids and respect her work.

Sandy became a superintendent following a fifteen-year career in human resources as executive director and five years as a secondary teacher. In her early years, Sandy negotiated contracts for districts. Sandy believes having an HR background has been invaluable because it has allowed her to understand people and learn how to lead a building of common purpose. However, Sandy admits had she known she wanted to assume the superintendency, she would have chosen a career path that allowed her to serve as a principal.

One career challenge she faced was being seen as less effective because of her gender. Being addressed as, "Hey girlie, aren't you a cutie" was a problem for her. However, she felt that this necessitated her working harder to attain credibility. One female who looked her in the eye at an interview and asked, "Just how tough are you?" later became one of her strongest advocates. She also faced pay inequity in her roles and was brought in at a lower salary than her male predecessor.

Sandy believes in helping youth build their leadership and end discrimination. She advocates for giving students a voice in the world and help to model democratic practices. Although she never had children of her own, education fulfilled her need to serve children. That satisfaction is a great part of her satisfaction with her role as superintendent.

Despite their differences in experience, in relation to their continued professional learning, all superintendents felt the importance of handling diminishing finances, assessing educational outcomes, understanding strong community and board relations, and finding new ways to help close the achievement gap. And what skills are needed to get this job done? Who better to ask than the superintendents themselves?

Brunner & Grogan (2007) presented a self-assessment of skills that superintendents said they needed to perform their job. It is interesting to note the emphasis that superintendents placed on specific qualities that correlate with their career. The findings were as follows:

1. Interpersonal skills   87%
2. Responsiveness to parents and community   83%
3. Ability to maintain organizational relationships   82%
4. Emphasis placed on instruction   61%
5. Knowledge of instructional processes   59%
6. Knowledge of curriculum   57%

Knowing the primary work of schools to be instruction, the findings are telling in a male-dominated profession. Women leaders in this chapter seem to have a diametrically opposed rank of importance in their self-assessment from those who participated in Grogan and Brunner's (2007) survey. Knowing the importance of every area, these women each shared the emphasis they placed on instruction—sometimes to their detriment. Female leaders more often stay focused on the work of the organization: teaching and learning. Their emphasis on instruction also influenced their participatory leadership style, and women more often worked in partnership with staff as opposed to using a top-down management style.

That being the case, they more closely mirrored and included responses from fifty-one female superintendents. Female leaders liked feeling that they made a difference and provided focus and direction to people in the community. As superintendents, they appreciated available improvement opportunities and actively worked to create meaningful change in their schools and communities.

The importance of women sharing their stories was noted by Brunner (1998). Research demonstrates the lack of material in this area, for we know women are reluctant to tell their stories; the primary reason for this is the possible threat to their future career advancement. But the gap does exist, and this chapter was written in hopes of serving the purpose of documenting some of the challenges women face.

These stories are important for a number of reasons and can serve as tools for reflection for aspiring women leaders as they anticipate their direction and the challenges that lie in their paths. Women leaders highlighted a number of obstacles to advancement shown in the research; yet what emerged in the research for this chapter was when recognizing these challenges, each woman adapted and pursued advancement. Recognizing this reality did not change the participants' direction; it merely required a change of focus. For example, one woman stated that if she knew her leadership path would lead to the superintendency, she would have changed her career path and served as a principal. Another stated she never pursued advancement; she only sought to widen her sphere of influence, yet she became a critical leader through her hard work and relationship-building skills (albeit under the mentorship of another female leader). In every case, these leaders had strong mentors in place who often were men in the field. The participants also learned how to create networks that secured them access to information they might not have otherwise been privy to.

These women pursued advancement through sheer determination and refused to be deterred. The drive to make a difference was so compelling, each felt achieving her individual purpose was nonnegotiable. The stories of students who served under these leaders were heartwarming. Female leaders opened vistas/worlds to young women who saw new possibilities in their futures as a result of having female principals and superintendents.

Examples such as networking, mentorships, and equal access to search consultants were highlighted, and each served as important tools that were critical for career advancement. The tragedy lies in women having to "go the extra yard" and work harder to achieve the same results as their male counterparts. However, in participating in leadership, each woman gained unique opportunities, not the least of which was the chance for women to share their legacy. That was perhaps the greatest benefit to every participant.

References

Brunner, C. (1994). *Superintendent selection: Lessons from political science.* Paper presented at the American Educational Research Association annual meeting, New Orleans, LA, April 4–8, 1994.

Brunner, C. (1998, April). *Benefit or bane? Critique of the usefulness of research about women superintendents.* ERIC Document: ED424647.

Brunner, C. (1999). *Sacred dreams: Women and the superintendency.* Albany: State University of New York.

Brunner, C., & Grogan, M., (2007). *Women leading school systems: Uncommon roads to fulfillment.* Lanham, MD: Rowman & Littlefield.

Pavan, B. N. (1988). *Job search strategies utilized by aspiring and incumbent female and male public school administrators.* ERIC: Report ED302879. Apr.1988.

Skrla, L., & Young, M. D. (2003). *Reconsidering feminist research in educational leadership.* Albany: State University of New York Press .

Skrla, L. (2003). Normalized femininity: Reconsidering research on women in the superintendency. IN M. D., Young & L. Skrla (Eds.), Reconsidering feminist research in educational leadership (pp. 247–63). Albany, NY: State University of New York Press.

Van Tuyle, V., & Watkins, S. G. (2009). Women superintendents in Illinois: Gender barriers and challenges. *Journal of Women in Educational Leadership, 7*(3), 135–51.

Young, M., & Skrla, L. (2003). *Reconsidering feminist research in educational research.* Albany: State University of New York Press.

11

This I Believe: Teaching in Color

Carmen M. Johnson

The world is defined by Color. As a visual arts teacher, it has been my life's work to teach kids how to use Color. I have spent countless hours explaining what Color is and how it is used to enhance artwork. I illustrate the art of Coloring, how to stay in the lines and Color all the same direction. As life has shaped my artistic experiences, I have developed a better understanding of Color. Color should not be forced in any direction but should be allowed to go where it wants, do what it wants, and become who it wants to become.

This I believe: Color is not blind, nor should it be nearsighted or farsighted. Color is clear. It is alive and conscious. Color moves, breathes, and has many names. Color is emotional, experiencing both joy and sorrow. Color laughs, cries, believes, hopes, dreams, wins, and loses. I believe that Color is a phenomenon of light and a visual perception. I also believe that Color is the defining badge that stands for bravery, courage, honor, defeat, and disgrace. Color characterizes freedom as personal liberty and bondage as slavery. Color has forced nations to conquer nations whose Color made them weaker. Color is the first thing that we see and the last thing that we see, the reason we are and the reason we are not. The reason we can and the reason we cannot. Color is powerful.

Because of Color I am beautiful; I am ugly; I am loved and I am hated. Because of Color I am chosen and because of Color I am passed over. Color has inspired me to be brilliant and Color has perceived me as dumb.

Color has provided me with opportunities and Color has left me with nothing. Color has made me who I am, and Color has made me who I am not. Color is permanent.

Personally, I believe that Color should be uncomplicated like a box of crayons full of options, possibilities, and dreams. The only limitation to each Color in this box is the inspiration and creativity connected to the hand that is using the Color. As the Colors swirl around on the paper, they radiate vision and expectation while at the same time reflecting the innocence of childhood. I recognize that Color is important, but I never realized it would be the reason that I am important. Color has made me afraid, left me lonely, forced me to conform, and demanded me to concede. I have accepted that the world is defined by Color and that it always will be. Color is prescribed.

I believe we are like a child's artwork, all of us fighting to be chosen for the perfect masterpiece. Some of us are always selected because our Color is universal, matching with everything. There are those of us, however, who tried everything to get noticed like changing our name, lightening our tone, even mixing with other Colors. In the end, the unchosen Colors remain alone, dreaming of possibilities not yet attained, hoping for a moment of untainted artistic liberty to come along so that we can express our true Color with pride and celebration. Color possesses me. It possesses all of us: our thoughts, our actions, and our intentions. We don't have to pursue Color because Color is. . . . This I believe.

What is belief? Belief is an assumed truth that has been created in our minds based on our personal experiences and understanding of the world around us. The beliefs expressed in the following chapter were formed, shaped, and stretched by the experiences of a person who views the world through the eyes of a woman of Color. This belief has transformed into truth. This truth has motivated me to investigate the current state of our nation's public education system and the gaping chasm of failure inequality and institutional racism that so many unforgotten children have fallen into. The failure of public education, in my opinion, is a direct reflection of what we believe. As Freeman (2004) states:

> I favor integration on buses and in all areas of public accommodation and travel. . . . I am for equality. However, I think integration in our

public schools is different. In that setting, you are dealing with one of the most important assets of an individual—the mind. White people view black people as inferior. A large percentage of them have a very low opinion of our race. People with such a low view of the black race cannot be given free rein and put in charge of the intellectual care and development of our boys and girls. (n.p.)

A very large part of me agrees with Samuel Freedman, while another large part of me wants to scream, *"No way. It is not true!"*

My conflict comes from deep within me. I was *raised* to believe that I could choose whatever I wanted to do and be whoever I wanted to be. Conversely, I was *taught* to believe that my reality was not based solely on the choices I make for myself but rather limited to the opinions and decisions someone else makes for me. For the child of Color, educational assumptions about them are made from the minute they step foot in their first school. Assumptions are made about their socioeconomic situation, their home life, their parental involvement, and their future. Teachers and administrators alike make a decision as to how much time they should spend pouring into a kid whose future doesn't appear to be promising. One could argue that assumptions are made about every child, and I'm sure that is true to an extent; however, statistics tell us that black boys make up more than 60 percent of all students expelled from school and as a result are twenty times more likely to end up in prison (Cottman, 2010).

My Story Begins

I am a teacher, like so many other eager young teachers, for all the cliché reasons: I wanted to make a difference; I wanted to change the world one student at a time. I love the art of teaching. While all that is true, it is not the reason I chose to teach. Teaching chose me. At a very young age, I realized that teachers had the ability to help some kids while at the same time hurt others. I began to understand that education was neither fair nor equal; I started to see myself through my teachers' eyes and I realized their perception of me had far-reaching consequences. As a result, my personal expectations were very low. I came to realize that the piece that was missing in my own education was a relationship with a teacher who knew what it felt like to be me. It was then that I embraced my purpose. My teaching career began twelve years ago in a middle-class school district in Michigan. I was interviewed and hired "on the spot." I was so excited to begin my career at the middle level. I was one of four teachers of Color out of a staff of fifty. At that time in my life I was very naïve and assumed that because students were treated equitably in my classes, they received the same kind of treatment in all classes. I learned very quickly that social class has very little to do with expectation when race is involved. Students of Color are viewed the same regardless of education or financial status. I intentionally began to advocate for students of Color, making myself available to listen and empower. This decision completely changed the way I viewed education. Students must be able to relate their learning to their own experiences in order for retention to begin. I recognized that my own perceptions of my students were being tainted by the opinions of negative teachers and administrators. The very system that qualified me to teach all children has promoted underachievement for many students of Color by ignoring the strengths of their cultures.

I Chose to Be a Culturally Responsive Teacher

As Gay (2000) indicates, "Culturally responsive teaching can be defined as using the cultural knowledge, prior experiences, frames of reference, and performance styles of ethnically diverse students to make learning encounters more relevant to and effective for them" (p. 20). This decision revolutionized the way I view education. My very presence brought hope to hopeless, marginalized children, and their families. I also was able to engage a community of professionals in conversations that promoted positive change and successful outcomes. Teaching became the vehicle that I used to transform self-image and empower future leaders. I recognized myself in my students and I realized that I was not smarter or more talented or even privileged; the fundamental difference between myself and the students that I was teaching was that I believed that I could achieve.

My career as an educator has led me to many different locations. I have taught in predominantly white schools as well as predominantly black schools, and I have noticed that there is a need for culturally responsive teachers everywhere. Students need to be taught to live in a world of differences, to appreciate the blending of cultures into a world of mosaic beauty. This is why I teach.

Courage

> I wanted you to see what real courage is, instead of getting the idea that courage is a man with a gun in his hand. It's when you know you're licked before you begin but you begin anyway and you see it through no matter what. You rarely win, but sometimes you do.
>
> —To Kill a Mockingbird, Lee, 1982, p. 116

I had been teaching for eight years when I transferred to the school at which I currently work. I was so excited about working at the middle school level once again, as I truly connect well with that age group. I knew going into the school year that I would be the only person of Color in that building. This wasn't surprising, however, because at that time I was one of only eight employees of Color (five of those being teachers) in a district of 1,100 teachers. I had heard such wonderful things about this particular school and its warm, welcoming culture of acceptance. I was a little intimidated at first by the coldness of the veteran staff, the strange looks I received from them in the hallway, and the subtle hints they would give off letting me know that things were done a certain way in the building and they were happy with status quo. However, as always, teaching for me is like riding a bike, new, exciting, and natural. Once you learn to control the bike, the only thing you have to worry about is where you are riding it.

I had been there approximately one month when I was checking the mail in the teacher mailroom on a Monday morning. I was surprised to find a sealed business envelope in my mailbox because it was too early for interschool mail to have been delivered. I immediately opened the envelope and was surprised to find a transfer letter with my name on it. I was shocked! A flood of emotions began to consume me as I was trying to process what I was reading. Was I being fired? Did my job get eliminated? Had I done something to offend someone? As I looked closer at the document I noticed that the ink was wet and had rubbed off a little on my hands. As I examined the form I realized that it was an old document that was no longer being used in our district. My mind was racing. I had read about people being targeted for racial hatred but that had never been my story. Immediately, fear began to crawl up my spine as I realized that I was alone in this building. I understood with my head that I must report this incident to my administrators, but I knew in my heart that it wouldn't make a difference.

As one would expect, my principal appeared to be outraged and said that he would get to the bottom of this. He reassured me that this had not come from him or anyone in administration. He also agreed that the actions appeared to be racially motivated but he was comfortable handling the investigation himself at the building level. (I knew what that meant.) My principal did launch an investigation; however, when he realized that in order to uncover the truth, he would have to side against his veteran staff, he immediately stopped the inquiry. He assured me that he knew exactly who the staff member was but that he didn't have enough evidence to confront him; one can imagine what it felt like to hear him say that. I looked across the desk at him and realized that I was truly a victim. I made a decision that day, as I could see my own reflection in the eyes of my principal. From now on, I would deliberately use education as a bridge that would connect his reality with mine. This was the first time in my professional career that I had experienced institutional racism on a personal level. The choice to belittle the feelings and experiences of one individual to avoid conflict and tension with others was the choice that propelled me to action. I knew at that moment exactly what it felt like to be a student of Color in this building and I realized that the only thing that separated me from my students in the eyes of my colleagues was my education. That day I *became courage.*

My Purpose

The word *purpose* is defined as "that which a person sets before himself as an object to be reached or accomplished; the end or aim to which the view is directed in any plan, measure, or exertion" (http://www.thefreedictionary.com/purpose). The skin I'm in is my purpose, the reason I teach, the reason I learn, the reason I listen, and the reason I write. My skin is my honor, and it is my responsibility to defend my honor. I can confidently say without hesitation that education is not inclusive nor is it fair, and it often employs the ignorant. These words are difficult for me to write to describe this profession that I love. Extraordinary education emanates relevance and inclusivity. In my career, I have known and respected diverse educators who were bold, courageous, and conscientiously equipped to reach all kids. Unfortunately, the number of highly qualified culturally relevant educators is small, as evidenced by the racial achievement gap. My purpose is to share my life with everyone because I believe it is significant to *truly* know a person and value what they believe in, to understand how they make choices and how they feel about themselves. I recognized ignorance in my principal that day as I stood in his office, but I understood that it was well intentioned. When we truly understand a person, and we have a relationship with them, their affliction and hardship becomes authentic. My purpose is to educate the well intentioned through ongoing courageous dialogue.

Racial Consciousness

Metapedia defines *racial consciousness* as "the understanding of the uniqueness of one's race compared to other races". In particular, a racially conscious person is aware of the physical characteristics, history, culture, traditions, and mores of his own race and how those things differ from other races. *Race* is a word that has to be taught and celebrated in education. I decided that in order for my colleagues and students to appreciate my thoughts and opinions, they needed to understand the rich tradition from where they came. I am multiracial; this is a term that I now share openly. My mother was white, of German descent, but my father came from the Dominican Republic; that makes him equally African and Spanish. As I child I was urged to choose a race (I think so that other people would feel better), but I quickly realized that in so doing I would have to deny part of who I am. So I identify with all three races. I believe that it is important to identify oneself with a racial group because it forces connection to history. History in its entirety needs to be taught, remembered, and valued in education today.

I have always known that I was different; my racial consciousness started with my first memories. I was adopted as an infant and raised by white parents. I was constantly comparing myself to my parents. I wondered why my skin was darker, why my nose was wider, and why my eyes were so much bigger. I often asked my mother why my hair was straight when it was wet and but curly when it dried. I wondered why people would stare at us when we were out together and why all of my baby dolls had white skin. As I grew I rarely saw kids who looked like me and when I did they made fun of how I spoke, saying "I sounded too white." I didn't understand what that meant. In school, the teachers tried to label me and put me in groups where they thought I would be more successful. They never seemed to expect very much from me. I was in high school when I was told I was pretty for a black girl. It was then that I realized that no matter who I chose to be friends with, what sports I played, who I dated, where I went to college, or what career I selected, I would always be a black girl.

Beverly Daniel Tatum, in her book entitled *Why Are All the Black Kids Sitting Together in the Cafeteria?,* writes:

> All Black People, irrespective of their Color, shade, darkness, or lightness, are aware from a very early age that their blackness makes them different from mainstream white America. It sets them apart from White immigrant groups who were not brought here as slaves and who have thus had a different experience in becoming assimilated into mainstream American culture. The struggle for a strong positive racial identity for young Black Afro-American children is clearly made more difficult by the realities of Color prejudice. (p. 44)

Blackness, I have discovered, is greater than skin Color. It is a perception of lifestyle and limits that lies on the outskirts of white privilege. Blackness, for the black child, is defined by what he or she doesn't have and can't achieve. It is a life of comparison and want, often mixed with poverty and welfare. The one thing that never changes regardless of one's situation is blackness.

As an educator I am constantly reminded of the borders that public education has created for black students. We refer to the borders as standardized tests, common assessments, and formative assessments. These borders have stained education with a permanent gap in achievement produced by a specific race of people and perpetuated by isolation and lack of cultural relevance. In order to break through the borders in public education, teachers must have the courage to question mainstream knowledge. Nieto (2005) writes, "Challenging mainstream knowledge and conventional ways of doing things in general, is not easy. We who do this work, are caught in a conundrum, working within the system to create change" (p. 210). We need to spend less time asking questions in education and more time teaching our teachers and our students to consider. Consider what is essential, consider what is true, and consider what is measurable.

It is safe to assume that many educators have not had regular interactions with people from diverse backgrounds, nor have they been taught about people who are different from them. Therefore, we should not be surprised that negativity and racist attitudes will be projected onto their students. While this behavior should not be accepted, educators have to be willing to engage in open, honest dialogue and self-examination so that sustained change can happen.

Hope

Hope is the feeling that what is wanted can be had or that events will turn out for the best. I wish I could conclude my story with a feel-good moment that causes one to believe that racism and inequality are rare and isolated misunderstandings. The reality is, however, that my story is very common. People of Color at some point in their lives will experience moments of racial tension and discrimination. They will be treated with hatred and viewed as statistics and stereotypes. The question is how will they respond?

One year after I made the decision to transform the racial consciousness in my building, I had several complaints filed against me with the union by my colleagues for starting a step team, defending students of Color at staff meetings, publically advocating for students and parents of Color, and taking on too many leadership roles in the school. My actions created hope for my students and aroused fear in my colleagues. I learned to embrace the pressure because I recognize that pressure leads to change and change leads to hope. Hope is a forgotten student who learns to smile, a parent who hears an encouraging word, a colleague who listens to her students, and an administrator who diversifies his staff. Hope is a teacher that is determined to challenge mainstream knowledge and transform school culture by teaching people to consider.

I am Color; I am hope. And this I believe.

References

Cottman, M. H. (2010). Education: Black boys set up to fail. Retrieved September 26, 2010, from http://www.blackamericaweb.com/?q=articles/news/moving_america_news/21682.

Freedman, S. G. (2004, May 16). Still separate, still unequal. *New York Times*. Retrieved October 7, 2010, from http://www.nytimes.com/2004/05/16/books/still-separate-still-unequal.html.

Gay, G. (2000). *Culturally responsive teaching: Theory, research, & practice*. New York: Teachers College Press.

Lee, H. (1982). *To kill a mockingbird*. New York: Warner Books.

Nieto, Sonia (Ed.) (2005). *Why We Teach*. New York: Teachers College Press.

Tatum, B. D. (1997). *Why are all the black kids sitting together in the cafeteria*? New York: Basic Books.

12

Both Sides of Mentoring: A Leader's Story

Lynn Kleiman Malinoff and James E. Barott

Sinetar (1998) described mentoring as a spiritual art:

> Mentoring is a timeless function. Its elements reside in our heart. . . .
> The word *mentoring* has mythic roots. It means "guide." . . . Productive mentors are productive types—wholesome guides who, by their way of being ignite our vision, our hope, our self-respect. . . . Both mentors and the mentor's spirit fire up vigor of thought and zeal to reach our true purposes: inner peace, liberty, the soaring heights of some specific goal. The mentor's spirit fuels our determination to flourish as fully integrated individuals. (p. 21)

The mythic archetype of the Good Mother is a fitting description of my experiences of being mentored and of my mentoring. Described as "one of the most powerful mythic figures of all" (Schechter & Semeiks, 1980), the Good Mother provides emotional support as well as spiritual and physical sustenance. Though *mother* is a female-specific term, in my experience this mythology represents an archetype universally embraced by my mentors, regardless of gender.

I am deeply committed to the process of mentoring from both sides, the richly rewarding experience of being the protégé and the art of being a mentor. When I agreed to write this chapter, I accepted the challenge of writing about mentoring and its role for women in educational leadership. I had never identified mentoring as a gender-specific practice, and my own mentors are a combination of people in different settings from different backgrounds, male and female, sharing their experience, strength, hope, and wisdom with me. I asked one of my mentors how I might frame this work given the purpose of the book in which it would be published. He reminded me that I was a woman, a leader in education, and so my story was important and fit perfectly in a book on women in educational leadership.

Mentoring is about the relationship between mentor and protégé. Sometimes it is parent to child, teacher to student, colleague to colleague. Mentoring has played a significant role throughout my life—in my youth, as a daughter and student, in my growing-up years in college, and throughout my adult and professional life. In addition to my parents, I have, since first grade, had mentors guiding me, teaching me, supporting me, and loving me. There were no strings attached, nothing owed to my mentors, simply my own commitment to pay it forward. And so I am committed to being a mentor, to continuing to have mentors, and to embracing mentorship as my primary leadership style in education.

> Stories are the womb of personhood. Stories make and break us. Stories sustain us in times of trouble and encourage us towards ends we would not otherwise envision.
>
> —Mair, 1989, p. 2

I believe there is great power and wisdom in each person's story, in his or her perceptions of the experience of being mentored, and my in own perceptions of the effects mentoring has had on me in multiple contexts and forming me as a leader in the field of education. Narrative continues to play a major role in my leadership, engaging staff, parents, students, teachers, and community members in sharing their stories with each other in order to create meaning, develop compassion, explore outcomes, and improve practice whether it is in leadership, teaching, parenting, active citizenship, or any other context. As Crossley (2002) indicates, "Human life carries within it a narrative structure to the extent that the individual, at the level of tacit, phenomenological experience, is constantly projecting backwards and forwards in a manner that maintains a sense of coherence, unity, meaningfulness and identity" (p. 11).

Mentoring is an act of leadership. Through this process, one helps unleash the potential of one's protégés by empowering them to act, to find meaning, and to stand for what they believe in. When they do so, amazing things happen. This is the magic of mentoring. Mentoring, more than any other practice, contributes to my skill and success as an educational leader. And it comes with an awesome responsibility.

Being a mentor demands that I practice what I preach and lead by example. Heider's *The Tao of Leadership* (1985), adapted from Lao Tzu's *Tao Te Ching*, addresses the spiritual nature of leadership, "The leader acts as a healer and is an open, receptive, and nourishing state. That is the feminine or Yin aspect of leadership" (p. 55). He asks, "Are you doing this work to facilitate growth or to become famous?" (p. 87). I contend that the practice of mentoring provides practice in humility, openness, caring, and love. Mentoring is a significant spiritual practice.

Educational leadership has many facets—understanding and navigating systems, supporting staff, professional development in leadership and for those one leads, goal setting, visioning, practical knowledge about teaching and learning, curriculum and accountability, using data, developing community. What the university left out of my education courses was the importance of mentoring, building relationships, developing strong people skills, and passing it on—that this is integral to being a leader. These are the skills I use most often as an educational leader.

Methodology

Volumes have been written about mentoring, coaching, guiding, teaching, and supporting others. In the United States, a grand movement of mentoring was and continues to be supported as a strategy for helping at-risk youth, improving teaching, and growing more effective educational leaders. But I was unable to find literature that provided a thematic analysis of the stories and experiences of mentors and protégés.

People act based on the meaning things have for them; and these meanings are derived from social interaction and modified through interpretation. According to Blumer (1969), in symbolic interaction, the researcher becomes the instrument of the research, studying the problem in its natural world. Its great strength is empiricism. This tradition treats theory as something that needs to be brought in line with the empirical evidence of peoples' experiences. Understanding a human event involves the study of the interaction of people, assuming that each individual's action fits into the action of others.

Derived from the work of George Herbert Mead, Charles Cooley, Herbert Blumer, and, more recently, Howard Becker, and others, symbolic interactionists use qualitative research methods to study interactions, identifying symbols and meanings.

In order to study the relationship between mentor and protégé, I had many questions, including:

> What happens between a mentor and her protégés?
>
> How is this interpreted by the protégé?
>
> What symbols and interactions define this relationship?
>
> What happens to the mentor as a result of these relationships?
>
> How does mentoring influence my leadership in education?

Data consisted of two sets. In the first, I wrote vignettes about my experiences with ten mentors. I wrote each as I remember the relationship, focusing on my experience of the relationships, the pivotal experiences, and the impact on my personal and professional growth. I analyzed all ten, though I have included only six in this chapter.

The second set of data consisted of writing I collected from my protégés. I invited twenty-one of my protégés to write about their experience of our relationship. This included colleagues, friends, students, and women who I sponsor in twelve-step recovery. The only instructions I offered came in the form of an e-mail in which I asked my protégés to write the answers to two questions:

1. What was your experience of our relationship? Tell your story.

2. What are you doing now? Describe.

I received eighteen stories that spanned the past two decades of my life. These relationships were both professional and personal. I analyzed all eighteen stories to develop this writing and have included only some of them in order to tell the story.

Once the data were collected, the analysis began. First, I wrote about the lessons learned from my mentors and the lessons I taught my protégés based on their written accounts. The themes and process emerged. It was uncanny (as it often is with qualitative work) to see the themes emerge and the consistency from one experience to the next that was embedded in the diversity of these experiences.

The mentoring process that emerged is the process that was so familiar to me, so much a part of my actions in these relationships, that I could not have explained it without the data. There is, in this mentoring experience, a combination of science, spirituality, and magic in the relationships that evolves. And it is, for me, the essence of my leadership work.

In the sections that follow, I will discuss the relationship between mentor and protégé. In the first section, I tell the story of my mentors and the lessons they taught me. Then I share the stories from my protégés, in their voices, and the lessons I taught them. The conclusion describes the process as it emerged from the voices of protégés who describe their experiences being mentored.

This is *our* story of the magic and science of mentoring.

My Mentors

In this section, I explore my relationships with some of the key mentors in my life, and describe the lessons they taught me. I have had mentors in multiple contexts—my parents as guides and mentors, teachers, principals, colleagues, and sponsors. I have had many mentors whose stories are not here but whose teachings are embedded in my practice and in this writing.

Miss Roseman, My First Grade Teacher

I held the necklace in my hand . . . not to my taste, but it did belong to Miss Roseman (there was no Ms. in 1957), my first grade teacher. My mother bought it at the estate sale that liquidated Miss Roseman's belongings after she passed away some time in the 1980s. My mother knew Miss Roseman was an important figure in my life, and as I contemplated writing about women in education as mentors and leaders, my experience with Miss Roseman stands out as one of my earliest mentors who changed my life.

I was afraid to leave home and attend first grade. My father had been ill, as had my brother, and as young as I was, I knew that it was risky to leave home for the day. My father carried me kicking and screaming into the classroom and Miss Roseman politely invited him to leave me and continue with his day. An old friend, Sue Johnson, still chuckles when she reminds me of the spectacle of my tantrum as my father left and my classmates looked on, puzzled.

In the privacy of a quiet hallway, Miss Roseman asked me if I liked dolls. I'm guessing I shrugged, but she quickly convinced me that a visit to her collection would be filled with wonder as the dolls were from places far away. Within days, in her lace-filled dining room, she served me tea and cookies, living only blocks from the neighborhood school and within walking distance of my house. She was a gracious hostess and very excited about the beautiful collection of international dolls. They were not like Barbie; each had characteristics of the faraway land from which it came. My fear of school and abandonment was replaced with confidence and excitement. Miss Roseman built trust, showed compassion, and opened up the world to me through her doll collection. I still have my own dolls from faraway lands, having begun the collection soon after that visit. This was the beginning of believing in mentoring and the power of relationships. She *was* the Good Mother, offering me sustenance and hope.

My passion for school and learning ignited. I felt safe in that classroom. I felt like I was somebody. I moved to a new school in third grade. I remember stopping by Miss Roseman's house to visit and her welcoming, caring hand was stretched out. Another peek at the dolls . . . another cup of tea.

Lessons Learned

Something very important happened when I tried to quit school in first grade. Miss Roseman understood the fear and welcomed me into her world of dolls, and, in that experience, the world beyond my hometown. This story is a powerful testament to the importance of relationships. She met me where I was, validated me, and empowered me to embrace school. I was no longer alone and grew much less fearful about school. I knew Miss Roseman would be there to greet me and teach me. And this doll collection became my passion. I hated baby dolls when I was young, but these international replicas of people in faraway lands provided fodder for dreams of travel and exploration that became, in my college years, a big part of my story. I am sure there is a connection. And I still have the dolls.

Carl, My Undergraduate Professor and Advisor

Carl is the smartest man I have ever known. He was my professor in a freshman course, Logic and Language, that was, to this day, the most challenging class of my education. We had seven philosophy books, the likes of Kant and Hume, along with an entire mathematical logic text. It was trial by fire for the freshmen at the University of Michigan Residential College. I learned to ask for help and met with Carl on several occasions to get a private tutoring session and see if I could make sense of the material. I passed the class, and most importantly, developed a mentoring relationship with Carl.

When it was time to declare a major, I was confused and undecided. I loved art, culture, people, psychology, and sociology. What could one do with this? I met with Carl and he sent me reading and researching possible majors. There was nothing on the UM list that allowed me to combine all these areas. And so, with Carl's guidance, I designed an independent major in art therapy. He saw no reason why I could not use what I learned in art and dance classes to work with children and solve problems. Art therapy had been pioneered at the U of M hospital, so he was familiar with the emerging field.

Carl opened doors for me. He taught me to navigate the vast and rich curricula of the university. He empowered me to take charge of my undergraduate education, and together, we mapped out a course of study that included studio art, dance, psychology, sociology, and practical experience using art and dance to engage children at Ypsilanti State Hospital. He *always* had time for me, and likewise, he posed critical questions to help me move along my path deliberately, courageously, always learning, always growing, and fueling it all with passion—passion for the subject, passion for the youth, passion for new ideas and learning. Passion became a significant factor in all that I do as a leader.

Lessons Learned

Carl demonstrated great passion for teaching and learning, putting emphasis on questions that were not only challenging but to which there was no one right answer. As my professor and later my advisor, Carl always made time for me. He demonstrated the power of developing individual relationships with one's students. He took me on. He became my advisor, my guide, my mentor. He handed me the responsibility for my studies and allowed me to design my own major. I developed a passion for self-driven learning. It was fueled by Carl's ability to help me identify and clarify my interests and by being my guide as I navigated the University of Michigan. Carl's deep questioning, careful listening, and strong belief in me and what I could do carried me through my undergraduate studies and on to the school of education to pursue my master's degree in teaching. I had no idea that this was my passion until I experimented within my independent major. I was on my way to becoming an educational leader.

Jane, My Boss's Boss

Some fifteen years into my teaching career, the new assistant superintendent for instruction, Dr. Jane Kuckel, summoned me to Central Office. By that time, I had wheedled my way into being the unofficial district grant writer, and she wanted to know more about the grants I wrote and managed, as well as my work at the alternative high school. At Tinkham Alternative High School, I was a teacher consultant with a caseload of thirty students and wore multiple district-level hats, including being the Safe and Drug Free Schools Coordinator and the district's front person for the Youth Mentorship Program (YMP) located at The Henry Ford, a magnificent museum and history attraction in Dearborn, Michigan.

Although I worked frequently with folks at Central Office in developing grants, Jane was different. She cared about me personally. I was awestruck by this caring and the time she took to find out about me—my work, interests, and abilities. It was as if she drilled into my core, and I left connected to her and her work with a mission to carry out for the students of the district. The mission was to continue to seek ways to connect the schools and community in the interest of those at-risk kids who usually fall through the cracks. I left that meeting with a desk at Central Office, a phone, and a secretary. Until then, I had done every aspect of the grant-writing process without support.

That meeting launched a five-year mentoring relationship in which I learned some of my most important skills and lessons in educational leadership. Jane led with great energy and passion. She understood people, cared for them in important ways, acknowledging their strengths and accomplishments, empowering them to lead, holding them accountable, and supporting them in times of personal challenge.

Jane, at my invitation, came out to The Henry Ford for a family night. We had twelve students in the program, all turning a corner in the direction of school success after having been a sneeze away from dropping out of high school. As she introduced herself to the students, Tim invited her to take a walk to the horse stables in Greenfield Village, his placement, to meet his charges and witness the work he now did with the animals. It was a rainy, muddy hike to the barn, but Jane was not fazed by these conditions. In spite of her high heels and business suit, she and I followed Tim all the way to the barn, where she petted the horses, complimented Tim on the grooming, talked with him about his future, and praised his ability and accomplishments. By the time we returned to the family night event, wet, covered in mud, with our hair pasted to our faces, she had a deeper understanding of the program that she then used to support it throughout her time in the district. Most importantly, she reinforced with Tim and all the students there that she knew they were making a difference, doing important work in the village and museum, and that she looked forward to watching them grow in their education. To this day, Tim, now thirty-one, asks about Jane and reminds me of that day. She was never above the students and their families. Their education and futures fueled her work, as they did mine. She understood her role as steward, not just in her work with me but in all she did.

At this time, the district had multiple community advisory groups. They were needed for federal, state, and foundation grants as well as to advise the board of education, curriculum committees, and superintendent relative to local issues. I asked Jane to consider collapsing them into one advisory group, the Health and Welfare Advisory. In this way, people could serve on one committee, meet monthly, and advise the district on any issues that would arise. She helped me develop the concept and insisted that no matter what, people had to leave the meeting with a common project, something to work on that they cared about and felt would make a difference in the community. We reflected on the group process and outcomes after every meeting. Within a few short months, the group took on literacy in NorWayne, the most transient and challenging neighborhood in the district. We created kindergarten backpacks and the Red Wagon, a program that resulted in distributing thousands of books each year to children in NorWayne, fueled by the committee and local volunteers pulling Red Flyer wagons in the neighborhood each week.

Each summer, Jane invited the department of instruction to her home on a local lake to celebrate the year. She cooked casseroles, barbecued, made desserts, and steered the boat for anyone wishing to have a ride. She laughed with us and made us feel like a family. We felt safe. We felt important.

Lessons Learned

That day I met Jane at her office, she saw something in me. She invited me into the world of educational leaders and handed me a membership card in the form of a desk, phone, and secretary. One of the great skills she taught me was to focus on actions. Whenever facilitating a group of advisors (which I did because it was a requirement of grants), help them identify something they really care about and want to contribute to . . . then help them develop a project. Help them find a reason to be together. There was power in this process. It is in the working together that the community is strengthened. Relationships can unfold. Conversations begin with the common cause but blossom into collaborations, shared vision, and shared resources. Action is key.

Jane was never above those around her. She was comfortable chatting with students and lunching with the custodians and secretaries, and she provided frequent opportunities to laugh and celebrate together. Humor was important. Humility was an essential ingredient. She did not wield power and she empowered others. And this is how she led. I wanted to lead by serving.

I followed Jane to an educational specialist program that she and two other female colleagues were facilitating for a local university. She taught one-third of the classes, and this gave me an opportunity to spend more time with her and to observe her in action as teacher/mentor to a group of about thirty educators from around the Detroit Metropolitan area. Her style was to give you something to read, watch, or observe and to ask questions and provide groups of people with whom you could discuss your experience. I loved this style of learning. I remembered what I learned when I had a chance to apply concepts to my work and to listen to others do the same. She was really great at getting her students to think and to apply learning to actions at work. Her teaching deeply affected the way

I taught from then on, using applied learning in every classroom in the hopes that student learning would be cemented.

Beverley, My Doctoral Program Professor

I called Beverley to ask permission to take her personnel class at EMU in the ed leadership department. Enrolled in an education specialist program at Wayne State University, I would be a guest student and therefore needed special permission. After a brief conversation, she agreed to allow me to join the class. She was, from day one, animated, sharp in her expressions, and very intelligent. I stayed late that first class to complete paperwork, and in our first conversation, it was clear that we had much in common both personally and professionally. We made connections immediately: both of us had been Safe and Drug Free Schools and Communities directors, both spoke French and had travelled extensively, both had dealt with alcoholism in our families and both of us were rather bold, assertive women. The course was not my area of expertise or interest, but I loved watching Bev teach, often taking on the role of personnel director, applicant, and principal in an interview, changing expressions, voice, and content as she switched from role to role. She had the attention of her students. She asked good questions, she questioned often. We pursued a relationship beyond the classroom. I knew she was someone I could learn from.

The conversation I remember early in our time together over lunch was the time she asked me why I did not pursue my doctoral degree in educational leadership. I was stunned. At age forty-seven, this had not crossed my mind. I remember her saying, "but we *need* you in our program and the schools *need* you." Within weeks, I was pursuing my application to the program. When I discovered the GRE was required, I scheduled a meeting with Bev. I had not taken a standardized exam since the SATs in high school. Mortified at the thought of taking the test, I tried to back out of the pursuit. Her comment, "After all you have experienced in your life, all the crazy junk you have dealt with, and you are afraid to take the test? You will do fine. Just take the test." She reframed my fear and gave me courage. I took the test. I got into the program. She encouraged me every step of the way. Bev retired before I finished, but she continued to support me with encouragement, meals, coffee, and frequent check-ins to see how I was progressing. She continues to do this.

Lessons Learned

Beverley opened an important door for me, that of the doctoral program. I was forty-seven years old when I took her class and applied for the doctoral program at Eastern Michigan University the following year, with her blessings and encouragement. That journey never crossed my mind until she invited me into her world. She retired soon after I entered the educational leadership program, but she remained a strong mentor and friend. She went on to become a superintendent and explore new vistas herself, and this she did in retirement. It is no surprise that in my "retirement" I am on to new experiences in education, directing out-of-school-time programs, forging community/university partnerships, and mentoring young educators.

Jim, My Dissertation Committee Chairman

Know whose shoulders you stand on.

—Jim

Jim is big in stature, but this is nothing compared to his ability to think in large pixilated pictures, where he connects each dot so that the images make sense. Speaking in metaphors, asking probing and difficult questions, and drawing pictures and diagrams require me to think, ponder, question.

Jim was my dissertation chair. I came to the doctoral program in educational leadership thinking that the experience would be like most graduate school experiences, plus the big research project that is the dissertation. I was wrong.

Aside from classes I took with Jane, graduate courses were not particularly motivating. I was often bored. I was looking for a challenge and a guide through the doctoral process who would challenge me. I needed a mentor with special skills and found that mentor in Jim.

In our early meetings, Jim repeatedly told me that my research, ultimately, would be a self-study. "You will do this research, not to change the nature of education as a result of your study, but to change you as a leader. You are really, in the end, the unit of study." I didn't believe that at first. I came to understand that everything I experience comes to me through my filter and is colored by every experience I have had. As a leader and a researcher, I had to learn how to tame this subjectivity, because it is *always* there.

Jim taught me that research must begin with the right questions. Developing questions became a challenge and required much practice. I often asked questions to which I knew the answers and questions that would have answers I could support through my work experiences. This was not wrong, but it was not going to lead to new understanding. As I worked on questions, Jim was (and still is) always available to help me work out the language and develop clarity and the courage to ask. A good question is often a difficult one.

During the dissertation process, Jim provided support, making it safe to talk about my findings and their implications. During the research process, I often found myself in a fog, and with Jim's support, I became comfortable with not knowing, with being lost in the data and my thoughts about them, not seeing clearly. My early response was that I just wasn't smart enough to see what was in front of me. As the process progressed and being in the fog became a more regular experience, I learned that this is part of deep thinking learning. It turns out that life is filled with foggy times, both personally and professionally. I learned to be in the moment . . . without answers. I learned to wait for the answers to emerge. I learned that there were times when no answer *was* the answer. I have passed this along to so many of my protégés, the skill to find one's self. This skill is foundational in leading in education. It is, like many important skills and actions, counterintuitive.

Lessons Learned

I learned the importance of asking the right questions. This is key to teaching and mentoring. I remember presenting a possible dissertation topic to Jim, a topic I knew better than anyone else. I wanted to write my dissertation about the Henry Ford Youth Mentorship Program (YMP). I had wanted to write about this successful intervention for years and to get the word out about mentoring. Jim suggested I study the system in which the YMP was born, the school district, the people, cultures, and history, how the politics play out. He explained that I would then be able to explain the YMP and *all* my programs. I would develop new skills and really, if one understands the system, one can explain the relationships, programs, and events within the system. This made sense. I embarked on a study of 177 years of history, culture, and school evolution in the Wayne Westland area. I studied the complexity of systems and interactions, the power of history and culture. By the end, I deepened my understanding of the system and could see more clearly. I became a pebble in the sands of time and my humility grew.

Jim repeatedly told me, "The answers to the problems of the community lie in the community." That meant I did not have the answers. My role was to question, to support, to help find resources, not to solve the problem. I did not have any control over the problem or the solution. This was at once freeing *and* terrifying. It required practice.

I had been given, by the school district's administrators and by the parents and children, a great deal of power. It had been my practice to give it right back. I never knew that is what I was doing. Jim helped me to understand this process.

Learning to identify assumptions—my own, those of my colleagues, and those that lie within systems, communities, and cultures—is an important skill Jim taught me. I came to this work with a full set of my own assumptions. Key to being good at leading was being good at recognizing my assumptions and those of others. This process is filled with conflict. Having been a conflict avoider—fearful of it my entire life—I was given the gift of understanding that conflict is a motivator, a driver, a big part of history, of life. Jim often took me from fear to understanding. He still provides that kind of support. It is powerful. It creates safety for me to take risks in challenging my own assumptions as well as those of others.

My Protégés

The stories that follow were written by my protégés. I asked them to write about their experience of the relationship we have and what they are doing now. Each story is followed by a brief analysis of the lessons taught.

Vera

Lynn's mentorship is based on attraction rather than promotion. She mentors younger and older women by example and through stories of her own life's journey. Throughout the most difficult decisions in my life, she has guided me through my own previous experience and has allowed me the dignity to make my own decisions—whether they were right or wrong. The guidance has been always to think about the greater good—to act honorably and with integrity—to take the harder path. When mentoring others, lift my mentees as I climb and *never* climb over them. Lynn taught me that boundaries with those we love can be flexible and those who we have difficult interactions with can be respectful but firm.

These words of wisdom have allowed me to flourish in my career as the director of thoracic oncology in a tertiary medical center. Even when I have made mistakes, she has allowed me to see the humor in them, and *never* once criticized my own personal educational/learning pathway. Lynn's mentorship has been in an arena of exercising her own well-marked personal boundaries that in turn have taught me to do the same.

Lessons Taught
With Vera, I have shared my own experiences on so many occasions, especially in times when she was greatly challenged. Ours is a relationship built on a spiritual foundation of trusting that there is something bigger than us out there. This higher power allows us to take responsibility for our choices and actions and know that we are not in control of outcomes, especially for others (colleagues, children, spouses, friends, etc.). She makes commitments and checks in with me to be accountable. Setting clear boundaries has been a major part of our discussions throughout the years. Humor has been important as well as taking personal inventories.

Suzie

I met Lynn nine years ago. I was twenty-two and fresh out of college. I was hired as the program facilitator for a program called the Youth Mentorship Program that Lynn started eleven years earlier. I was excited and had no idea what was in store for me. What I would soon find out is that I was embarking on an amazing adventure, which wouldn't have been possible if it wasn't for Lynn. Not just because she hired me (which she did), but because she believed in me—even when I was a complete mess (which I often was).

Lynn has the perfect balance of teaching by example and letting you figure it out through practice. I love this about her. She would coach me when it was appropriate and often apparent that I was lacking confidence and skills, but she would let me run with ideas that others laughed at. She always made a point to highlight my assets and strengths while giving me ideas to improve my deficits.

She let me test new ideas in a safe/low-risk environment and processed with me after. I have never learned so much. She taught me so many valuable lessons. I have "Lynnisms" running through my head daily. They often get me through tough situations.

Having Lynn as a mentor has been so impactful. I understand education and mentoring from a local and state perspective. I have been exposed to professional opportunities (trainings, conference workshop presenter, and college guest lecturer, to name a few) because of Lynn's gift of letting others shine and helping people see their potential.

I love the days that I spent watching Lynn work. She works tirelessly to improve the lives of kids and families. She is a champion, an advocate, and has a gift of navigating systems and finding a way to meet people where they are. She knows that the key to everything is to start on a community level and build up. She has a deep respect for all people and fights for basic and inherent rights of children to have access to quality programming and experiences. She works tirelessly to provide resources that create environments where people thrive. She knows that if you provide people with the tools for success, they'll be successful. Because of her guidance, I've seen incredible things grow in communities that had been written off.

I am so fortunate to have worked with Lynn at such a critical time in my career. It is in large part due to her example and instruction that I feel confident building community and continuing in this field. She is an amazing boss, teacher, and friend.

On a personal note, Lynn came into my life just a few years after my mother lost her battle with cancer. We joke that I was her telephone stalker and quasidaughter (because I was), but the truth is, I am so unbelievably lucky to have Lynn in my life. She never made me feel bad or uncomfortable for broaching subjects that were far from professional. She always listened, gave advice, and made me feel supported and loved. She helped to fill some of the big gaps that were left in the aftermath of my loss. She didn't have to. It's just who she is.

Lessons Taught

I believed in Suzie. I still believe in Suzie. When I met her I saw the light within. I knew she had great potential locked inside and that it is possible to unleash that power and set her on a path to her own greatness; however, she would define it. I let Suzie know she had the potential to learn and grow and become the person she wanted to be. I worked with her to identify her strengths and provided safety so she could look at areas of weakness. I often asked what it was she wanted to learn, improve, change. I gave her space to do that. I encouraged her to take risks and use mistakes as great teachers. I did not solve Susie's problems as they emerged (both personal and professional). I listened, asked questions, and encouraged her to seek solutions. Then I supported her efforts with opportunities to reflect and plan.

I invited Susie to follow me around for a few months. I took her to meetings and then we talked (usually over a soda or meal) and worked to find meaning in these experiences. I am committed to walk the talk. I shared my passion for working with at-risk youth and my commitment to providing opportunities for them, opening doors wherever possible. I demonstrated acceptance, caring, and love for our students. I was not from the community in which we worked and had learned to meet folks in their territory and accept them where they were. I allowed my students to teach me about their culture, and Suzie would learn about it the same way. We are all students.

With Suzie, my role became, at times, that of a nurturing mother. She had lost her mom *and* she was adopted. She was seeking parental support and was very direct with me about it. I told her she could be my adopted kid whenever she needed it. This opened the door for her to ask for help as needed. Over time this included meeting her fiancé, discussing living arrangements, how to manage debt, and all kinds of life skills and personal issues. So many mentors *and* my parents had taught me what I know. I was willing to pass it on.

Stacy

The thing of it is, I never knew I needed a mentor. I didn't know I was supposed to have one . . . or want one. No one told me. Where do you pick up one of those?

I had just finished a very expensive master's degree and I was ready to take on the world. I had my diploma. I just needed a wall to hang it on. But there wasn't one available. No one had taught me what to *do* with that diploma. No one had showed me how to use it. No one had translated theory and concept into practice. Now what?

Then one night in August of 1995, I found myself at one of Lynn Malinoff's patchwork quilt dinners. They were quite a creative collection, you never knew who would be there, but there was always someone who was in some kind of "recovery." I suppose that I felt oddly comforted by the fact that Lynn always seemed to be surrounded by people who were somewhat "flawed." I grew to love those dinners over the years, but on this night, I had come along as a friend of a friend, not even a first-tier guest.

Lynn greeted me from across the table, "So Stace, you got a job yet?" She wasn't much for pleasantries and she was about as subtle as a sledge-hammer. This is gonna be fun. I'm glad I came. "Um . . . nope."

"Huhm." *I later learned to be cautious of that sparkle in her eye, but on this night, I was without insight.* "You should come work for me at the museum."

"Doing what? I could pretty much do anything except work with teen-agers." *I was vaguely aware of what Lynn did for a living.* "I can't stand teenagers."

"Well, we can work something out." The first of many "Lynn phrases." I would never say Lynn taught in "bumper stickers" because she was certainly not a cliché. But. She had learned to boil down her wisdom over the years to succinct phrases—phrases she almost left you to figure out on your own if the meaning wasn't readily apparent. This first phrase, that was Lynn-speak for *I've just made a decision and I'll let you in on it later when it's too late for you to back out.*

I realized years later that was my moment, a true pivot point: a dinner that would steer the rest of my life . . . a *relationship* that would end up molding my thinking, shaping my ideas about myself, influencing my politics, building my career. This relationship would bring about a maturity and sense of self in me that had somehow gotten lost on my journey through adulthood. I finally arrived in my late twenties, better tardy than never showing up at all. It is my relationship with Lynn that I credit for every good relationship that was to follow in my life.

I was never really sure why she went out on that particular limb that night. Because I had zero experience in her field; it was as much a com-mitment for her as it was for me. Why did she pick me? Was she at the bottom of her barrel too? She didn't really know me that well. I'd always assumed it was due to her fondness for my friend, but if I've learned one thing about Lynn, it's this: Lynn doesn't gamble. She must have seen something worth the risk in me. To this day, I'm not really certain what it was, but somehow, I don't care.

This is the first true characteristic of a strong mentor—*know where to invest your energies.* You can't really be a good mentor without knowing what one is, and we've idealized and socialized this word to death. It now *buzzzzzzzzes* around with all the rest of the edu-speak in Washington like a fly caught in a pair of industrial mini blinds banging its body repeatedly against the glass.

If you've experienced this relationship, however, you know. It is clear. A mentor is a bridge, a link between what you know and what you *think* you know but don't. They're a translator, a tour guide, a seeing eye dog. They watch the road ahead and send back better directions than the map you arrived with. They're Sacajawea and you're the know-it-all explorer. They speak the language, know the customs, and know how to barter. And what's most important? They're willing to show *you* how to do all that.

But it's not a gift. It's a partnership. They expect something in return. They expect you to try, move outside your comfort zone, sometimes *stay* outside your comfort zone. They expect you to try, oh and they expect you to try. They see you as having value. Different is unique, and they are interested in anything that makes them smarter. Different makes you wise. This arrangement isn't meaningful, however, unless you want it to be, or, in my case, need it to be.

On day one of my insane job with Lynn I was treading water . . . on another planet. I was definitely working with teenagers, but not ordinary teenagers. These people were the pinnacle of pain in the ass. These were the young people who had already been thrown away. They'd been used up already, by everyone who should have taken care of them, and tossed out; Lynn Malinoff, for some reason that I didn't readily understand, was there with a catcher's mitt.

You see, I grew up in June and Ward's house. I had two married parents who didn't do drugs, had stable jobs, and always put healthy food on the table. We weren't wealthy, but we had enough for a comfortable middle class life and often some extras like vacations or singing lessons. I *liked* school and always respected my elders.

"What choo say your name is?"

"Stacy, and yours?"

"My what? Hah. You don't need to know." This oddly tough-looking girl with freckles was looking me up and down and rolling her eyes at my appearance to her friends. I was, I'll be honest, afraid of her.

"Daaaamn Stacy. Them shoes is ugly." She cackled and walked off down the hall.

Oh god, someone please help me. *Lynn would be proud that I was attempting to access a higher power on day one.*

Every kid in that program pushed my buttons every day. Lynn once told me in her not-so-gentle but direct way, "You need to put them (your buttons) away, stop wearing them out there where they can get to them all." *It took me the better part of a year to learn this skill.*

I ran a *mentoring* program for "at-risk youth." I connected my young people with older, more educated, more experienced, patient, and kind teachers in the hopes that they would see a better life ahead and have a personal bridge to it. And it worked. It worked a lot. It would be working so well, and I'd be floating with happiness, gloating in my Angelina Jolie fog over all the *children I'd saved,* and then they'd get arrested for breaking into trailers and stealing, paging me from Wayne County jail at two in the morning.

"Yee-uh. Um . . . can you bail me out?"

And I did. I made a lot of poor decisions in that first year. Once I'd accepted that this was my job, I loved them. The emotional momma took over, and so the first lesson I had to learn was to have boundaries. I didn't learn this one right away. Lynn knew that on some level, I just couldn't help myself. She made me go to twelve-step meetings. I remember being so angry. "Why? Why would they do this? Everything was going so well; they're getting off probation, getting good grades in school, showing up every day, *finally* on the right track. This makes no sense to me."

It was called *sabotaging your success.* It is my second "Lynn phrase," and it was explained to me this way. "Failure is familiar to someone who's never experienced success. Success is scary. Success is uncertain. Success feels foreign. Success brings pressure and expectation, but failure, failure is familiar. And familiarity is comfort."

I thought that was the dumbest thing I'd ever heard. My righteous, white, middle-class indignation could not wrap its head around such a ridiculous concept. Why would *anyone* find failure comforting? Well, it's hard to disappoint someone who expects nothing from you, or who disappoints you. I saw student after student sabotage their success over the years: do something stupid that derailed them every time. That continuously occurring phenomenon taught me to re-evaluate my understanding of the term *success*, for them and for me.

Lynn lesson number three. "You just never know the impact you might have. You do not know what it will be or when it will manifest, but it will." She would always follow this particular sage wisdom with colorful stories of kids I didn't know, she always thought I did, and where they were now and what they were doing. *A good mentor should be a good storyteller because let's face it, sometimes they have to convince you that what they have to offer is something worth having.*

She would follow up this particular nugget of wisdom with another of my favorites, Lynn lesson number four: "You gotta love 'em where they are." This one required lots of research on my part. I had to "let go" of my reality a lot and allow myself to truly see the world they lived in; otherwise, I would always be an outsider, someone who just didn't understand and I needed to. I needed to understand why Tim would buy a $200 leather jacket when his family had been without electricity for two weeks or why Sorinthea's mother would dump all of her things out of a garbage bag into the lobby screaming, "Here. If you love her so much, *you* keep her." I had to be able to move past the feelings of *who would do that to their child?* Because pity is not a useful emotion. I learned to see each young person separately. I learned to measure them against their own yardstick instead of some ambiguous national silhouette for success. With this lesson, I learned perseverance, and with that came great rewards. I hung in there even when they didn't want me to.

"Uh. Stacy. Why do you keep hugging me? I hate you."

"I know, but I love you Tonya."

"I *seriously* hate you. I tell you that every day. Why don't you get it?"

"I know, but I love you, and I'm gonna tell *you* that every day." She cried the hardest the day I left.

Our young people *did* succeed, and I did too. Like anything, there's a range. Scott dropped out of school and disappeared for a while, but I visited the museum before I left Michigan. I'm walking through the village when I hear "Stacy," and up pulls Scott driving a carriage. He drives my family and me back to the carriage house and he runs inside to come out with a framed document—his GED. He is still living in Westland, still working at the museum. But he's sober. He has a job where he feels appreciated and a part of something; his coworkers helped him study for that test. He is happy and I cried like a baby all the way home, that image of those twinkling eyes burned into my head.

Last month our college hosted an all-faculty forum to discuss "student success," which our state's legislature is defining narrowly. "Success" is: the percentage of students who earn an A, B, or C in a class. Period. And our faculty were up in arms. I've become close to our vice president since I've been here, and she was in my office lamenting how to handle the bomb she felt was coming down the road. "Put a human face on it. Let the faculty know that although that definition of success is certainly out there, it's not the *only* definition that we value. Let a student speak [I learned that from Lynn]. And I have one in mind."

So she took a gamble on my idea and one of my students, Jacob, spoke to the entire college's faculty in a crowded auditorium. This young African American man told the story of the semester he spent in my class—the semester his only parent, his mother, was extremely ill with failing heart disease. He spoke of how he would take the bus to the hospital every day from school and do his homework by her bed until she fell asleep, then return to school the next day and do it all over again. He talked about losing their insurance, her death, being kicked out of their home, and his last straw: a tuition due notice that brought him to my office, a place he considered a refuge. This young man was an honors student, always articulate and composed. He handed me the bill and quietly asked if I had any ideas about where he might get some help. He sat quietly while I started with my phone calls. I was polite but firm not accepting "no" from anyone (another skill I learned from Lynn).

Within fifteen minutes that same vice president had promised the tuition would be taken care of. Great. He lingered. I said, "Can I help with anything else?" He hesitated. "No, it's just been a bad day." The tears finally started to fall. "This is the kinda thing I woulda talked to my mom about." And then I sat quietly for the next couple of hours and just listened and handed off tissues. He eventually told my colleagues about that afternoon, the next day when the English faculty member moved his things into storage in her garage, and the history teacher who connected him with a mentor at the hospital. I showed them pictures of all the people who, behind the scenes, had worked together to make sure *this* young man would get through this and then he thanked each and every one of them with the most poignant sincerity I have ever heard. I told them where he was, a successful graduate of our CNA program, and entering our nursing program, a 4.0 student again, standing on his own two feet. "So I understand that the legislature wants you to value those numbers: 75 percent, and you should, but you should also value the number 4, which is my grade point average thanks to professors Omar and Florez, the number 750, which was the number that the college 'gifted' to me in the spring of 2009, and the number 2012, which is the year I will graduate thanks to. . . . " And we got the whole list. There was not a dry eye in that room that day and no one was up in arms or even in the mood to argue about numbers anymore.

"No one can say it better than the people you are trying to serve," Lynn lesson number five. I will admit, I "see" those young people in my classrooms more clearly and quickly than most thanks to my years with Lynn. I know what to do with them. I know how to reach them and I believe they deserve my help. But I learn from them too.

Lessons Taught

Mentor, teacher, trail guide, Stacy uses many labels for this work. When I hired her, I saw great potential. She had amazing skills and no direction. Stacy was able to revise, rework, create herself. She was given an opportunity to construct meaning, a desire that is innate in people. With each phase of Stacy's growth and development as the director of the Youth Mentorship Program, she gathered more information, reflected on her experiences, and constructed new meaning. This opened up new ways of thinking and acting. It was all built on her thirst to learn and to teach.

Stacy was a performer, a forensics champion in college. She was not afraid to speak out, but she was searching for meaning, for a cause, for something to speak out about. And she found it in the youth at the YMP. They terrified her, endeared her, and ultimately loved her as she loved them. It was a strange and challenging dance at first that evolved into a well-developed community with a highway to new possibilities for Stacy and the youth she served.

In relationships, developing boundaries provides great safety, clarity, and opportunity. By knowing where you begin and end, you can learn to stay in your own hula-hoop. It isn't that you ignore the situation of your protégé. You pay attention. But you give them the dignity of owning their own problems and challenges. You provide safety so they can try things out, risk failure (and benefit from the lessons that follow). You help your protégé set goals and then provide a system of accountability. You do this without controlling for outcomes. You just ask them to check in periodically. Ask how it is going. Ask if they are pleased with the direction in which they are headed.

Stacy picked up on the importance of voice. I gave her a voice by listening and allowing her to use her voice in her work. She gave the youth voice. She gave them back their power as I had done with her. She continues to do this as a community college professor.

Betsy

When I first met Lynn, I was in the bind I often found myself in—all the interesting work I did was unpaid, and all the paid work was uninteresting. The previous August, I had graduated from U of M with a master's degree, a teaching certificate in English, and the sneaking suspicion that while I cared deeply about education and young people, I didn't care much about teaching English. This seemed to be a problem. In the meantime, I had cobbled together a series of paying jobs—as a sub in Ann Arbor, as a writing tutor for U of M athletes, as a babysitter—and a series of unpaid jobs—creating online forums for high school and middle school students to write poetry, to follow an Arctic expedition, and helping my former professor to conceptualize an online dictionary of education. It was thrown together and it was getting more desperate—I had regular meals of brown rice and honey for breakfast and brown rice and spinach for dinner, and my fellow graduates were having similar struggles finding work.

And then, my professor called to say that this woman named Lynn would be calling about a job and that although he did not know much about it, I should take it because she seemed like someone I would like working with. Within minutes Lynn called, we talked on the phone, and the next day she picked me up and on the drive to Westland offered me the job. I wondered how she could have possibly offered me something so suddenly. A few things were clear: Lynn was a woman of action, she expected big things, and she expected me to have questions.

In time, I realized that I had lucked into the perfect teaching job for me— working with nontraditional students in an intensive and nontraditional way where I got to focus on them and their learning rather than on me and what I was required to teach them. At that time, at that school, the motto was, do what's best for the student. Here was my first lesson from Lynn—"It's easier to beg forgiveness than to ask permission." Time and again, we did what was right and hoped that it worked. But that's not exactly the lesson that I was learning—the real lesson was "if you are doing work that matters, failure is expected." I saw Lynn make mistakes, admit them, learn from them, and try again. For me, this was the most freeing thing I could learn as a new teacher—not only is it ok to make mistakes, but it is required. I couldn't possibly be pushing the edge enough if I wasn't messing up and in fact, if I wasn't regularly messing up.

I messed up often, regularly and with great gusto. I didn't confront the student who showed me his white power tattoos, I talked to them about religion and abortion in a conservative community—like all new teachers, I was negotiating the balance between mentor, teacher, supervisor, and friend, but without the classroom structure, that line was even harder to define. Lynn told me what she would do, how I could clean up my mess, and sent me on my way. But more often, Lynn led by example. She took me along to meetings I didn't need to be in, trainings that weren't directly relevant, events at the school. Through all of that, I learned how she worked and how I should work. I learned how to resolve conflicts between students, how to lead support groups, how to talk about difficult topics, and how to work with administration and staff.

I was lucky enough to live around the corner from Lynn, so from the start, there were dinners and lunches and walks in the park together. For me, it just accelerated how quickly I grew to trust and respect her. From the beginning she made it clear that I could talk to her about any and all mistakes and questions that I had. I did not have to cover anything up or make it sound better. I could bring my confusion and it did not change her belief in me.

The biggest lesson I carry, though, is the one Lynn was clearest about—"it's about the relationship." Relationships grease the wheels of systems—but not in a corrupt, favor-swapping way—in an authentic, "I believe in you" way.

Much like my first job with Lynn, I have only worked in nontraditional settings, teaching nontraditional classes with the aim of permanently changing the system. Right now, I supervise twenty teachers across twenty middle and high schools and have the opportunity to play the same role that you played for me. When I left the classroom, I wondered if I would get the same level of satisfaction from adults. In Peer Resources, we tend to attract young teachers or teachers who are dissatisfied with traditional teaching, and I have the opportunity to help them figure everything out. At this point, I am supervising one of my former students who is a current teacher. It is incredibly moving to work with him as a colleague and a new teacher and to support him as he makes all his mistakes and to celebrate all his successes. In mentoring new teachers, I am consistently reminded of what I learned from you and I often think about how I can foster that in my relationship with teachers.

Lessons Taught

In Betsy's telling, she identifies many of the consistent lessons I learned from my mentors and shared with my protégés. Take risks, ask for forgiveness, not permission, and embrace the journey, including the mistakes. Create the safety to take risks. Pushing my protégés is about pushing the edge, about finding freedom in thought and action because the work is founded in a higher order. The relationships, the people, who they are, their cultures and communities, in other words, the context, are to be respected. Always act with honor and integrity. *Walk the talk*. Find your passion and follow it.

There is often an element of being a career counselor. I don't give my protégés tests to identify a career path. I do ask them about their unique abilities and what they care about. I always tell them they might as well find something they love doing *and* get paid for it. We all spend a significant chunk of our lives in the workplace; why not be somewhere that taps your passion and your skill?

Jason

My relationship with Lynn is a kind, loving, and constantly growing relationship. It started in 1994 when I was placed in alternative education after being expelled from junior high school. At this time I was at risk, a confused teenager who thought the world was against him, who had no control over anything. I came from a low-income family that constantly fought alcoholism and drug abuse.

Lynn found me in the hallways of school and always had time to listen no matter what my frustrations were and how mixed up I was in the head. She always had another side of the situation to present to me. We had group meetings where I learned conflict resolution, anger management, and a lot about myself through discussion. By experiencing this, it has helped me learn about myself and has helped me keep control of situations when normally I would explode and get myself into trouble or potentially hurt others.

As I spent the remainder of my junior and senior high school years working with Lynn, my outlook on life changed drastically. I wasn't so hard on myself anymore or full of anger. I was finally in control of my life, and the decisions I made were mine and had consequences. I learned to think things through so when my choice was made I knew I analyzed all possibilities to rule out error on my part and make the best judgments.

I went from being a failing student to actually applying myself and getting a 3.0 GPA for the remainder of my time at school. I was returned to the regular high school and was able to play sports and associate with the population of kids that someone my age should be with. I took pride in my work. I felt normal. I was a kid again, not someone with a chip on his shoulder and the whole world against him.

After high school, I completed a two-year vocational school for aviation maintenance and joined the Air Force. I have been serving for almost nine years now. I am a licensed technician with an associate's degree, and I am almost finished with my bachelor's degree in project management. The skills that I have learned from the relationship with Lynn I use every day and they have been the key to my success.

I love the fact that I can call Lynn from Iraq or Korea, and she is always there to dust me off and point me in the right direction. My parents have been dead for the last eight years, and to have someone recognize and praise me for my accomplishments makes everything that I have ever done worth it. The thing about being a great mentor is to never judge, to listen and also to be able to give constructive criticism and to be patient. These were the things that I was missing in my home life, and I have received through my relationship with Lynn. I am proud to say that I am one of Lynn's hundreds of children and I have brothers and sisters out there that she has dedicated her time and compassion to as well.

Lessons Taught

Jason, a student at my alternative high school, came to the program all puffed out, macho, and ready for a fight. He was, really, a gentle loving guy. I saw the light inside. His hard crust was not a deterrent, but it was a challenge to crack and I accepted the challenge with gusto. Listening was key to building trust. Reframing his thoughts and ideas was a major strategy. Helping Jason accept himself and giving him the power to take control of his life paved the way for his very amazing development professionally and personally. I know that for Jason, and for all the folks I've worked with, I left the door open for a continuing relationship. When his brother was dying of cancer during his senior year, he came back for support, the same when his mother died and his father reappeared. He has sought parenting, guidance, counseling, and feedback. He is a seeker. He has taught me about the culture of the Westland community, the military service, and the world of flight. He has made himself available to write letters of support for the Youth Mentorship Program, the alternative school, and projects like these. Jason has continued to pass it on to others in his work in the U.S. Air Force, teaching others, and in his neighborhood with boys whose dads are overseas.

Fifteen years have passed since I met Jason, and our relationship has continued to grow. We experience mutual admiration. Sometimes teacher, sometimes parent, sometimes student; this is a relationship I cherish.

Katie

Sixteen years ago, and in my ninth grade of education, it seemed as if all hope and/or possibility of attaining any potential had been given up on; the teachers/school officials up to that point never seemed to believe as if there was any hope for me to begin with, and I finally started to agree with them. My hope and faith in my own potential and ability were restored when I met Lynn. Lynn is the first person in my life who demanded excellence from me. Lynn refused to accept the mediocrity that others praised me for, insisting that I perform at a higher standard than "good enough"; sixteen years later, she continues to motivate and encourage me.

I am a fighter, I am a survivor, and I have always valued "doing the right thing." I root for, and ferociously defend, the underdog, at times to my own disadvantage. I believe in the nobility of the "righteous cause" and likewise, tend to hide behind it, in order to avoid my own self-evaluation; I learned to do this at a very young age. I will reach the heights of my potential, and a large part of the credit for my ability to even imagine the reality of this goal belongs to Lynn. She taught me to exceed expectations, especially my own.

Lessons Taught

In Katie's case, I saw immediately that she was underachieving in every aspect of her life (except, maybe, taking care of her mother). She had been tossed by the system. She was smart and lazy. She had potential and someone or multiple people had convinced her that she was incapable of success in school. She is ADHD and has a learning disability (writing . . . she asked a friend to write this with her), and she was truant. The folks in the schools gave up on her. I remember calling her on mornings when she did not show up and with Stacy, we would sing show tunes and threaten to do it every time she did not show up. One day she showed up on time. We grabbed the Polaroid, snapped a photo (under the clock), put it on the front office door for all to see. We celebrated a small step in Katie's taking charge of her life. We raised the bar, and raised it and raised it and raised it.

Carolyn

I met Lynn through an e-mail. Lynn came across a newspaper story about my journey through college and the various obstacles I faced along the way and my career goals. Growing up, my family experienced poverty and homelessness—while attending college, this was still the case. A writer from the Associated Press decided to write a story about me, a story that one of Lynn's colleagues suggested she read. After reading a brief synopsis of the article, Lynn invited me out for coffee. We chatted about my background, how she became an educator, and her mission behind after school programs. In our meeting she said that I reminded her of former students who defied the odds of success given adverse circumstances. At the end of our conversation, Lynn asked me to speak to her class about the importance of mentorship in education. I agreed, and afterwards she offered me a part-time position with her program

Bright Futures. I initially worked as a student tutor, but over time, Lynn gave me more responsibility and allowed me to develop a parent engagement initiative for her after-school program.

Regarding my professional development, I have appreciated Lynn's willingness to allow me to take the reins on projects and initiatives. Over the past two years, she has vested a lot of discretion to me in working with her programs and taught me a lot about decision making. I've learned the importance of trial and error. Lynn has shown me that developing programs is an iterative process; perfection doesn't happen overnight, nor is always feasible on the first try. It is important to understand that processes, experiences, mistakes, and failures create great formative opportunities. I've learned to lighten up and to apply some wisdom and practical know-how to my ideas and ambitions.

Lynn's mentorship has also challenged me to mature in my professional relationships with others. Specifically, she's taught me how to work with people to accomplish goals. I've learned how to practically gauge others' needs and working styles and to develop working relationships accordingly. As a result, I've become a more effective leader and communicator.

Personally, I have really valued the conversations I've had with Lynn. She's been exceptionally transparent and honest about her own personal hurdles and offered advice on working through difficulties. She offers a refreshing bigger-picture perspective to even the most minute details of life. For instance, over Starbucks one evening, I expressed my frustrations with feeling strapped for cash. I confessed to her that I really wanted more financial wiggle room to do some special things for myself, like a manicure or new earrings. She suggested I play a little trick on myself by setting aside small amounts of money, one to five dollars from time to time, into a "splurge" account. Though seemingly unimportant, this small insight taught me the principal of delayed gratification. I haven't had many mentors over the course of my life who have been willing to give such candid yet simple advice.

I am currently a third-year doctoral student in a combined Ph.D. program in political science and public policy at the University of Michigan. I am currently developing prospective dissertation topics and intend to defend my prospectus by May 2011. I plan to have completed my degree by fall 2012.

Lessons Taught

My friend Cindy sent me a ten-line news clipping with Carolyn's story of growing up in poverty and overcoming odds to graduate from college with honors and attend U of M on a full ride in a Ph.D. program. Cindy had a sticky note attached that said, "She sounds like one of yours." So, I looked her up since I was teaching at U of M at the time. She had a few teachers who helped her see the possibilities in life if she took her studies seriously. She knew a lot about mentors and the role they played, but she did not have any mentors here. I offered to meet with her until we could figure out what it all meant, but in the meantime, invited her to speak to my undergraduate students and tell her story of mentors and mentoring, since my undergrads were mentoring K–12 students in low-income schools.

Ours is a newer relationship, but as Carolyn approaches her dissertation work, we have much to talk about. This is an area in which I have experience. And it is new territory for her. We also share an interest in families in poverty and seeking ways to provide hope and new experiences for them as well as seeking resources to help them take care of the basics. She is now working with me on developing the family component of our out-of-school-time programs. I hired her. We are talking about money management and basic skills, as she missed some of that growing up. We are talking about families we serve and what they need. We discuss culture and the challenges that I, and some of my Caucasian staff, have in working in communities where the predominance is people of color. We talk about faith-based communities, spirituality, hopelessness, and hope. We talk about academia and Carolyn's future. Ours is a relatively new relationship that is filled with energy and possibility.

Amber

I had Lynn as a professor for Education 360. Education 360 enabled student athletes to tutor and work as a mentor with elementary, middle school, and high school students in the Detroit metropolitan area. I enrolled in Education 360 because I thought it would be cool to work with young students. I usually worked with the less motivated/troubled students. Fortunately, my personal experiences enabled me to connect with the students and function as a role model. I do regret not staying in touch with the students, but I began to battle more with issues of my own.

After education 360, I would run into Lynn at the Athletic Academic Center every once in a while. And during these times we would speak cordially. However, we did not have our first real heart to heart until five months after the course. I was applying for a scholarship and I asked Lynn if she would write me a letter of recommendation. Since we had never had a conversation, and I did not feel that she knew me well enough, I thought she would refuse. Fortunately, she agreed. She requested that I submit to her a personal statement.

After reading my personal statement, Lynn seemed to really open up. She may have always been open, so the truth may be that I began to open up to her. I am a very private person, and I am hesitant to share my life story because I do not want to be judged by it. My life has not been the worst, being that I have a father who is dedicated to my well-being and I have family and friends who have protected and provided for me. However, there are some things that I am confused about, and that make me feel less worthy when I am around those who seem, in my eyes, to be more privileged and more affluent. Therefore, when I shared a small smidge of my personal story, I felt like a wall had been lifted from between Lynn and me. The impression I got from Lynn in Education 360/362 was that she was brilliant, scholarly, and went straight by the books. I would never have thought that I would be able to share any of my background with her, because I thought that she was the very type of person who would judge, or try to classify me based on my life experiences. But I could not have been further from the truth.

Lynn is now a very influential part of my life. She is a great mentor, and she helps me with understanding and working through my faulty thoughts and misconceptions about people and life in general. Lynn is very intelligent; however, I really admire her drive to continue learning. She is well versed and knowledgeable about many areas. But she does not portray that she knows more than what she really knows. I really appreciate this attribute of hers, because as a result, I feel that we have a mutual learning/growing relationship. I learn a lot more from her than she learns from me, but it feels good to know that I am able to educate when I share my problems, rather than just whining and complaining.

I feel very fortunate to have Lynn as a mentor, and I appreciate all of her efforts and cherish our mentor/mentee relationship.

I will be starting my second year at the University of Michigan Law School this upcoming fall, 2010, and I am a tutor/mentor for undergrad students at the University of Michigan. I am interested in working with a mentoring program for young high school students, educating them on how to prepare, apply, and get funding for college.

Lessons Taught

From our first encounter, I really admired Amber. When a door opened to a mentoring relationship, I opened it wide and invited her in. She was extremely motivated, in fact driven. She was going to go to law school. She was accepted at the University of Michigan to one of the most prestigious programs in the country. What an amazing woman.

Amber is very self-conscious. Early in our meetings, she was guarded. Then something changed. We shared our stories. I told her I have more questions than answers in my life. I told her I would be her support, but only if she wanted that, and that she always had a choice about it.

Transitioning from her urban schooling to the University of Michigan and then to U of M Law School, the cultural divide was enormous. After a semester in law school, we met for lunch. She confided in me that her most fearful experiences during the first semester of law school were speaking in class. She was concerned that she would botch the grammar, having grown up with Ebonics. When called on in class, she was afraid . . . and in law school, being called on is part of the experience of learning to speak as a lawyer. We meet on campus for lunch and talk about school, scholarships, work, her fears, her dreams, her path.

Amber has a scholarship from a firm owned by some Jewish lawyers in Detroit. She worked there this summer and we have had many conversations about that experience. There were other law students, Jews (like myself), who the partners took to lunch. They did not take her. She did not ask. We talked about all the black kids sitting together in the cafeteria and why people sort themselves out. We talked about implications in the world of law and lawyers.

Since this project began, Amber got a job with one of my teammates from my 1980s softball team, The Great Pretenders. All I did was introduce them. This is often an outcome. I provide resources and a network and support to my protégé to reach out to the opportunities that are opened through relationships.

In her writing about us, she writes about my willingness to be open and humble. She, too, is willing. She also talks about the mutuality of our relationship. We are both teachers to one another. It is growing. It is powerful. She picked me, really. She asked for help. In the helping, I decided to offer to be an ongoing support. And so it unfolds.

The Mentoring Process Explained

> The wise leader stays in the background and facilitates other people's process.
>
> —Heider, 1985, p. 131

What is leadership? It is *not* followership. It involves identifying what one stands for (personally, as a team or school staff, as a department) and leading self and others to take action. These powerful relationships, mentoring and being mentored, provide practice in skills that are essential to leadership. These are skills in developing relationships, empowering others, guiding, supporting, and reflecting together. While the process is not altogether linear, there is a logical order to it. The steps that follow reflect the experiences of mentor and protégé alike. They are the result of the analysis of my narrative regarding lessons learned and the narrative provided by my protégés.

The Instrument of Self

I have been searching for the key: How do I explain this magical process of mentoring and the blossoming of both mentor and protégé? I used scientific methods to identify the mentoring process. While the science allowed me to tease out the elements of mentoring, these steps in the absence of the key will not work. And because I have worked so hard on my humility, the key was hidden from me and not from those I mentored.

What makes this work in my world of mentoring is my passion, caring, and love for people, all expressed with no strings attached. And it is a huge commitment of my time and energy. There is no doubt that the returns are much greater than the investment in spite of the enormous amount of time it takes, or maybe because it does take time and patience and trust.

Trust. It is not about trusting the process. It is about trusting each other. It is essential to the process to develop mutual trust, and this is done by first trusting my protégé. I have faith in her, believe she will do what she says she will do, and then hold her accountable. I make promises and I keep them. I make coffee dates and appointments and I show up. And I expect her to do the same. I make mistakes and own them and allow my protégé to make mistakes and own them. We learn and grow together.

When I made the list of my mentors and protégés, I was going to write about context. However, in the analysis, the context was not that important to the relationship. I am attracted to people, all kinds of people from all walks of life and many cultures. What attracts me is their uniqueness, their *light within*, the wisdom and potential they possess, sometimes locked up and awaiting the key.

I am clear on the amazing things that happen when very different people come together, so I make it a habit to mix things up as often as I can. I invite several protégés, family members, and friends to dinner at the same time. The conversations are highly charged, and the results are unpredictable. Sometimes someone gets a job, a connection for entrance into a college program, or simply shared stories that enrich us all.

This is life. Not things, but people. Not trophies, but conversations and shared meaning. Not being in charge, but simply being. From this grows opportunity and discovery, and an opportunity to identify what it is we really care about, what we stand for. This prepares us all to lead. This is the magic.

Seven Steps to Mentoring

1. Make a commitment
2. Connect
3. Validate
4. Take a personal inventory
5. Plan and act
6. Reflect and construct meaning
7. Readjust

1. Make a Commitment

Commit your time and energy and share your passion. In this process, I take an interest in my protégé. From this flows great energy. It fuels my passion for learning and my commitment to serve. I learn every bit as much as the people I mentor.

2. Connect

Early in the process, we make contact and discuss interests. Coffee, tea, lunch, or on a park bench, this is an informal process. In many of the stories, food was a social lubricant. In some of the relationships, these meetings had rituals, like meeting on a given day at a given place each week or month. The rituals seem to provide comfort and safety. Throughout this process of connecting, it is important to: listen, be available—make time for this process to unfold. Accept without judgment where the protégé is in her/his life. Demonstrate compassion. Seek common interests or experiences. Share your story—give your protégé an opportunity to know you, warts and all. Use humor. Take turns asking questions.

3. Validate

There is a process of validation, of meeting people right where they are, accepting them as they are without judgment. I acknowledge their existence and express my belief in them. They all stand for something, care about something. They all want to construct meaning. They all have passion for something. Early on, my role is to validate their interests and fuel their passion. I unlock the box and free them to pursue their interests. It is the beginning of building hope.

I acknowledge how they feel and then move them toward action. I believe people act their way into feeling right, not feel their way into acting right. Action, however, requires courage. Fear can be paralyzing, so I provide them a safety net to take the plunge. There are simple strategies for validating and supporting one's protégés: listen, nod your head, ask good questions, and be curious, let your protégé know you believe in her or him. Say it in direct terms—"I believe in you" and "I know you can do it." Talk about choices. Connect dots for them using your experience and knowledge. Begin the process of helping your protégé develop or strengthen her or his personal control; the locus is within the individual.

4. Take a Personal Inventory

A business that takes no inventory is likely to go broke. So I make this an integral part of the process. In this process, we identify interests, passions, and skills. Sometimes it is formal and I ask my protégé to make lists of assets and challenges, describe where they are currently. Sometimes I just use questions: What are you doing now? What do you want to be/do when you grow up? What do you *care* about? This process helps people find themselves on a life map of sorts.

This is the beginning of identifying perceptions of self, others, situations. Often, my protégé's early perceptions are skewed. They are built on what people have told them and norms that surround them. My role becomes helping them gather empirical data that will challenge their perceptions and help them to construct new meaning. I help them take an inventory of themselves and the situation. For example, Katie was told she was not capable of being successful in school; this is a young woman with an admirable IQ and great creativity who believes she is worthless because others told her so, and these are people to whom she gives power. My role was to provide her with more information. Find something she is good at (inventory), where she wants to improve (inventory), and then support her in her academic work by teaching her to study, to write, to express herself. I support her in discovering herself as a learner, as an intelligent woman.

5. Plan and Act

Action is extremely important in this relationship. The reason my protégé is willing to develop a plan of action is because I have modeled doing this. I share my own reflection and personal inventory and the kinds of actions that I plan as a result. The plan can be simple or complex. It often entails some study, some data gathering, and several meetings to develop the plan. The plan becomes a commitment to take action. Within this process, I create safety to take risks, as the plans are often filled with risks and hindered by fear. My mentor's mentor, George Brown, always said, "There are no mistakes, only negative and positive results." When fear arises, I often ask, "What is the worst thing that can happen if you try this?" Rarely is there an answer that keeps my protégé from making an attempt. A good plan is one that has some form of accountability. How long does she need to take the action and when will we get back together to discuss the experience? This helps her push through the fear, take a deep breath, do it in spite of her reservations.

At this juncture of the journey, I often find myself teaching skills. Most commonly: setting boundaries, navigating the system, networking, resource development/money management, how to ask for help, how and where to get the data needed in order to make the plan, career exploration strategies.

We are guides to our protégés. We help structure their plans, encourage risk, and open doors. We empower them to act and then get out of the way. There is an art to this dance. We start out the leader and then release our protégé to the process, their choices, and the outcomes. We give them permission to take charge and be deliberate, to act based on acquired information and knowledge, dreams, and life goals.

The actions my protégés take become the material and resources with which to construct meaning. Experiences count. They have power. They give energy to ideas, help one sort out what works and what needs to change. The action may even result in a life-changing experience, though it may not be identified as life changing in the moment.

6. Reflect and Construct Meaning

"The wise leader does not try to protect people from themselves. The light of awareness shines equally on what is pleasant and on what is not pleasant" (Heider, 1985, p. 9).

This is where the learning takes place. This is the juncture that defines the progress the protégé is making. This process allows us to move between optimism and realism, back and forth, until we can figure out our next move. We examine ourselves in the context of experience, seeking to construct meaning that will move us forward. *Reframing* is an integral part of the process. The most negative experience can provide the richest lessons and inform our next move. What seems negative at the time may be a significant opportunity. Reframing involves looking at an experience through multiple lenses—one's own values, the culture that surrounds the person, gender, theory, natural order, and so forth.

7. Adjust

That is, use the data and newly constructed meaning to adjust beliefs, interests, and goals. Return to step four and review the inventory work done so far. Search for new information. Ask questions and gather more data. If stuck, go back to step three and validate your protégé's thoughts and feelings. Help your protégé see new options and choices. Be sure the safety net is well established and support your protégé in taking action, even if it is baby steps. This process is cyclical. The journey is never really over, though it morphs and changes. This is true in the mentoring relationship and in our roles as leaders. The process is not complex, but the skills required make it as much an art as it is a science. This is not a linear map but a circular, never-ending process.

Mentoring as Leadership and Legacy

> The greatest use of a life is to spend it on something that will outlast it.
> —William James

The art of mentoring is very clearly described in my protégés' stories. The common themes described behaviors and actions that brought meaning, safety, and sustainability to the mentoring relationship.

How is this leadership? This is transformational leadership at the grass roots. Transformational leadership is defined as a leadership approach that creates valuable and positive change in the followers with the end goal of developing followers into leaders. As a leader, I am not a goddess or a queen but rather a steward of the people I lead. This process is not about creating followers. It is about passion, commitment, action, and reflection. It results in empowering others to lead—with passion and by example. And as my protégés become mentors, the energy, love, and hope are carried on to the next generation.

I am looking in a mirror at a reflection of myself in the mirror behind me and the image keeps going and going and going. This is the mentoring experience, and in that mirror is everyone who has ever mentored me and everyone I mentor. It's quite a crowd, a lineage that keeps on going long after I die. This is my legacy.

Conclusion

This writing is a labor of love. The stories shared about my mentors describe the foundation of my passion, skills, and commitment. These people moved me, energized me, taught me to take risks, take a stand, and move to action. My gratitude to them is expressed in my actions mentoring others in order to carry on this rich tradition.

The stories my protégés wrote touched me deeply. I am only sad that I could not include them all. There is no way I could write this chapter without their voices. It is not about me, it is about them, their courage, their passion, and their commitment to this process. I am overwhelmed by the amazing accomplishments of my protégés, but not surprised. They know what they stand for, they are moved to action, and they are selflessly paying it forward.

References

Blumer, H. (1969). *Symbolic interactionism: Perspective and method.* Englewood Cliffs, NJ: Prentice Hall.

Crossley, M. L. (2002). Introducing narrative psychology. In C. Horrocks, K. Milnes, B. Roberts & D. Robinson (Eds.), *Narrative, memory and life transitions* (pp. 1–13). Yorkshire, England: University of Huddersfield.

James, W. (n.d.). The quotations page. Retreived 1 March 2011 from http://www.quotationspage.com/quote/23543.html.

Heider, J. (1985). *The tao of leadership.* Atlanta, GA: Humanics New Age.

Mair, M. (1989). *Between psychology and psychotherapy.* London, UK: Routledge.

Schechter, H., & Semeiks, J. G. (1980). *Patterns in popular culture: A sourcebook for writers.* New York: Harper & Row.

Sinetar, M. (1998). *The mentor's spirit.* New York: St. Martin's.

About the Editor and Contributors

Editor

Jennifer L. Martin, Ph.D., has worked in public education for fifteen years, thirteen of those as the department head of English at an alternative high school for at-risk students in the Detroit metropolitan area. She is also a special lecturer at Oakland University, where she teaches in the Education Specialist Degree Program and in the Women and Gender Studies Program. As an educational leader, Dr. Martin has been an advocate for at-risk students and has received several district, state, and national awards and recognitions for her advocacy, mentorship, and research. She has served as a mentor to high school, undergraduate, and graduate students, as well as to new teachers in a variety of areas such as writing and publishing, career and leadership development, and advocacy. Dr. Martin has conducted research and published fourteen book chapters and numerous peer-reviewed articles on bullying and harassment, peer sexual harassment, educational equity, mentoring, issues of social justice, service learning, the at-risk student, and other educational topics. Dr. Martin has been an invited speaker at universities and non-profit organizations on the aforementioned topics. As Action Vice President of Michigan NOW, she engages in volunteer Title IX education and legal advocacy work. Through this work, she has been asked to comment on proposed Michigan legislation on National Public Radio.

Contributors

Elizabeth J. Allan, Ph.D., is an associate professor of higher education at the University of Maine, where she is also an affiliate faculty member with the Women's Studies Program. She received her Ph.D. in educational policy and leadership with a women's studies emphasis from The Ohio State University in 1999. Her research focuses on campus cultures and climates and has included studies on classroom teaching practices, diversity, student group experiences, university women's commissions, and the methodology of policy discourse analysis. Her professional experience includes a visiting professorship at Universidad de las Americas in Puebla, Mexico, and five years of teaching women's studies at The Ohio State University. She is author of more than twenty articles and is the recipient of the Outstanding Publication Award by the American Educational Research Association's Division J. Her book *Policy Discourses, Gender, and Education* was published by Routledge in 2008, and she is co-editor of the 2010 text *Re-constructing Higher Education: Feminist Poststructural Perspectives,* also published by Routledge.

James E. Barott, Ph.D., has served as a Professor of Educational Leadership in the College of Education at Eastern Michigan University (EMU) for the past twelve years. Dr. Barott began his academic career at the University of California, Santa Barbara (UCSB) where he was mentored by Drs. Laurence Iannaccone and George Brown. His previous academic positions include serving as a Lecturer and Academic Program Leader in the Confluent Education Program at UCSB, Assistant Professor in Educational Leadership at the University of Utah, and Associate Professor in School Administration and Supervision at the University of Texas Pan American. Dr. Barott has focused his career on the development and mentoring of educational leaders. He specializes in teaching organizational theory, the politics of education, and field study research methods. During his tenure in higher education, Dr. Barott has had the privilege of mentoring and serving as dissertation chair of numerous students. He has also worked closely with a number of specialist and master's students. He views his greatest achievement as the important contributions made to field of education by his students. Dr. Barott has published numerous articles and presented a number of papers with his former students and continues to serve as a mentor and advisor and friend to these students. He has received awards for his teaching and mentoring from the University, the College, and the Department at EMU.

Christa Boske, Ed.D., is an assistant professor in pre K–12 educational administration at Kent State University. Christa works to encourage school leaders to promote humanity in schools, especially for disenfranchised children and families within America's public educational system. Her scholarship is informed by her work in residential treatment and inner-city schools as a school leader and social worker. She recently co-edited the book entitled *Bridge Leadership: Connecting Educational Leadership and Social Justice to Improve Schools*, published by Information Age, with Autumn K. Tooms. Christa's work can also be found in the *Journal of School Leadership, Journal of Research, Leadership and Education, Multicultural Education and Technology,* and the *International Journal of Educational Administration*. She serves as Kent State University's Plenum Representative for the University Council of Educational Administration.

Deb Clarke, Ed.D., has a passion for excellence in both developing and administering programs and believes that all children can achieve. Using a team-based approach in partnership with school leadership, parents, and community, Dr. Clarke credits the amazing efforts of staff in their commitment to continuously closing the gap and raising student achievement. By example, one creative, energetic, and hardworking staff developed a program implementing significantly higher standards and accompanying student supports and was recognized at the White House as a National Exemplary School and Michigan Blue Ribbon High School. This school was also recognized as one of the top one hundred high schools nationally and one of the top ten high schools in the state. Honored by the U.S. Department of Education, she received an Outstanding High School Principal Award. While an assistant superintendent for curriculum and instruction, the staff was recognized by *60 Minutes* and at the White House for its work with robotics. While she was a superintendent working with an economically challenged, minority, underperforming district, 100 percent of the seniors in her third year went to college, most on scholarship. The district was also recognized as a Governor's Network School recipient and earned two state championships. Her doctorate in early childhood education has shown promise in testing a new theory that built upon pre–K/3rd grade research for reducing and/or eliminating the Head Start Fade effect. Currently an educational consultant and leadership coach, Dr. Clarke uses her extensive background in professional development to work with some of the finest educators in the nation. She has facilitated teacher team presentations on improving achievement and data-driven achievement practices in Boston, San Francisco, Charleston, and at state conferences.

Lindson Feun, Ph.D., is the research and evaluation consultant at Oakland Schools (ISD). He has been evaluating educational programs, conducting research, assisting schools in AdvancEd (NCA) accreditation, and helping doctoral students with their dissertations for the past twenty-two years. He is also a lecturer in the Education Specialist department and Professional Development department at Oakland University. He has been teaching for the past nineteen years. His publications and interests are in leadership and organizational development, school improvement, and professional learning communities (PLCs). He is currently cowriting a book on the evaluation of Title 1 programs.

Shannon R. Flumerfelt, Ph.D., is an associate professor of educational leadership in the School of Education and Human Services and the director of Lean Thinking for Schools, Pawley Lean Institute, Oakland University. Her publications focus on leadership and organizational development. Previously, Dr. Flumerfelt worked for twenty-six years in public school administration and teaching. Her research interests include leadership and organizational development, school improvement, and lean and e-learning.

Valjeaner Ford, Ed.D., has been an educator for thirty-six years and holds a bachelor's degree in U.S. history and political science from Fayetteville State University, Fayetteville, North Carolina, a master's degree in human relations and management from Webster University, St. Louis, Missouri, and a doctoral degree in educational leadership from Fayetteville State University, Fayetteville, North Carolina. Valjeaner began her educational career as a social studies teacher in South Boston, Massachusetts, during the early 1970s busing era. She returned to North Carolina, where she taught at South View Jr. High School before traveling to Bamberg, Germany, with her husband and taught for the Department of Defense (DOD)/Community College: Big Ben Community College, University of Maryland and Temple University. She then traveled to Ft. Leonard Wood,

Missouri, where she taught at the Truman Army Education Center, teaching English as a second language to non-English-speaking military personnel. After a return to Fayetteville, North Carolina, in 1984, she began an eighteen-year tenure in Hoke County teaching U.S. history at Hoke County High School. She served as an assistant principal and curriculum specialist. She has published numerous articles, with a primary focus in gender equity. Valjeaner is currently an associate professor at the University of North Carolina at Pembroke, teaching graduate school in the School of Education, where she continues to make a difference in the lives of her students. She serves on numerous educational boards (state as well as national), where she imparts knowledge from her illustrious thirty-six years and counting in the field of education, her passion.

Rachel Grimshaw, B.A., is currently a graduate student in the English department at California State University, Stanislaus, concentrating on both composition and literature as part of her degree. She is an active member and officer in the local chapter of Sigma Tau Delta, the International English Honor Society. She plans to pursue her Ph.D. degree in the field of literature, with a focus on contemporary or modern works. Her research interests include gender and sexuality in literary texts and social contexts, societal and cultural literacy, feminism and political activism in the classroom, identity constructs inside academia, and portfolios and ethnographies as a means of assessing and articulating student performance and concerns. She will be teaching her first college composition course during the fall 2010 semester and has designed the course around the theme of censorship.

Lisa P. Hallen, M.Ed., is a doctoral candidate at the University of Maine. She has served as a contributor to the Mitchell Institute's study on Barriers to Postsecondary Education in Maine (2007). She currently serves as a director of guidance/school counselor at a Maine public comprehensive high school. Her dissertation is entitled *Socioeconomic Status, Curriculum Placement, and Constructed Realities Carried by High School Course Guides: A Policy Discourse Analysis.*

Carmen M. Johnson, Ed.Spec., is a visual arts educator who has worked in public education for fourteen years. Carmen currently serves as the visual arts teacher at a middle school in the Detroit metropolitan area. Her research focuses on cultural relevance in education, pedagogy, and practice. As an educational leader, Carmen is an advocate for minority students, creating valuable opportunities for students of color to be successful in school. Such activities include a districtwide diversity council, mentorship opportunities and cross-curricular learning experiences, and communitywide partnerships. Carmen is committed to educational leadership and teacher development and has served the district as a contributing member of the Equity Team, Visual Arts Task Force, Inclusion Task Force, and the Breaking Ranks at the Middle Level team. Along with her colleagues, Carmen presented her award-winning photojournalism project entitled Behind the Lens at the MCTE and NCTE conferences; Carmen believes that teaching is challenging, controversial and collaborative work. This mindset has compelled her to share her story, ideas, and life with students, colleagues, and parents to create a sustained equitable and relevant educational experience for all children.

Susan S. Klein, Ed.D., is the education equity director of the Feminist Majority Foundation, focusing on fully implementing Title IX. She is also VP for programs at the Clearinghouse on Women's Issues and co-chair of the National Coalition for Women and Girls in Education (NCWGE) Single Sex Education Task Force. She joined the Feminist Majority Foundation in 2003 after thirty-four years in the research offices in the U.S. Department of Education, where she worked on gender-equity issues whenever she was allowed to do so. She created the Department of Education Gender Equity Expert Panel to identify promising and exemplary products and programs to advance gender equality. As the general editor of the 1985 *Handbook for Achieving Sex Equity through Education* and the 2007 *Handbook for Achieving Gender Equity through Education, 2nd Edition,* Sue coordinated the contributions of more than 200 gender-equity experts. Sue earned a doctoral degree in educational psychology from Temple University in 1970, a master's degree from the University of Pennsylvania in 1967, and a B.S. in education from Temple in1966. She has received a variety of awards for her close to 200 publications and leadership. Sue has known Dr. Bernice Sandler since 1969, when Sue conducted a pilot test for her dissertation on *Student Influence on Teacher Behavior* in a class that Dr. Sandler was teaching at Mount Vernon College in Washington, DC.

C. Robert Maxfield, Ed.D., is an assistant professor of educational leadership in the School of Education and Human Services at Oakland University. He is also the director of the Galileo Institute for the Study of Teacher Leadership, Oakland's representative on the Southeast Michigan Galileo Consortium Board, and a member of the Stakeholder Steering Committee of the Learning Achievement Coalition–Oakland (LACO). He and Linda Tyson are cohosts of a weekly podcast series entitled Podcasts for Leaderful Schools. Prior to joining the Oakland faculty, he was a teacher, principal, and superintendent in several Southeast Michigan school districts. His research interests include teacher leadership, reforming school organizational structures, new models of school finance, and systemic approaches to addressing achievement disparities in schools.

Lynn Kleiman Malinoff, Ed.D. is the director of Eastern Michigan Universities 21st Century Community Learning Centers Bright Futures out-of-school-time programs. A member of the project team at EMU's Institute for the Study of Children, Families, and Communities, Lynn's current work focuses on positive youth development in low-income schools along the Michigan Avenue corridor in the heart of the failing auto–industrial complex. Lynn's career is dedicated to mentoring, academic-service learning, and the development of youth voice in the K–12 environment. Lynn has worked for more than thirty-five years in K–12 education as a general and special education teacher, grant writer, program developer, and change agent. She has taught at all levels and developed grants and programs for at-risk youth, with a focus on mentoring and service learning. She coaches administrators and consults on the implementation of the Youth Program Quality model for positive youth development. Lynn received her doctorate in educational leadership from EMU, where she studied the culture, history, and politics of local communities along the Michigan Avenue corridor in southeastern Michigan. She continues to use her entrepreneurial skills and systems knowledge to build bridges between higher education, the K–12 schools, and the community. She has two grown sons, a husband, and three Shetland sheepdogs, teaches graduate courses at Eastern Michigan University, and is passionate about photography.

Cheryl McFadden, Ed.D., an associate professor in the Department of Educational Leadership at East Carolina University, has worked as an educational consultant in both higher education and the public and private school sector. Her research interests include principal preparation, program evaluation, leadership styles and behaviors, online education, and civic engagement. She has presented her research at more than a hundred state, national, and international conferences and has published more than thirty articles and book chapters in these areas.

Jennifer O'Connor, Ph.D., has taught graduate students in the field of education at Suffolk University, Northeastern University, and Kaplan University. She received her undergraduate degree from Amherst College and her master's and doctoral degrees from Boston College in higher education administration. She teaches classes on student development theory, research methodology, ethics in education, and diversity in higher education. Her research and publications focus on gender and social class equity in higher education. She recently published her book, *Working-class Students at Radcliffe College 1940–1970: The Intersection of Gender, Social Class, and Historical Context.*

Michele A. Paludi, Ph.D., is the author/editor of thirty-four college textbooks and more than 170 scholarly articles and conference presentations on sexual harassment, campus violence, psychology of women, gender, and discrimination. Her book, *Ivory Power: Sexual Harassment on Campus*, (1990, SUNY Press), received the 1992 Myers Center Award for Outstanding Book on Human Rights in the United States. Dr. Paludi served as chair of the U.S. Department of Education's Subpanel on the Prevention of Violence, Sexual Harassment, and Alcohol and Other Drug Problems in Higher Education. She was one of six scholars in the United States to be selected for this subpanel. She also was a consultant to and a member of former New York State Governor Mario Cuomo's Task Force on Sexual Harassment. Dr. Paludi serves as an expert witness for court proceedings and administrative hearings on sexual harassment. She has had extensive experience in conducting training programs and investigations of sexual harassment and other Equal Employment Opportunity (EEO) issues for businesses and educational institutions. In addition, Dr. Paludi has held faculty positions at Franklin & Marshall College, Kent State University, Hunter College, Union College, and Union Graduate College, where she directs the human resource management certificate program and management and leadership certificate program. She is on the faculty in the School of Management.

Marjorie Ringler, Ed.D., is an assistant professor in the Department of Educational Leadership at East Carolina University (ECU). She teaches in the master's, specialist, and doctorate programs in school administration. Her areas of research include English language learners, professional development, and leadership at international schools. Dr. Ringler began her career as a high school math teacher and an administrator in Florida. She then coordinated a professional development grant funded by the Florida Department of Education to effectively deliver professional development in several K–12 instructional practices. Dr. Ringler obtained her Ed.D. at the University of Florida (UF), her master's in educational administration from Stetson University, and her mathematics education degree from Florida International University (FIU). She grew up in Barranquilla, Colombia, where she completed her elementary and secondary education.

Index